Reflection
on America's
Great Loop

A Baby Boomer Couple's
Year-Long Boating Odyssey

By George and Patricia Hospodar

REFLECTION ON AMERICA'S GREAT LOOP: A BABY BOOMER COUPLE'S YEAR-LONG BOATING ODYSSEY

Copyright © 2012 Atlantic Publishing Group, Inc.
1210 SW 23rd Place • Ocala, Florida 34471 • Phone: 800-814-1132 • Fax: 352-622-1875
Website: www.atlantic-pub.com • Email: sales@atlantic-pub.com
SAN Number: 268-1250

Library of Congress Cataloging-in-Publication Data

Hospodar, George, 1946-
  Reflection on America's great loop : a baby boomer couple's year-long boating odyssey / by George Hospodar and Patricia Hospodar.
     p. cm.
  Includes bibliographical references and index.
  ISBN 978-1-60138-901-5 (alk. paper)
  1. Atlantic Intracoastal Waterway--Description and travel. 2. Reflection (Motor yacht) 3. Hospodar, George, 1946---Travels. 4. Hospodar, Patricia, 1946---Travels. 5. Atlantic Coast (U.S.)--Description and travel. 6. Canals--Canada, Eastern. 7. Great Lakes Region (North America)--Description and travel. 8. Rivers--East (U.S.) 9. Gulf Coast (U.S.)--Description and travel. 10. Boats and boating--Atlantic Intracoastal Waterway. I. Hospodar, Patricia, 1946- II. Title.
  F106.H67 2012
  910.4'5--dc23
                              2012015774

Printed in the United States

Printed on Recycled Paper

INTERIOR LAYOUT: Antoinette D'Amore • addesign@videotron.ca
COVER DESIGNS: Jackie Miller • millerjackiej@gmail.com

A few years back we lost our beloved pet dog Bear, who was not only our best and dearest friend but also the "Vice President of Sunshine" here at Atlantic Publishing. He did not receive a salary but worked tirelessly 24 hours a day to please his parents.

Bear was a rescue dog who turned around and showered myself, my wife, Sherri, his grandparents Jean, Bob, and Nancy, and every person and animal he met (well, maybe not rabbits) with friendship and love. He made a lot of people smile every day.

We wanted you to know a portion of the profits of this book will be donated in Bear's memory to local animal shelters, parks, conservation organizations, and other individuals and nonprofit organizations in need of assistance.

– *Douglas & Sherri Brown*

PS: We have since adopted two more rescue dogs: first Scout, and the following year, Ginger. They were both mixed golden retrievers who needed a home.

Want to help animals and the world? Here are a dozen easy suggestions you and your family can implement today:

- *Adopt and rescue a pet from a local shelter.*
- *Support local and no-kill animal shelters.*
- *Plant a tree to honor someone you love.*
- *Be a developer — put up some birdhouses.*
- *Buy live, potted Christmas trees and replant them.*
- *Make sure you spend time with your animals each day.*
- *Save natural resources by recycling and buying recycled products.*
- *Drink tap water, or filter your own water at home.*
- *Whenever possible, limit your use of or do not use pesticides.*
- *If you eat seafood, make sustainable choices.*
- *Support your local farmers market.*
- *Get outside. Visit a park, volunteer, walk your dog, or ride your bike.*

Five years ago, Atlantic Publishing signed the Green Press Initiative. These guidelines promote environmentally friendly practices, such as using recycled stock and vegetable-based inks, avoiding waste, choosing energy-efficient resources, and promoting a no-pulping policy. We now use 100-percent recycled stock on all our books. The results: in one year, switching to post-consumer recycled stock saved 24 mature trees, 5,000 gallons of water, the equivalent of the total energy used for one home in a year, and the equivalent of the greenhouse gases from one car driven for a year.

Disclaimer

This book is designed to entertain and provide information about cruising America's Great Loop. It is not intended to be a complete guidebook. Although every effort has been made to provide accurate information, the authors do not take any responsibility for errors, incorrect information, or omissions. Conditions at marinas, anchorages, and on waterways are constantly changing. It is the captain's responsibility to verify all information found in this book to ensure accuracy. The authors and publisher have neither liability nor responsibility to any person or entity with respect to any loss or damage caused, or alleged to be caused, directly or indirectly by the information contained in this book. The purpose of this book is to tell the story of a personal adventure and to give the reader some guidance.

Authors' Dedication

To our parents who are forever in our hearts, to our family members who are also our friends, and to our friends who are also like family: Thank you always for your prayers, love, and support.

Acknowledgments

We first wish to thank Lou and Judy Ianniello and Ed and Karen Rajsteter for generously assisting us as the crew on our boat's inaugural journey from Florida to New Jersey. You always have a place in our hearts and aboard *Reflection*.

We are also deeply grateful to our "support" crew: Evelyn and Tony Christiano, Ernie and Kay Giordano, Susan Luciano, and Bob Smith, who made the America's Great Loop trip possible for us by looking in on Pat's mother, taking care of our mail, and watching our home during our absence. You are terrific neighbors and friends.

Next, we would like to recognize Pat's mom, Anne Robak, Pat's brother, Father Tony Robak, our many trip followers who kept us in their thoughts and prayers, George's cousin, Bob Boehs, and those who showed they cared by phoning or emailing us on a regular basis just to make sure we were all right. Thanks to you all; we were blessed by the best.

In addition, we are truly indebted to our exceptional "onboard" crew: George's sister and brother-in-law, Pat and Al Mackay, Charlie and Helen Dambroski, and George and Linda Telschow, who traveled considerable distances to share some segments of this incredible journey with us. You will always be an important part of this story because you were there!

Thanks also goes to the wonderful people who welcomed us with hospitality as we visited their locales: Mike and Sue McGirr in Chicago, Illinois; Joe and Linda Dahm, our niece, Angela Mackay, great nephew Charlie, and great nieces Allie and Anna in Manistee and Holland, Michigan; Werner and Grace Lohmann and Joan Shields in Marathon, Florida; Bo and Cindy Trossbach in Palm City, Florida; Ed and Andrea Boubol and their family and Florence Grant in Boca Raton, Florida; Gus and Linda Barberi and Nancy Husbands in Vero Beach, Florida; Andrew and Clare Zeigler in Savannah, Georgia; and Judy Hagerstrom in Deltaville, Virginia.

We also appreciate the help of: Ken MacDonald of Bay Port Marina in Midland, Ontario for his graciousness in spending time going over charts with us and outlining premier stopping points on his beloved Georgian Bay; and Roy Eaton for his travel advice and the incredible assistance he gives to all boaters in the North Channel area of Lake Huron through his radio show, "The Little Current Cruisers' Network." You are two of Canada's finest gentlemen.

Reflection traveled with several special "buddy" boats along the way: *Maya Lisa, Houlegan, Falkor, Freedom,* and *Holiday VII.* Thank you Hank and Ceci Bassford, Ray and Caryl Houle, Al and Gayle Binnington, Andrew and Sallyann Newton, and Richard Walker for all the memories and your friendships.

We would also like to particularly acknowledge Christine Magyarits for her honest suggestions and critiques in the writing of this book, Raymond Barton for his insightful guidance in the development of its structure, Sharon Starling for her photos of us, and Les Levy for the fortuitous conversation at the Halifax River Yacht Club in Daytona, Florida, which led to the publication of our story. You all helped to make the idea a reality.

Table of Contents

Foreword by Gary Jobson

*M*ost maritime literature seems to be about crossing oceans, surviving storms, horrific shipwrecks, winning races, or chasing whales. It is refreshing when a new boating topic comes along. George and Patricia Hospodar's voyage around "The Loop" is an engaging tale of American life witnessed from a boat. This well-written narrative moves along swiftly and includes helpful hints at the end of every chapter. Once you start reading, two things happen: You will not stop, and you will start thinking about planning your own adventure.

The Hospodars' story begins with the purchase of a 26-foot boat for mostly day sailing around Barnegat Bay on the New Jersey Shore. They boldly name their first boat *Adventuress* and eventually venture to the Chesapeake. As retirement loomed, this baby boomer couple thought about circumnavigating the Great Loop, which is a 5,000-plus-mile trip up the Hudson River, followed by endless locks through canals into Canada, down the Great Lakes and the Mississippi, along the Gulf Coast, and eventually passing Florida before the return trip up the east coast to their home on Barnegat Bay.

There are many stories in this volume, some predictable and others surprising. I am not going to give away any here, but you feel like you are on board for every wide-eyed event that takes place. Most people see our vast country from their car windows, occasionally from an airplane or even on foot, but I think the best way to understand America is to see it from the water. Early settlers moved about via waterways. Bold entrepreneurs built canals to move commercial goods and people. These waterways are still in use. The Hospodars' boat, *Reflection*, made a convenient home as the couple and some of their friends visited huge cities such as Chicago and many small, remote towns. As an added bonus, *Reflection* visits Canada, which is a significant part of the journey. We learn about some of the differences between the United States and Canada.

Along the way, the couple meets other mariners. They refer to one another as "loopers." George tells us their sacred time is happy hour. The nice thing about being within sight of land most of the time is that you get to stop each night and savor the experience, whereas in the ocean, the watch-standing routine never ends. The Hospodars are sailors at heart but wisely purchase a powerboat for the adventure.

As one can imagine, there are equipment breakdowns, navigational challenges, and occasional hardships. At one point, George declares the word "boat" stands for "break out another thousand," a fact to which every boat owner can relate. They were especially appreciative of courtesy cars that were available at some marinas so they could venture inland or go food shopping.

George and Pat make a good team. He calls her "Admiral," and she calls him the "Captain." George describes Pat as "the conceptualizer" and he "the actualizer." In other words, she comes up with the ideas, and he makes them happen. This theme continues throughout the story. Along the way, they visit 98 places during 324 days aboard and consume 3,547 gallons of fuel. Their longest respite was a five-month stop in Marathon, Florida.

Throughout the text, appropriate pictures are included that amplify the stories. Many of the photos are taken from the bridge with the bow of *Reflection* in the lower part of the photo. This made me feel that I was on board the boat with Pat and George, and they seem like the kind of people you would want to cruise with for a week or longer. This extended cruise was all about having a good time, seeing new things, and meeting like-minded people who shared their passion for adventure.

The list of suggestions on navigation and how to make life easier at the end of each chapter are practical tips based on actual experience, which many can apply to any cruise. One of my favorites was their encouragement to stay in a marina on the Jersey side of the Hudson because the New York side is too expensive. There are many suggestions on how to navigate narrow channels, and sometimes I wondered if there was an unfortunate experience backing up the suggestion.

Many aspiring sailors consider such trips but never realize their dream. The example the Hospodars' voyage around the Great Loop set proves this is a doable dream. There are setbacks and unexpected problems, but a good attitude and determination helped this couple overcome them. These tales are told here in detail, and you get the feeling they want to help future "loopers" avoid some issues they experienced.

Like George and Pat, I am also part of the baby boomer generation. I grew up sailing on Barnegat Bay, so I can understand how they aspired to venture toward new horizons. Although most of my career has been trying to reach the finish line ahead of other boats, I have cruised extensively with my family in Maine and Nova Scotia and completed several ambitious expeditions to the Arctic, Antarctic, and around Cape Horn. An expedition is a cruise with a purpose, yet until I read *Reflection on America's Great Loop*, I never considered that an expedition like this could be taken on coastal and inland waters. Now, I have another item for my long bucket list, and you will, too.

Gary Jobson

Gary Jobson is a world class sailor, television commentator and author based in Annapolis, Maryland. He is President of US SAILING, the National Governing Body of Sailing. Gary has authored 17 sailing books and is Editor at Large of Sailing World and Cruising World magazines.

Jobson has been ESPN's sailing commentator since 1985. He won an A.C.E. (Award for Cable Excellence) for the 1987 America's Cup. In 1988 Jobson won an Emmy for his production of sailing at the Olympic Games in South Korea and won an Emmy for the 2006 Volvo Ocean Race on PBS. He has covered the Olympics five times for NBC. Gary Jobson has won four Southam Awards and one Telly Award. His newest book is Gary Jobson: An American Sailing Story. Jobson has produced a new film, Energy on Trial (**www.energyontrial.com**).

He has won many championships in one design classes, the America's Cup with Ted Turner, the infamous Fastnet Race and many of the world's ocean races. In College at SUNY Maritime he was an All American sailor three times and was twice named College Sailor of the Year.

In October 2003 Gary was inducted into the America's Cup Hall of Fame by the Herreshoff Marine Museum. In 1999 Jobson won the Nathanael G. Herreshoff Trophy, US SAILING's most prestigious award. This trophy is awarded annually to an individual who has made an outstanding contribution to the sport of sailing in the United States. Gary has been the National Chairman of HYPERLINK "http://www.leukemiacup.org/" The Leukemia Cup Regatta, The Leukemia & Lymphoma

Society's sailing program, since 1994. These events have raised over $35 million to date. Jobson was awarded a Doctor of Letters from the State University of New York Maritime College in 2005.

Over the past thirty-five years Gary has given over 2000 lectures throughout the world. He started his career as a sailing coach at the U.S. Merchant Marine Academy and the U.S. Naval Academy.

Gary is also an active cruising sailor. He has led ambitious expeditions to the Arctic, Antarctica and Cape Horn. He currently races a Swan 42, Mustang, and an Etchells, Whirlwind.

Gary and his wife, Janice, have three grown daughters, Kristi, Ashleigh and Brooke.

For more information log on to: **www.jobsonsailing.com**

Gary has received 52 awards from 1966 to the present including:
- Membership in the National Sailing Hall of Fame
- Winning Tactician in the America's Cup Race
- Numerous Emmys for broadcast coverage of Olympic Sailing and other Yachting events
- The John Southam Award for his Expedition to the Arctic

Books by Gary Jobson
- *Gary Jobson: An American Sailing Story,* 2011
- *Classic Yachts,* 2008
- *A Cats: A Century of Tradition,* 2005
- *Championship Sailing,* 2004
- *Fighting Finish: Volvo Ocean Race 2001-02,* 2002
- *An America's Cup Treasury The Lost Levick Photographs, 1893 - 1937,* 1992
- *The Winner's Guide to Optimist Sailing with Jay Kehoe,* 1997
- *Championship Tactics with Tom Whidden and Adam Loory,* 1990
- *World Class Sailing with Martin Luray,* 1987
- *Sailing Fundamentals,* 1987
- *Revised Yachtsman's Pocket Almanac,* 1985
- *Speed Sailing with Mike Toppa,* 1985
- *Storm Sailing,* 1983
- *The Yachtsman's Pocket Almanac,* 1981
- *Gary Jobson's How to Sail,* 1980
- *The Racing Edge with Ted Turner,* 1979
- *U.S.Y.R.U. Sailing Instructor's Manual,* 1978

Chapter 1

You Want to do What?

"I own a boat!" I proudly bragged to Pat, my future wife, on the night we first met in the early 1970s. However, rather than getting the enthusiastic response I was used to hearing from other young women when I made that announcement, she simply nodded that it was nice and acted totally unimpressed. However, little did we know at the time what a chain reaction that simple statement would eventually make in our lives.

As we got to know each other, she found out that having a boat (even a small one) was important to me and that it was the fulfillment of a dream I had held from when I was a child and could only watch vessels go by from the beach. I learned that she had little experience on the water and that she had led a somewhat sheltered childhood filled with books and music because she had some physical limitations in her right leg and foot caused by her bout with polio at age 6. Could or would we be able to mesh our two backgrounds? Well, love does amazing things, and as our romance continued to blossom during our first summer together, my non-athletic girl decided that I should teach her how to sail. We eventually spent numerous weekends going out on *Rum Dum*, my 14-foot Goldfish sailboat, on different lakes and bays in New Jersey. With my encouragement, I happily watched her confidence and boating abilities grow.

Within a year, we were married, and a short time later, Pat decided that carrying this boat around on top of our car and trying to find places to launch it was too much of a hassle. She suggested buying a bigger boat, "maybe one with an enclosed head, a small galley, and room to stay overnight." And so it began: "Boat escalation." If you have never owned a boat, this is what happens: You start out with a small, easy-to-maintain, modestly priced boat, and after a year or so, you say it would be nice to have something else. Before you know it, you have a boat loan, boat storage, maintenance, launching, and dockage bills. It is a "law" of nature, and you can't do anything about it. Rarely does someone say he or she bought a smaller boat, because that simply goes against all logic!

So, not to defy this universal "law," we went to a local boat show and, much to the horror of our parents, ordered a brand new Bristol 26 sailboat to be custom-built for us. We named her *Adventuress*. She had it all: head, galley, sleeping cabin, icebox, fresh (pumped by hand) water, an outboard motor, and all the expenses mentioned above. We were on our way! This was also how our shipboard roles became defined: The Admiral (Pat) would conceptualize, and the Captain (I) would actualize. To put it another way: She would get an idea, and I would make it work.

We sailed *Adventuress* for five wonderful summers around Barnegat Bay and even made a trip to Chesapeake Bay, but at the end of the fifth summer, Pat heard about a new boat the Bristol Company was building. It was bigger, 30 feet long (you must not go against the "laws" of nature), faster, and had more goodies onboard, including hot and cold pressurized water, an enclosed shower, and an inboard diesel engine. It did not take long before we ordered *Temptress* to be built for us. The escalation continued; however, this is where the escalation ended for about 30 years.

During that time, I obtained my 100-ton captain's license and had a variety of careers — everything from designing computer systems for a major bank to selling real estate — while Pat taught music and directed an award-winning middle school chorus in Irvington, New Jersey. However in 2004, Pat retired and began to mention a cruising adventure she had read about called "America's Great Loop," suggesting that this once-in-a-lifetime trip could be something we might like to do.

The Great Loop, or just The Loop, as those who travel it know it, is a circumnavigation of one-third of the United States with portions of Canada thrown in for good measure. It is a journey of between 5,000 and 6,000 miles, roughly covering an area from the Atlantic coast, to the North Channel in Canada, to the Mississippi River, to the southern tip of Florida. This is no weekend getaway. It commonly takes most boaters at least one year to complete the trip, but some others take several years to make it all the way around, depending on individual circumstances or desires.

I hesitated a bit in signing onto this idea because I knew a trip like this could not be easily made on our beloved *Temptress* and that it would probably mean we would need to sell our cherished friend and buy a powerboat. To many people, buying a powerboat might not be a big deal, but to someone who had only owned sailboats, this was a sacrilege! The decision to give up sailing and buy a "stink pot" instead would take some serious soul-searching on my part. It seemed ironic that my wife, the girl who when we first met cared nothing about the water, now wanted to embark on a major boating journey. Be careful what you wish for!

However, like in our early days, love prevailed, so I finally relented and told Pat she better start looking for a boat. That was all she needed to hear. She had her marching orders, and off she went. She began searching the Internet for a boat — but not just any boat would do. It had to be big enough to carry the two of us in comfort and to accommodate guests who would join us along the way as we traveled on our newest adventure, the Great Loop.

We decided that to get the biggest bang for our buck, we would look for a used boat, rather than go "new," and as Pat's list of requirements for creature comforts grew, so did the size of the boat. It had to have two separate staterooms, each with its own head and shower, and no "V-berths" for our guests — only an inline double bed would do. The list included a spacious salon with a bar, a full galley with a dining area, and an aft deck for entertaining. This was a far cry from our cozy, 30-foot sailboat. Cue the escalation music!

After looking at nearly 100 boats online, a list of possible candidates soon developed. The boat locations spanned the states of New Jersey, Pennsylvania, Maryland, the Carolinas, Georgia, and Florida. We then embarked on several road trips to view the contenders in person and learned that pictures can be deceiving.

Once home, after looking at 25 vessels in person, we decided that there was only one boat on our list of possible contenders: She was a 48 Symbol Cockpit Motor Yacht with a 14-foot-6-inch beam and 4-foot draft we found in Palm City, Florida. We called the broker and made an offer. After some negotiation, we settled on a price with a closing date in mid-January. As part of the deal, the owners (Bo and Cindy) were kind enough to let us keep the boat at their home until April when we would move the vessel north to our home in New Jersey. This was an important point for us because the words, "January," "New Jersey," and "boating" do not belong in the same sentence.

After the marine and engine surveys revealed that the boat was in good condition, we closed the deal on Jan. 25, 2008. During the next few months, we made trips back and forth to Florida and were so busy getting the boat in shape for the trip home in April that we were able to take her out only once during the day and again only once to anchor out overnight. That was some shakedown!

To put this in perspective, operating this boat would be like going from driving a sports car to driving a Mack truck. Now we were about to drive this truck 1,350 miles north to our home, having only limited experience in its operation and little road testing of its reliability. We would also be doing much of this trip on shallow, unfamiliar waters. This did not give us a warm feeling!

However, we did have a few aces in the hole going for us. First, the engine and general marine surveyors felt that the boat was in good condition. Second, the previous owners took obvious pride in the care of their boat. Third, we were bringing in a crack crew to help us move the boat. The crew consisted of our friends Lou and Judy, who had years of experience operating boats of this size, and my cousin Ed, who had crewed with me while moving our sailboat on various voyages from New England to Norfolk, Virginia, for more than 30 years. The stage was set for the voyage, starting on April 11.

Chapter 2

Bringing Home "Baby"

We got to the boat ahead of the crew to make final preparations and to bring on provisions. We picked them up at the airport, got everyone settled onboard, and had a farewell dinner and cocktails with the previous owners, Bo and Cindy. The conversation was light and filled with laughter, but by 10 p.m., we were all in our bunks and ready for our predawn departure.

Everyone was up early the next morning and excited about getting underway. We said our goodbyes to our hosts, and at first light, we headed down the narrow canals that lead to the Saint Lucie River and the Intracoastal Waterway.

I was hoping for light winds, calm seas, and clear skies to start this journey off right, and I was not disappointed. As the warm sun rose, it was obvious that this was going to be a picture-perfect day on the water. Soft breezes and tiny wavelets greeted us as we entered the open waters, and a pod of dolphins escorted us down the river. It was going to be an excellent day.

Everything was going smoothly until early afternoon when the port engine started losing power. "So much for the perfect day," I thought. After several phone calls to Bo and to our engine mechanic, Lou and I determined that the problem was most likely a clogged fuel filter. With the port engine shut down, the crew kept the boat heading north on the starboard engine, while he and I made the repair under way. Within an hour, we had the engines running again and continued toward our evening anchorage near Cape Canaveral.

We anchored in a quiet spot near the NASA Parkway about an hour before a glorious sunset, settling in just in time for happy hour. I regard happy hour as a sacred time of peace and quiet, which means no sound coming from the running of the generator. Fortunately, the boat is equipped with an inverter that converts battery power into alternating current to run the refrigerator and the icemaker (my favorite appliance) without the need of the generator or its noise.

Once our happy hour ended, we fired up the gas grill, threw on some steaks, and had a relaxing dinner on the aft deck. At about 10 p.m., we all hit the bunks for an early morning wake-up to get started for our next port, Saint Augustine, and I fell asleep feeling grateful for such a beautiful day.

All was quiet until about midnight when something woke me up. There was no noise but just a sense that something was wrong — and there was. The AC power had gone out, which meant that the refrigerator and icemaker had stopped working. I can put up with a lot, but I have to have my ice! With no ice, there would be no cold drinks tomorrow, and as the Captain, I will not stand for that!

Luckily, the generator started right up and we had power, but this also meant we would not have a quiet night's sleep after all. It was not until we got the boat home and investigated the wiring that I discovered the power had gone out because the "house" batteries were the wrong type and were not holding a full charge. Also, the engine alternator that charges the batteries was not working. These kinds of things on a used boat are expected, even on one that has been well maintained.

The next day broke with beautiful sunshine, and the weather "gods" were still smiling on us, but the question was how long would it last?

That day's trip through the Intracoastal Waterway to Saint Augustine was somewhat uneventful until late in the afternoon when the wind started blowing out of the north between 15 and 20 knots. Forget calm seas and light winds. As we approached our slip across the harbor from Saint Augustine near the Bridge of Lions, we realized a strong current was running through the marina with a brisk crosswind in front of our assigned spot. Docking was going to be an unexpected "thrill," to say the least.

I set aside my pride and asked our far more capable friend Lou to back the boat into the slip. This was going to be a heart-pounding experience.

A 33,000-pound boat with no bow thruster backing into a narrow slip with gusty winds pushing it one way and the current another — my heart was in my throat as it looked like we might crush the sailboat in the next slip. "I hope the insurance is paid up," I thought. Lou yelled for Judy to jam a fender between the two boats to avoid any damage. Ed, Pat, and I feverishly tossed lines to other boaters on the dock who were helping out by holding the boat off as we backed in. We put on quite a show that afternoon for the folks in Saint Augustine. Happily, thanks to Lou's skill, the crew's hard work, and help from the boaters on the dock, we got tied up after several thrilling attempts with no harm to our boat, any other boat, or anyone onboard. Isn't boating fun?!

Now that the boat and crew were safe and our hearts had stopped pounding, it was time for a serious cocktail hour. Lou and Judy were meeting one of Lou's cousins for dinner, so Ed, Pat, and I headed across the Bridge of Lions to the A1A Ale House, which was jammed with people of all ages. We found seats at the bar, and once we looked around, determined rather quickly that we were in for an interesting evening.

The band was playing some great music, and the "people-watching" was terrific. Next to Pat, an older guy was trying to pick up a much younger woman — a futile attempt at best. A wedding party was celebrating; young people were trying out their best pickup lines on each other, and a 20-something-year-old guy offered to buy Pat a shooter and shots for Ed and me. What luck!

The food was excellent along with all the entertainment the patrons and band provided, and after a few hours, we walked back across the bridge to the boat, wondering what tomorrow's adventure would bring.

During the night, a cold front passed through the area, leaving behind brisk north winds, cool temperatures, and rain. The light winds, calm seas, warm temperatures, and sun were now only pleasant memories as we continued north through the Florida Intracoastal Waterway and into Georgia.

Traveling the Georgia Intracoastal Waterway can be challenging for several reasons: Boaters encounter tidal ranges that can run 10 feet or more. There are swift-running currents and numerous areas of shallow water. That day, though, luck seemed to be smiling on us because we uneventfully crossed each area with skinny water at mid-tide or greater.

The wind continued to blow strongly from the north, and the sun finally came out as we neared the dock just off Saint Simon Sound for our evening tie-up. As we approached the dock, it was evident that this was going to be another white-knuckle docking. The strong wind was blowing us off the dock while a swift current pushed the boat around like a toy. Once again, after a hopeless attempt by me, I turned the helm over to the more experienced Lou to bring the boat in.

We put on another show that day for the folks on the dock, with the dock mistress impatiently yelling sarcastic instructions as we repeatedly tried to throw her our dock lines. After several passes, Lou finally maneuvered us safely in.

This kind of stuff was getting old fast, even after only a few days. Our routine included the entire crew getting up and dressed at 6 a.m. I would check the engines, we would quickly eat breakfast, and the boat would start moving by 7 a.m. We then traveled about 100 miles with the wind on the nose, pounding through waves, and taking water over the bow. After spending a long day in these less-than-pleasant conditions and arriving at our stop for the night around 5 p.m., we would struggle to get into the dock safely. Worn out from the day's adventure, we would eat dinner and retire early, only to start the process over again the next day. This was not exactly my definition of a fun trip.

By 7 a.m. the following morning, under sunny skies and temperatures in the low 50s, we were underway and once more continuing our pilgrimage north. We wound our way through the shallow Georgia Intracoastal Waterway, and as Lou and Ed, who were on the bridge while I napped below, approached Sapelo Sound, they decided that this would be a good time to take a run up the Atlantic Ocean. With the wind out of the northwest, the seas had calmed, and we made good time on this pleasant diversion from the shallow waters of the Intracoastal Waterway. However, as we entered Wassaw Sound, the weather conditions rapidly deteriorated, and by the time we arrived at our destination for the night, the Savannah Yacht Club, it was overcast, windy, and cool.

I was finally able to dock the boat myself without putting on our customary "show" — a most pleasant experience. Our hosts at the Yacht Club, Andrew and Clare, who were friends of Lou and Judy, drove us into downtown Savannah for dinner and groceries, and we all enjoyed a lovely evening of true southern hospitality. On our return to the boat, however, Lou and I were not feeling too well. We would see how we felt in the morning before going on to Charleston, our next port.

The next day, we awoke to temperatures in the low 40s, overcast skies with gale force winds out of the northwest, and a possibility of showers. Neither Lou nor I had improved overnight. I was fatigued, and Lou had some kind of "bug". Yet, being the "tough" men that we are and with the knowledge that we had additional capable crew aboard, we decided to move on.

The trip to Charleston was cold, windy, and occasionally wet. By the time we docked (again without incident), the sun was setting. I was feeling better, but Lou was feeling even worse. Here we were in beautiful Charleston, but we were all so tired that no one wanted to go out to eat. Forget seeing the sights and enjoying this charming southern city. However, we had two excellent cooks onboard who took over dinner preparations. While Ed made his wife's recipe for barbecued chicken, Judy was in the galley baking an apple crisp.

Unfortunately, awhile later, we discovered that drippings from the barbecue grill, which was mounted on the aft deck just above the master cabin, had run down the back of the boat, through an open window, and onto Pat's pillowcase and our new satin bed coverings. Cries and sobs emanated from our cabin as the tearful Admiral made the discovery. She called out, "They're ruined! They're brand new, and they're ruined!" Looking good has always been one of her priorities, but even I had to admit that as much as I liked barbecue sauce, having the smell and stain of it on my pillowcase was a bit much. She finally calmed down after I convinced her that we could get them dry-cleaned after we got home and in the future we would close our cabin's window before grilling. This was just another part of the learning curve as we became accustomed to the nuances of our new boat. Dinner was good though, and as usual, we retired soon afterward.

The next day we followed our typical routine: up at the crack of dawn and on our way by 7 a.m. I felt all right and Lou was questionable, but we were determined to push on. Temperatures were again in the 40s with a brisk north wind. Spring seemed to be coming late to the south.

Part of our morning routine was rolling up the center window of the flybridge enclosure to improve visibility. These windows were made of flexible, clear vinyl. However, as they age, they become dried out, stiff, and difficult to open in cold weather. That day, while we were rolling it up, it shattered and became irreparable. Forget the enclosure providing any protection. We decided we were going to replace all the flybridge canvas anyway.

After we left Charleston Harbor and headed up the waterway toward our next stop, the winds began to subside, and the temperature rose to about 70 degrees — a delightful change from the past few days.

We arrived a few hours later at Pawley's Island, South Carolina, where Ed's wife, Karen, joined our crew. She had been visiting her sister, Bonnie, and brother-in-law, Mike, who live in the area and they had invited us to their home for dinner. Once again, we had another enjoyable evening with good friends. As we sat there, however, I was thinking that tomorrow would be an interesting and challenging day. I would be losing my safety net because our most experienced crew members, Lou and Judy, would be leaving us to drive home to New Jersey.

The next day started out cool and dry as we headed north for South Harbor Village Marina in Southport, North Carolina. The trip went along without incident, and by 2 p.m. we were safely docked. After grateful goodbyes to Lou and Judy for their assistance and friendship on the first half of our journey home, we went out for dinner at a nearby Italian restaurant with Ed and Karen. Afterward, we turned in early, and I went to bed wondering how I would do now that Lou was not there to back me up.

We awoke early, and by 7 a.m. we continued heading north in the North Carolina Intracoastal Waterway. That day, fortunately, there seemed to be a break in the weather because we had lighter winds, partly cloudy skies, and warmer temperatures.

Traveling the Intracoastal Waterway is not always easy because of the various shallow areas that can creep up on you, especially if you are unaware of them. Onboard we were relying on waterway guidebooks and information from the Internet for assistance about some of the worst trouble spots.

Everything was going well that day until early afternoon when Pat called me to come below. "Houston, we have a problem!" The aft head (toilet) was clogged, and though water could come into the bowl, nothing would pump out.

Before going on, let's talk about the marine toilet for a moment. The head can be compared to a beautiful white orchid: both are lovely to look at, they must be treated gently and with great care because they are each delicate, and if they are neglected or mistreated, the results can be unfortunate. I have had considerable experience with heads (not so much with flowers), and on every boat we have ever owned or chartered, I have spent numerous hours with my head in the head, repairing the head, and sometimes the Admiral suggests I'm even sick in the head! It is almost like an art form: Some men work with clay or marble — my specialty is porcelain. If you are a boat owner and claim you've never had an intimate relationship with the head on your boat, you're either a liar or haven't owned a boat for long. Sooner or later, you will have that "pleasure."

I sent Pat up to the flybridge to relieve Ed, who had taken over the helm when I went below to attend to the head issue. "Have Ed come down here and give me a hand. I wouldn't want him to miss out on all the fun." Now we would face a challenge above and below deck. Although the Admiral had spent more than 35 years steering our sailboats, she had limited experience at the helm of this one, and Karen, whose boating experience could be measured in nanoseconds, would now be our navigator, guiding Pat at the helm through the often narrow and sometimes shallow Intracoastal Waterway using the GPS on our laptop computer. I felt a minor "twinge" in my head at this prospect.

The Intracoastal Waterway can be compared to Dorothy's path to the Emerald City, but instead of following the Yellow Brick Road, boaters follow the magenta line on the navigation chart. If you stay on the line, you will travel through the best water — at least in theory.

I was not overly concerned about Pat's helmsmanship because Karen had her eyes glued to the computerized chart, and if the Admiral strayed off the magenta line, Karen would be quick to call for an immediate correction. I also trusted that if they had any problems or questions, Pat was experienced enough to call for assistance.

Going back to the head, without any idea of what was wrong, Ed and I started taking things apart. After some time had passed with the bowl out and resting comfortably in the salon, we determined that there was a clog in the plumbing between the head and the holding tank. We suspected that the discharge hose, where the clog might be, passed from the head through the engine room before passing back through the vanity on its way to the holding tank. So it was time for me to climb down into the engine room for a look-see.

On working my way to the rear of the engine room where I thought the suspect hose could be found, I discovered that the port engine packing nut, which prevents water from coming up the propeller shaft, was leaking profusely. "Houston, we have another problem!" I got a wrench and attempted to loosen the lock nut that held the packing nut in place. Suddenly the engines slowed to idle, and their transmissions went into neutral.

Ed called down to me that I was needed on the bridge right away. I left the leak and hurried to the bridge to see what was going on. An old wives' tale is that things happen in threes. Well, here was No. 3.

Once on the bridge, I spotted the dilemma. Pat had wisely stopped the boat because she had spotted an uncharted buoy in what appeared to be the middle of the channel. The last thing we wanted to do was to pass a buoy on the wrong side in the Intracoastal Waterway because doing so could likely put us aground. As we approached the red buoy, we noticed that it did not have an official Intracoastal Waterway identification on it. I took my best guess that it was probably a temporary inlet buoy that had gone adrift from a nearby channel and maneuvered around it. After safely passing it on what we estimated to be its best side, The Admiral took the helm once again, and I went back to the leaking packing nut.

I made several more unsuccessful attempts at loosening the lock nut and finally gave up. The bilge pump kept up with the flow of water, and as long as the leak did not get any worse, we would be all right until we pulled in for the night.

I then went back to tracing the head discharge line through the engine room. After contorting my 6-foot-2-inch, 225-pound body into places and positions in which it was never intended to be, I eventually found the offending hose. Finally after some time and the use of numerous "colorful" words, I was able to disconnect the hose to find that it was packed solid with "debris." It could not be cleared underway, so this, too, would have to wait until we stopped that night.

Leaving the toilet bowl sitting in the middle of the salon, Ed and I got something to drink and went up to the bridge to enjoy the rest of the day. We just love boating — especially sewage jobs!

Around 4 p.m., we docked safely for the evening. Ed and I quickly left the boat, and with the determination of men possessed, we took turns literally beating the "crap" out of the head hose on the dock, a disgusting job at best. It was not long before the hose heaved out its contents all over the place. After cleaning off the dock and flushing any remains out of the hose, we hooked it back up in the engine room, and the bowl was returned to its rightful place in the head.

The leaking packing nut was another matter. I checked with the owner of the marina to see if he had a wrench large enough to free the lock nut on the propeller shaft. He did not but suggested an alternative — albeit unorthodox — method for removing it. "Hit it with a hammer!" he said. Taking his advice, I went into the engine room with hammer in hand and started whacking the lock nut in a clockwise motion. This was excellent therapy for me as the Captain. First I got to beat the head hose, and now I could beat up on the lock nut.

Much to my surprise, the locking nut began to turn, and in moments it was loose enough to tighten the packing nut. Once tightened, I set the locking nut back in place and beat it again, thus solving our leak problem and releasing some stress.

There was a celebratory mood throughout the boat. We had not gone aground, the Admiral's head was working, and we were not sinking! All was right in the world. Ed and I even talked about going into business together with our new-found talents. We later celebrated our triumph of "man over machine" with a toast and a quiet dinner aboard, and then as had become usual, we turned in early, having had another wonderful time on the Intracoastal Waterway.

The next day was somewhat uneventful as we continued to follow the magenta line through North Carolina, eventually passing through the Neuse and Pamlico Rivers, some of the largest waters on the Intracoastal Waterway. This was real sailing country, especially near Oriental, known as the "Sailing Capital of the U.S.," a title the town had given itself. As the day wore on, we could feel that the wind speed had increased as we made our way up the Pungo River to an anchorage just southwest of the Alligator River-Pungo River Canal. Luckily, the wind calmed down a bit overnight, and our anchor held securely.

The following morning under overcast skies with winds out of the southeast at 15 to 20 mph, we made our way through the canal. The canal was somewhat narrow with pine trees lining the shores, and it led us to the Alligator River, which empties into Albemarle Sound. Pat had been concerned about crossing this sound because of its reputation of being a nasty piece of water. However, this was not the case today because conditions on the Sound were overcast skies with only about 1-foot waves. The Admiral and the Captain were pleased.

As we moved into the Sound, we had to make the decision whether to follow the main Intracoastal Waterway route north along the coast or the secondary route that would take us through the Dismal Swamp. Being the adventuresome types that we are, we chose the Dismal Swamp route.

Construction on the Dismal Swamp was started in 1793, and it was not fully operational until 1814. George Washington was one of its original financial backers, and it is rumored that he was the original surveyor. However, there is no proof of that. It was dug entirely by hand to an original width of 40 feet and a depth of 4.5 feet, but years later it was widened and deepened. When you travel on the waterway, you are traveling through a piece of American history.

We followed Albemarle Sound to the Pasquotank River and headed for Elizabeth City, North Carolina. In Elizabeth City, there is free overnight dockage at the city pier, and if several boats stay for the night, the local folks provide a free wine and cheese party in the evening — my kind of town. When we arrived, however, the wind was blowing up the river right into those slips, and with a forecast of overnight thunderstorms, it would not be a comfortable place to stay. We felt it would be in our best interest to continue upriver for a short distance to a quiet cove just beyond a drawbridge, and we anchored securely there for the night.

In planning for the next day's passage, we would have to go through the South Mills Lock at the southern end of the Dismal Swamp Canal. The lock was about 17 miles from our anchorage and opened only at scheduled times, so we decided to shoot for its first opening of the day at 8:30 a.m. To give ourselves plenty of time to get there, we would get underway by 6 a.m. Otherwise, if we missed the 8:30 a.m. lockage, we would have to wait two and a half more hours for the 11 a.m. opening.

After a night of thunderstorms, we were up and on our way early on this dark, cold, and drizzly morning. In just a few short miles, the Pasquotank River narrowed considerably, and as dawn broke, the trees began closing in from the banks. The upper Pasquotank was snug and winding, and it felt like we were transiting a primitive area that time had forgotten, with just the sound of bird calls accompanying the sight of low tree branches hanging into the water, tree stumps lining the shores, and drizzle in the air. The scene was dismal before we even got to the Dismal Swamp!

To have a similar experience to Humphrey Bogart and Katherine Hepburn in the movie, "African Queen," head up the Pasquotank River. I was concerned that, like Bogie, I was going to have to get out and pull us through! As the river meandered along, it narrowed to the point that we were not sure what we would do if another boat our size tried to pass us coming the other way.

We eventually came to a junction in the river and spotted a small sign nailed to a tree, which pointed the way to the South Mills Lock. As we passed the sign and went around a bend, in front of us were the lock doors. It was 7:45 a.m. and the lock tender verified he would open them for us at 8:30 a.m. Because we were early, I asked him if there was any place we could tie up while we waited. He said we could tie up to a group of pilings just outside the lock or could just idle there until he opened. We chose the latter because the former did not look promising, and for the next 45 minutes, I kept maneuvering us in this narrow channel, keeping the boat away from the low-hanging trees and stumps and as close to the center line as possible.

Finally at 8:30 a.m., the lock doors opened and we got the green light to enter. As I guided the boat close to her designated spot along the lock wall, the sky opened and it poured down rain in buckets. Ed tossed a bowline to the lock tender, and Pat threw one from the stern.

The lock tender closed the doors, and as soon as we began our lift, a catamaran pulled up outside the lock, and the lock tender told him he would have to wait for the next lift. Timing is everything!

During the 8-foot lift, Pat and Ed had to man their respective lines by taking them in as the boat rose while the rain was coming down in torrents. I was not fairing much better than the deck crew because the Bimini top over the flybridge was leaking like a sieve, and with the center enclosure window gone, the rain poured in on me. Once we finished locking through, the rain subsided to a drizzle.

As we left the lock and entered the 20-mile Dismal Swamp canal, it was evident that it would live up to its name. Gray sky, drizzle, low overhanging trees, the narrow and shallow path (about 50 feet wide and 6 feet deep), and the dark cedar water added to the bleak atmosphere. The only things missing were alligators and dinosaurs to complete the picture.

The entire canal is a "No-Wake" zone, so at the slow speed we had to travel to be compliant, we calculated that we would miss the 11 a.m. lockage at Deep Creek at the other end of the canal. We slowed the boat to about 5 knots so as not to arrive too early for the 1:30 p.m. lockage and prayed that no other boat would pass us in the narrow waterway. This pace gave the crew time to take hot showers and put on dry clothes, and we moved the operation of the boat to its lower interior steering station, which allowed everyone to keep dry.

Once again we arrived early and held our position in the canal, while waiting for the next opening. As we entered this lock, in the words of Yogi Berra, "It's déjà vu all over again." It started pouring rain as hard as it did when we went through the first lock. Pat and Ed went back to their line handling on deck, and within a short time they were soaked again, and just like before, as we left the lock, the rain all but stopped. Times like these make you fall in love with boating!

After leaving the lock, the scene rapidly changed from primeval forest to industrial waterfront as we joined the main Intracoastal Waterway route at the Elizabeth River. By 4 p.m. we were tied up for the night in Portsmouth, Virginia, across from one of the many Navy floating dry docks that line the area. Although we were not in our home waters just yet, we were in familiar waters, having traveled to the Norfolk/Portsmouth area in the past on our sailboat.

We spent the rest of the afternoon drying out and cleaning up the boat and were ready for a travel break. Tomorrow's weather forecast was for rain and wind on the open waters of Chesapeake Bay. We had been traveling without a stopover for 11 consecutive days, so we thought that it was a good time to hold up and recoup.

The forecasters were right, and overnight, the wind came up and the rain came down, so we stayed put. We got some much-needed rest that day. The extra day also gave Pat and Karen a chance to do laundry at the marina and go grocery shopping using the marina courtesy car. That evening, we all went out for a lovely dinner in town.

We love courtesy cars. As cruisers, in our planning we look for marinas that have one and always call ahead to see if one is available at our next stop. The convenience of being able to drive to the local market, do laundry, or stop in at the drugstore instead of lugging our purchases or clothes back to the boat on a cart is wonderful. It also provides us with the opportunity to tour the surrounding areas near our ports. I am always amazed at the variety and condition of the vehicles. We have driven everything from fairly new Mercedes Benzes to pickup trucks with the floorboards nearly gone. As long as the brakes work, we are good to go. Today's model was a high-mileage Buick that shook and rattled as it rolled down the road, but it got us to our planned stops.

The following day, the wind lightened up and the rain stopped, so we headed up the Elizabeth River, past the Norfolk Naval Base, (the largest naval base in the world), through Hampton Roads, and into Chesapeake Bay.

While leaving Hampton Roads, however, the fog rolled in and our visibility dropped to nearly zero.

We picked up an image on the radar — a large image. Then we heard a blast from a ship's horn, and its radar blip was heading toward us about a mile and a half away. I quickly headed for the edge of the channel as a security warning came on the VHF radio for all vessels to stay clear of the approaching vessel. The radar image continued to grow larger, and then suddenly through the fog, we could spot Coast Guard and Marine Police vessels. The reason for the security zone became quickly apparent as a large cruise ship heading for Norfolk appeared out of the mist off our port bow. She was as high as a large apartment building and several football fields long and was something to which we did not want to get close in pea soup fog. Almost as fast as the ship appeared, it disappeared in the fog behind us.

Once clear of the ship, we headed north on Chesapeake Bay toward Solomons, Maryland. The rest of the morning was spent dodging other ghostly images that appeared on the radar, which were mostly tugs towing barges, but none were as dramatic as the cruise ship. By mid-afternoon, the fog finally lifted for the day and the sun came out through high clouds, which made the rest of our trip pleasant.

On arriving at Solomons, we fueled up and headed for our favorite marina where we thought we could tie up. As we approached our assigned spot, though, I got "the look" from the Admiral. The dock was old and not in the greatest shape, so tying up would be difficult, and getting on and off the boat would be a challenge. But being stubborn sometimes, I ignored Pat's wishes and attempted to dock the boat anyway. There is not much I will not do for Maryland crab cakes. The Admiral was less than cooperative in helping to bring the boat in, and after finally admitting to myself that she was right and it was not the best spot, she got her way and we moved to another marina. I, the Captain, was outranked again!

Bringing the boat into the next marina was easy, and I proudly thought I was getting pretty good at this docking business. Safely docked, we settled in for the night with our usual routine of cocktails followed by dinner. The next day we would head up to Chesapeake City on the Chesapeake and Delaware Canal (C&D Canal) at the top of Chesapeake Bay.

We were on our way again about 7 a.m. under partly cloudy skies with light winds. The trip north was tranquil, and we arrived at the small anchorage off the

C&D Canal in the mid-afternoon, got the hook (anchor) set in as far away from other boats as we could, and settled in for the night.

Early the next morning, our crew was up and ready before dawn for the 100-plus-mile trip to Atlantic City, our final stop before home. Entering the C&D Canal must always be done with caution, especially in the dark. There is large ship traffic in the canal, and when two ships are passing each other, there is little room left for pleasure craft. It has been reported that this waterway carries more commercial tonnage than the Panama Canal, so it is important to keep a sharp lookout. Fortunately, there are no locks on the canal, and on this morning, there were no ships.

We entered the Delaware River just after dawn. It is important to always travel the Delaware River and Bay in good weather. These waters can carry considerable current, and when you have an opposing strong wind and tide situation, a steep chop will build that can be extremely uncomfortable. As we headed downriver, the current was against us, and the wind was light. Soon the current changed, and we rode the outgoing tide southeast well into Delaware Bay with less than 1-foot seas.

As we approached Miah Maull Shoal Light on the bay, Ed was at the helm with Pat on watch, Karen was taking a nap on a couch in the salon, and I was emerging from the head. Suddenly Ed called down to me that there was a large ship heading toward us — and fast! I ran up to the bridge to find that the ship was still a few miles away but was quickly closing in on us. I took the helm and headed the boat outside the ship channel into safer waters, yet it was still a problem because the ship was throwing bow waves, each about 4 feet high. There was little I could do except to slow the boat to idle and hit the waves head-on.

This was by no means a dangerous situation. Our boat could easily ride over waves of this size, and she did. However, they were steep, and when we came down the backside of the first wave, we heard a crash come from the salon, and after the last wave passed, Pat ran below to see what had happened.

Next to the couch was a counter on which had rested an old-style heavy TV. However, when Pat got below, she found that the TV had launched itself off the counter when the bow waves hit our boat and had bounced off the couch, just missing Karen, and finally hit the deck. Luckily, Karen was not hurt, and neither was the TV or the boat.

There were lessons to be learned here: First, stay as far away as possible from fast-moving ships, and second, no matter how heavy an object is on a boat, make sure it is secured.

Shortly after the incident, we turned away from the shipping channel and headed for the Cape May Canal (another sea level waterway). The canal connects Delaware Bay to Cape May Harbor and the Atlantic Ocean beyond. We passed through the canal and harbor quickly and soon found ourselves heading north toward Atlantic City in the dark blue Atlantic. The ocean was kind to us with waves about 1 to 3 feet from the stern, which eventually became a gentle swell.

We arrived at Gardner's Basin Marina in Atlantic City about 3 p.m., and Cousin Ed and his wife, Karen, left the boat to begin the drive back to their home in New Hampshire. They were amazingly gracious in giving up their time to make this journey with us, and we were grateful to them for their help. Around 6 p.m., our friends Lou and Judy, who had started the trip with us, returned to the boat for our final push home the following day. Our other friends and neighbors Tony and Evelyn drove them to Atlantic City. We truly had a full support team.

We had dinner out that evening and celebrated our return to New Jersey. After dinner, Tony and Evelyn headed back home by car, and the rest of us turned in before 10 p.m. The next day would be a big one for us, as we were nearing our final destination in familiar waters with only another 64 miles to go. Pat and I were excited that at the same time the next day, our new boat would be docked behind our home.

There were two ways to get to our home off Barnegat Bay: one was the short route up the Atlantic coast to Barnegat Inlet — one of the most notorious inlets on the east coast but one we know well — and the second was to travel through the New Jersey Intracoastal Waterway, a longer but protected route that only vessels of 4-foot draft or less should transit. We chose the inside route that day because we found out that Oyster Creek Channel, which leads from Barnegat Inlet to the bay, had shoaled in spots to less than 4 feet at low tide. This condition has since been corrected through a dredging project.

Early the following morning, with temperatures in the 60s and under partly cloudy skies, we were on our way home. As we entered the New Jersey Intracoastal Waterway, we noticed that the tide was low and getting lower. It did not take us long to find out how low. Coming around a turn, the boat suddenly stopped, much to everyone's surprise. We had traveled 1,300-plus miles through shallow waters in several states but on our last day out we found the bottom in familiar waters. I checked the depth sounder and it showed that we were in 8 feet of water.

At first, we could not understand what had just happened. Nothing made sense. Then I realized that the depth sounder transducer was located about mid-ship, and when we came around the last turn, without realizing it, we went out of the channel. This meant that the bow was in less than 4 feet of water while the stern was in more than 8 feet. Luckily, the bottom in the waterway was soft mud, so all it took to get us back to deep water was putting the engines in reverse, and we easily floated off.

The rest of our trip home through Barnegat Bay that day was uneventful. We arrived home about 12:30 p.m. and were greeted by my sister, Pat, and her husband, Al, who were house-sitting for us, along with friends and neighbors. As we docked our boat after traveling 16 days and 1,387 miles, it was good to hear the sound of champagne corks popping. Let the party begin!

We celebrated that afternoon, and the party went on for hours with an additional dinner that evening, hosted by our neighbors, Tony and Evelyn. It was good to be home.

I felt happy and was content with the performance of the boat we had purchased. We had learned a lot on this journey about our vessel and ourselves, and except for a few minor problems, everything and everyone performed extremely well. I was looking forward to making upgrades to the boat, and I figured we would be heading out in early June to do the Great Loop.

The Admiral had other plans.

Chapter 3

Primping for the Big Date

at now informed me that before we set off for the Great Loop, she would like to modernize the boat. Because the boat was built in 1987, she felt that the interior and exterior could use some updating. Soon, a list of items as long as my arm emerged. It included everything from all new furniture and cushions to completely refinishing the laminate surfaces on the boat. The list seemed endless. To this I added updated electronics and new house batteries. The word "boat" stands for "Bust Out Another Thousand," and we did — many of them. My head was reeling! It was obvious that the boat was going nowhere this year.

We are not superstitious people, but we do respect certain nautical traditions. So in late June, we took a break from working on the boat to give *Reflection*, as she would be named, a time-honored champagne christening.

Pat was to do the honors because she had christened our previous boats. So with centuries of tradition behind her and more than 30 close friends and family looking on, Pat gave a short speech and struck the bottle across *Reflection's* anchor. Nothing happened, so she hit it again, and again, and again! It just would not break! (Luckily this was a boat, not a baby we were christening!) So now I gave it a try. I took the bottle in both hands and with all the strength I could muster, struck the anchor. The bottle finally exploded, and champagne and pieces of glass flew all over the bow and us. A long-awaited rousing cheer rose from those in attendance.

The rest of the summer we spent working on the list of upgrades, and in early October, we took *Reflection* to a local boat yard and had her hauled out of the water. After a quick inspection, it was obvious that sandblasting the bottom was in order.

By November, the sandblasting company made its appearance. I was there to watch the progress and was concerned when black marks appeared on the bottom after the paint was removed. Apparently, gel-coat blisters under the paint broke open during the sandblasting. However, under the gel-coat, instead of finding fiberglass and resin, an unknown hard black substance was uncovered.

The company doing the sandblasting told us how to take care of the blister problem: Give them $20,000 to 30,000 and they would strip the gel coat off the bottom and redo it. However, I was not naïve regarding boat repairs, so I took a pass on their suggestion and decided to do some research to figure out what to do.

In contacting a representative from the manufacturer of the boat, I was told that under no circumstances should I remove the black material. It was a barrier coat protecting the fiberglass from water intrusion. The gel-coat was merely a cosmetic covering. After some additional research, I found an excellent epoxy putty that would repair the voids left by the blisters.

Again boating, January, and New Jersey do not belong in the same sentence. The same goes for repairing the bottom of a boat outside during a New Jersey winter, but that is what we did. Throughout the winter, whenever the temperature rose above 40 degrees and the wind was light, I was under the boat repairing the bottom.

By March, the repairs were successfully completed, the bottom was sanded smooth and painted, and all the underwater gear was serviced. After launching in early April, *Reflection* came back home for her final outfitting before the targeted departure date for our Great Loop adventure — June 5, 2009. She was looking good, and although she would not be the youngest girl at the party, she could still turn a head or two!

While all this work on the boat was going on, we were also planning the trip around the Loop. We are not Lewis and Clark, but traveling through unfamiliar waters with a boat still new to the captain and crew would take some preparation.

First, there was the consideration of time and how long we could be away from home. We considered whether to complete the Loop in a year, continue to follow the sun and keep moving toward the warm weather, or make it a multi-year journey. We considered how far we would have to travel each day to find anchorages or marinas that could take a boat of our size. Other considerations were fuel capacity and range. We wondered if we could travel long distances between fill-ups. Then we had to consider bridge heights and our inexperience traveling through locks. We wanted to be safe and comfortable and considered how many open ocean and Great Lake crossings we wanted to make.

We decided we would complete the Loop in about one year. With that in mind, instead of attempting to plan the entire trip, we planned the trip by segment. For the first leg of the journey, we would have four possible routes that would take us from our familiar home waters in Brick, New Jersey, to our destination of choice: Trenton, Ontario, the beginning of the Trent-Severn Waterway.

The first and longest navigation route was to hug the Atlantic coast sailing past the spectacular sites of Nova Scotia. On arriving at this famed seagoing area of the world, we could then enter the Saint Lawrence Seaway north of Quebec, Canada, and follow the Seaway directly to Lake Ontario. The enticements to take this route were that we would view the beautiful sites of the New England coast topped off by the quaint ruggedness of Nova Scotia and visit the old city of Quebec and bustling Montreal. However, following this "Down East" route would add additional time to the trip, and more days on the open and unpredictable Atlantic Ocean. The Bay of Fundy in the spring might be spectacular, but no matter how majestic the scenery is, having had previous experiences on the North Atlantic, the Admiral was always looking to limit her days on those ocean waters.

The second route would direct us up the New Jersey coast through New York Harbor and along the Hudson River to Waterford, New York, where we would continue north through the Champlain Canal into Lake Champlain and on to the Saint Lawrence Seaway. Traveling through this area would be scenic and filled with early American history.

 The Hudson River is a beautiful natural resource running north and south through New York State. The lower Hudson River is a fjord with water depths reaching more than 100 feet and cliffs rising hundreds of feet on each side. The Champlain Canal runs along the foothills of the Adirondack Mountains through some of the most rural, remote, and picturesque country on the East Coast. Lake Champlain with its deep crystal clear waters, which some argue should be considered another of North America's Great Lakes, was the birth place of the American Navy.

Although this route sounded like a winner, it had one insurmountable problem: low bridges. Even with our radar arch lowered, we would not be able to safely sneak under many of the overpasses. Scratch another route off the list.

The third route would take us up the Hudson River again to Waterford, New York, but this time we would turn west through the 363-mile Erie Canal across New York State to Buffalo, New York, on Lake Erie.

Although traveling the full length of the historical waterway would be scenic and educational, the route had two major problems: The bridges on the western half of the canal would be too low for the height requirements of *Reflection*, and we would exit the canal in Lake Erie, not Lake Ontario, so another route bit the dust.

Finally, the fourth option would be to exit the Erie Canal about halfway across New York State into the Oswego Canal leading us directly to Lake Ontario. This canal opened in 1828 and is only 23.7 miles long. It connects the Erie Canal at Three Rivers (near Liverpool) to Lake Ontario at Oswego. The canal has a comfortable depth for a boat the size of *Reflection*, with seven locks spanning the 118-foot change in elevation. We ultimately chose this route because we knew there were no bridge height clearance problems for us and it would also be the most direct path to Lake Ontario and the Trent-Severn Waterway.

With our plans made, as late May rolled around, we were in our final preparations for departure. Our expected departure date was June 5, and with time running short, things got a little hectic because we were still making minor repairs to *Reflection* and provisioning her.

Pat's brother, Father Tony, who is a Catholic priest, came to see *Reflection* and blessed our vessel, praying for us and for our safe journey around the Loop. He left Pat with a bottle of Holy Water to carry with us if we were ever in a situation where we needed to ask God for extra help along the way. Pat immediately put it in her nightstand next to our bed onboard so she would always have it close at hand.

Our neighbors surprised us with a Bon Voyage party. We were grateful for their gifts and good wishes, and we felt especially blessed to have such terrific friends. The anticipation for our departure was building, and it began to sink in that this long-awaited trip was going to happen.

As the day of departure grew near, I knew how General Eisenhower felt before the D-Day invasion. The weather prediction for the Atlantic Ocean between Manasquan Inlet and New York Harbor was for northeast winds of 15 to 20 knots and seas of 3 to 5 feet with a 60 percent chance of rain. The next day's outlook seemed better with northeast winds of 10 to 15 knots coming south, seas of 3 to 4 feet, sunshine, and zero percent chance of rain. We were in a quandary as to whether we should leave as planned or wait for the better weather the next day, so I consulted with a local meteorologist to make the call. After weighing several factors, we decided the weather and sea conditions would be more favorable if we waited a day.

All the best leaders have to make tough command decisions. That is why I am paid the "big bucks" to be the Captain! We would leave in two days — or so we hoped.

Chapter 4

And So It Begins. . .

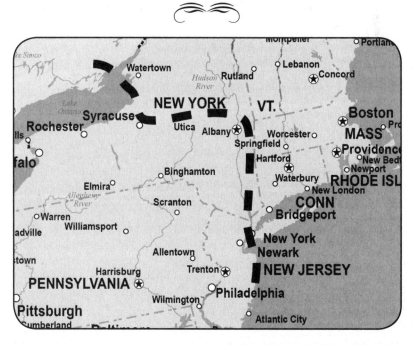

June 6 — 46 miles to Liberty State Park, Jersey City, New Jersey[1]

D-Day had finally arrived — the long-awaited departure day for our Great Loop adventure. After putting in more than 13 months of work on *Reflection*, she looked beautiful, and we felt that she was as ready as we could make her for the voyage. Leaving on this journey was not a casual undertaking. During this period, we had to make arrangements for banking and bill-paying, phone and Internet service, mail delivery, our home's care, and we also purchased and studied the guidebooks, charts, and other materials we would need to take the trip. The boat was loaded with clothes for all seasons, groceries, DVDs, and books to read, and by this time, we felt like racehorses at the starting gate. I thought, "We are actually going to do this!"

Joining us for the Hudson River leg of the journey was our friend Charlie. We were happy to have him along. Our neighbors were at our dock to share a champagne toast and to see us off. After hugs, kisses, and tears, we left at 10 a.m. under partly cloudy skies. As our friends waved goodbye from our dock, we waved back, and with a few blasts from *Reflection*'s horn, we were on our way. It was difficult to leave them and the home we loved so much (which they all would be keeping a watchful eye on during our absence), but we were relieved and thrilled to finally be out on the water as we headed north in Barnegat Bay, through the Point Pleasant Canal, and then out Manasquan Inlet on our way to New York Harbor.

Once in the ocean, the sea conditions were good with a 3- to 4-foot gentle swell from the east that rolled the table and chairs on the aft deck. Charlie secured the furniture, and without further problems, we continued up the Atlantic coast. By the time we passed Mount Mitchill and the Twin Lights at Highlands, New Jersey, the sun was shining and the seas became a gentle roll from the south.

 Mount Mitchill is the highest natural point on the Atlantic Seaboard between southern Maine and the Yucatan Peninsula of Mexico. It rises 266 feet above sea level, but few people are aware of this fact or have ever even heard of Mount Mitchill. Also located nearby is the Twin Lights Lighthouse situated 200 feet above sea level atop the Navesink Highlands. Although decommissioned, Twin Lights has stood as a sentinel over the treacherous coastal waters of northern New Jersey since 1828.

We entered Lower Bay and headed toward the Narrows with the Verrazano-Narrows Bridge clearly in sight and the magnificent New York City skyline gleaming in the distance.

 The Verrazano-Narrows Bridge is a double-decked suspension bridge that connects the boroughs of Staten Island and Brooklyn in New York City at The Narrows. The bridge is named after the Italian explorer Giovanni da Verrazzano, the first known European navigator to enter New York Harbor and the Hudson River, and for the body of water it spans, the Narrows. Unfortunately there is a spelling difference between the last name posted on the bridge, and that of its namesake!

As we arrived in the Upper Bay, we worked our way through a fleet of tour boats in New York Harbor to get a view of the Statue of Liberty before heading west for our anchorage behind the statue. Because I had worked in New York City for years, and Pat and Charlie also knew it well, we passed up another visit and opted instead for an anchorage with a magnificent view of the city.

The Statue of Liberty in upper New York Harbor

We anchored the boat in a spot alongside Liberty State Park, which is located behind the Statue of Liberty on the New Jersey side of the Hudson River. Once settled in, we celebrated our first day on the Loop with a champagne toast while the setting sun lit up the Manhattan skyline in a golden glow. We were thrilled to be there and were off to a good start.

June 7 — 82 miles to Kingston, New York

After a peaceful evening at anchor, we began the trip up the Hudson River by following the cruise ship *Norwegian Dawn* as she returned from the sea to her berth in New York City under clear skies this morning. The scenery changed dramatically along the way, from the skyscrapers of New York to the New Jersey Palisades, as we passed north of the George Washington Bridge, a double-decked suspension bridge that connects New Jersey to New York. A hefty toll is collected on the New Jersey side of the Hudson River crossings, and it is referred to as the New York City "cover charge."

The Palisades are a line of steep cliffs rising hundreds of feet along the west side of the lower Hudson River in northeastern New Jersey and southern New York. The cliffs were formed about 200 million years ago at the close of the Triassic Period and were originally connected to Morocco.

The Hudson River north of West Point
Technically, the river is a fjord, as is evident in the picture above.

As we continued north of the Governor Malcolm Wilson Tappan Zee Bridge to Haverstraw Bay, we encountered sailboats and even antique sailing vessels that were in the area to celebrate the 400th Anniversary of Henry Hudson's original voyage. The view along the way was lovely as we motored passed lighthouses, mansions, the U.S. Military Academy at West Point with its majestic buildings visible from the river, and lush foliage along the shoreline.

 West Point was founded in 1802 under the administration of Thomas Jefferson, and its graduates have fought in every war or conflict in American history since the War of 1812.

A lighthouse along the Hudson

We arrived at Kingston after a trip of 82 miles.

A small group of immigrants from Holland who moved from Albany first settled Kingston in 1652. In the summer of 1777, it became the first capital of New York, but in the fall of 1777, the British burned it down. Easy come, easy go!

As we approached the Kingston City Marina, we were instructed to tie up in a rather tight space between a tour boat and the end of the dock, and I maneuvered *Reflection* slowly towards it. We had not had to tie her up to a pier other than the one at our house for more than a year, and I did not want to put on a show for the locals. As I got close to the spot, Pat tossed her line to the dockhand but it fell short into the water. She retrieved it and then threw it again harder but she only achieved the same result.

The current in Rondout Creek kept pushing us off the dock, and I had flashbacks of our difficult docking experiences in Saint Augustine and Saint Simons the previous year. Finally, after more maneuvering, the dockhand caught Pat's line on her third toss. Charlie then successfully threw his line from the stern and we were in.

The Rondout area of Kingston where we stayed was quaint, and the marina was located in a park-like setting with restaurants and shops nearby. We had a lovely dinner that evening at the Mariner's Harbor Restaurant, which was only steps away from our boat and next to the waterfront. *Reflection* was two days into the trip, and all was well.

June 8 — 59 miles to Waterford, New York (Lock 1) [2-3]

We decided to travel 59 miles up to Waterford instead of anchoring in the Hudson River as we had originally planned because the weather report predicted heavy rain for the next day.

Approaching the Troy Lock

Despite a late start, we quickly made our way north, passing scenery that changed dramatically from rural to industrial at Albany. In 1797, the capital of New York was moved from Kingston to Albany, which is also New York State's sixth largest city. Farther on, we reached Troy Lock, which is also known as Lock 1, the first of 104 locks through which we would eventually pass. As we approached it, we covered the starboard side of *Reflection* with fenders (big, round rubber things known as "bumpers" to the folks in New Jersey) to protect her from the lock's concrete walls.

As we entered the lock, I remembered an aerial view of the lock and dam that I had seen on Google Earth. The dam and waterfall it created were impressive on the computer screen, and they were even more impressive in person. I kept thinking that once we exited the lock at the top there would be a 24-foot waterfall just a few hundred feet to port. This was unsettling because we had always traveled at sea level, so I wanted to make sure I kept us clear of it.

We were the only boat in the lock, which made maneuvering easy, but as lock newbies, we still gently bumped the starboard bow rub rail against the wall — a rookie mistake. This taught us a valuable lesson in that it was not the number of fenders we used but their placement that mattered. For the next 103 locks, we only needed three fenders to protect *Reflection*: one in the bow where we would touch the wall, one oversized fender amidships, and one in the aft quarter. This combination served us well for the entire trip.

After small maneuvering, Charlie was able to loop a line around a pipe recessed in the lock wall that would guide us to the top as the lock was flooded. Once set, it was a smooth lift up 24 feet to the top. *Reflection* would not return to sea level for more than five months.

Exiting the lock was easy, so by 5:30 p.m., we were tied up to the floating dock at the Visitors Center in Waterford.

 The village of Waterford is the oldest incorporated village in the country, having been incorporated in 1794 before the town was formed, and it has been host to "Canal Fest" and the "Tugboat Roundup" for years.

We were docked just yards from the first lock on the Erie Canal, joining several other boats that had arrived earlier who were also doing the Great Loop.

Identifying other loopers is easy. Most of us making the journey belong to the America's Great Loop Cruisers' Association (AGLCA) and fly a burgee with the association's logo (a map of the eastern portion of North America with the route of the Loop traced on it) and the letters AGLCA. When we see other loopers at the dock, it is customary to say hello and exchange boat cards (business cards for boaters). Our fellow travelers often share stories and valuable information, and if enough loopers are gathered, an impromptu dock party ensues.

June 9 — Waterford, New York[4-5]

After a rainy morning, the weather cleared enough for us to walk to nearby Lock 2, the first lock in the Erie Canal. (The Troy Lock is considered Lock 1, although it is not on the Erie Canal.)

 Proposed in 1808 and completed in 1825, the Erie Canal links the waters of Lake Erie in the west to the Hudson River in the east. It is an engineering marvel dug by hand to an original depth of 4 feet and a width of 40 feet, and when it was built, some called it "The Eighth Wonder of the World". It has been improved many times and now contains 36 locks and encompasses a total elevation differential of about 565 feet.

At Lock 2, we purchased our ten-day lock pass and had a conversation with Leroy, the lock tender, who gave us tips on safely negotiating the locks. We then got a personal tour of the tug *Urger*, which was tied up near the lock.

The tugboat *Urger* was built in 1901, went into service on the Canal in 1922, and is venerated as one of the oldest working vessels in the country that is still afloat. Stationed in Waterford, *Urger* served more than 60 years hauling machinery, dredges, and scows on the Erie and Champlain Canals until she was retired from service in the 1980s.

The tugboat **Urger** *on the Erie Canal with our friend Charlie getting ready to go aboard*

In the evening we went out for dinner at McGreivey's, a local restaurant where we toasted Charlie, who would be leaving us the next morning, and we looked forward to the arrival of my sister, Pat, and our brother-in-law, Al, who would join us tomorrow and stay aboard for several weeks.

June 10 — Waterford, New York

We rented a car early in the day and had a fabulous breakfast at Don & Paul's, an eatery packed with colorful locals drinking coffee, dining, and playing pool. Afterward, I drove Charlie to the Albany train station for his return home. Pat and I were happy and grateful that he was able to spend time with us on the beginning of the journey.

There were boats of all kinds from far-away places (Vancouver, San Francisco, Toronto, North Carolina, and Tennessee) at the dock getting ready to transit the Canal. We stocked the boat up with more supplies, picked up my sister and Al at the train, on which they had traveled up from Richmond, Virginia, and celebrated their arrival with a Chinese dinner aboard.

We had been sitting at Waterford for three days, and I was getting antsy to get moving again. Yet, I was apprehensive about the locks ahead after having bumped the wall at the Troy Lock. I was hoping that the old adage "Practice makes perfect" was true.

June 11 — 21 miles to Schenectady, New York (Locks 2-7) [6-7]

After another breakfast at Don & Paul's, we returned our rental car and departed the dock at 9:15 a.m. I maneuvered *Reflection* in front of Lock 2 and called the lock tender for an opening. We were about to begin the Waterford Flight, a series of five locks through which we would be lifted 169 feet in a 2-mile span. This was accomplished by entering each lock and looping an amidships line around a cable on the lock wall. While the lock was being flooded, Pat adjusted the line as needed during the lift, and my sister and Al used boat hooks to fend the boat off the wall, a process that worked well.

About a half-mile after exiting the fifth lock, we passed Crescent Dam. Just 500 feet to our port side was a more than 100-foot drop over a waterfall that the dam created. Similar to passing by the dam at the Troy Lock, this again was unsettling for us, but something we would soon get used to. After this series of locks, we passed through one more before arriving at the Schenectady Yacht Club in the early afternoon.

That evening, we enjoyed watching club members come and go from their Thursday night barbecue on the dockmaster's porch. Onboard, we had a luscious welcome dinner and toasted our trip with a cold bottle of Veuve Clicquot champagne. As Baroque music lilted from the CD player, I raised my champagne flute and thought wryly to myself, "Now, this is roughin' it!"

June 12 – 21 miles to Amsterdam, New York (Locks 8-10) [8]

After a heavy overnight rain, we got on our way by about 10 a.m. We passed through three locks as we traversed 21 miles on the Mohawk River area of the canal.

The Mohawk River had long been important to transportation and migration to the west as a passage through the Appalachian Mountains and is located between the Catskill Mountains and Allegheny Plateau to the south and the Adirondack Mountains to the north. The scenery is lovely and the water, quite placid, often mirrors the reflection of the sky and trees.

Reflection docked at Riverlink Park in Amsterdam, New York

Samira, an express cruiser owned by John and Donna from the Chicago area, accompanied us. They had begun the Loop in September 2008 and had enjoyed the trip so much thus far that they wanted to do it again.

We arrived in Amsterdam, New York, around 1:30 p.m. and tied up to the dock at Riverlink Park. Though a fee was supposed to be collected, no one ever came around to collect anything.

[8] *See notes on page 60*

The Dutch first settled Amsterdam in about 1710. The completion of the Erie Canal in 1825 was an economic boon to the city, and a dam on the Chuctenunda River, finished in 1875, allowed the city to become an important manufacturing area, primarily of carpets. Unfortunately, it has fallen on hard times.

After lunch, we took the pedestrian walkway from our dock over the railroad tracks into town. Downtown proved to be small and somewhat depressed. We passed the Professional Wrestlers Hall of Fame, but unfortunately it was closed. However, we invited John and Donna for happy hour and enjoyed a delightful evening listening to the stories they had about their Loop adventure.

June 13 — 23 miles to Canajoharie, New York (Locks 11-13)[9]

On this day, we lifted through three locks on route to Canajoharie. After we tied up at Riverfront Park, we walked around the town. The Beech-Nut Company had a large factory here, and the company was putting on a picnic for its employees and their families. We thought that was nice until we found out that the plant was closing and that the event was a farewell party! The Beech-Nut factory that had fueled the town's economy for decades was in the process of shutting down, and that situation, along with the community's difficult recovery from the flood of 2006, had affected the business life of the area. It was sad to see.

We toured the Arkell Art Museum, which was located inside the town library, and were pleasantly surprised to find that it contained works by many famous American painters. The museum's collection also included objects and archives related to the Mohawk Valley. The original founders of the Beech-Nut Company had funded the museum throughout the years so their employees would have the opportunity to enjoy fine art. Nothing like picking up a little culture along the way!

As we continued our exploration of the town, we purchased steaks for dinner at a combination of a butcher shop, furniture emporium, and handbag store — all under one roof. How those three things combined together as a business venture boggled the mind. As the weather began to go downhill, we returned to the boat and relaxed and enjoyed a sumptuous meal. There is a first time for everything, and this trip was already proving to be a learning experience.

June 14 – 18 miles to Little Falls, New York (Locks 14-17)[10-11]

We lifted through four locks today and had then climbed to 363 feet above sea level. The last lock looked particularly daunting as we entered it because it was more than 40 feet high. Although we had then passed through 17 locks, each was unique, and this one was no exception. Once inside the lock, we felt small as we looked up at the four-story walls.

The Admiral wearing her work gloves while locking through.

The scenery along the river was lush and beautiful, and it was amazing how few boats were out on the water compared to busy Barnegat Bay near our home in New Jersey. Other boats we had met in the past few days joined us in Little Falls, and we added a new boat from Georgia to our merry band of travelers.

Little Falls was first settled around 1723. The need to portage around the falls promoted the growth of a trading location on the site of the future city, and just as it did to other towns and cities along our route, the Erie Canal brought a boom to the area when it first opened.

[10-11] *See notes on page 60*

June 15 — Look out above — 21 miles to Utica, New York (Locks 18-19)[12-13]

Before we prepared to pass under the CSX railroad bridge just before Lock 19 on the Erie Canal, the check of our chart showed a clearance of 22 feet, which we could clear. With the antennas down, the highest point on *Reflection* is 20 feet 1 inch, which includes the anchor light mounted on a fixed, stainless steel tube above the radar dome. As we neared the bridge itself, however, its height marker showed just less than 21 feet, which we could still successfully clear. So we decided to move ahead slowly, but as we passed under the bridge, I remember looking up and thinking it was going to be tight. Then suddenly I heard a "crunch" and knew we had hit the bridge!

Somebody lied! We could clear 20 feet 1 inch, but the bridge height apparently was 20 feet ½ inch — not what was posted. All we needed was another half-inch to clear it! As we completed our pass, we could hear the anchor light banging off the bridge, but because I was not able to see the light from the helm station, I could not immediately assess the extent of the damage. Fortunately, all that happened was that we broke the plastic mount that fit into the tubing. We did not even break the lens, and the light still worked — amazingly. I later repaired it with electrical tape, and happily, it held together for another ten months until a more permanent repair was finally made.

The bridge that did the damage

The anchor light after hitting the bridge

We ended the day early in Utica, New York.

 Utica was first settled by Europeans in 1773. The town was located there because it was next to the shallowest spot along the Mohawk River, making it the best place for fording across to the other side. It was also situated at an Iroquois Indian crossroads, a spot that made trading exceedingly easy for local merchants.

To compensate for our day's earlier mishap, we had a nice lunch at a local restaurant on the canal and then took a tour of the Matt Brewery Company in town.

 As one of the few remaining American regional breweries, the Matt Brewing Company had prospered at the foothills of the Adirondack Mountains in Central New York for more than a century. Originally founded as the West End Brewing Company in 1888, it quickly became one of the largest and most successful of the 12 breweries operating in Utica at the time and since has earned a reputation as one of the most respected specialty brewers in the country by producing distinctive, flavorful beers.

After attending the tour, we were encouraged to sample as many beers as we desired until we found that one we wanted to drink. The samples were not small, and by the time each of us found the one we particularly liked, "some" of us were well on our way to a comfortable buzz. At this point, the barman would pour another pint or two of our choice. This was an excellent place. All was right in the world once again.

From left to right:
The Captain, his sister Pat, and brother-in-law Al having a beer at the Matt Brewery

June 16 — 29 miles to Sylvan Beach, New York (Locks 20-22)[14]

After having shared a tasty, substantial, thick-crust pizza for dinner followed by a good night's sleep, we got underway early, traveling through three locks on our way to Sylvan Beach. The first lock lifted us to the highest point we would reach on the Erie Canal — 420 feet. Henceforth, in the second and third lock, we began to reverse the process by dropping rather than lifting.

Samira accompanied *Reflection* through the locks, and we both docked at Mariner's Landing Marina in Sylvan Beach. Sylvan Beach was a cute old lakeshore community on Oneida Lake and was just a short walk from our slip. It had 4 miles of beach, cottages, restaurants, and even a small amusement park. As luck would have it, this was "Bikers on the Beach" night, when hundreds of bikers

---

[14] *See notes on page 60*

would converge on the town. We fit right in! None of us got tattoos, but we did have an enjoyable evening watching all the action while eating on the porch of Yesterday's Hotel, which overlooked the lake and the canal.

While sitting at the hotel, I reflected on the trip so far. It is truly a unique experience seeing the country by water and something that few people would ever experience. I am a lucky man!

The **Governor Roosevelt** *towing a barge on the Erie Canal*

June 17-18 — 22 miles to Brewerton, New York[15-16]

We started the day by heading across the first bit of open water we had been out on in days.

Oneida Lake is 20 miles long and lovely, and it is the largest lake entirely in New York State. The lake is a remnant of Lake Iroquois, a large prehistoric lake formed when glaciers blocked the current outlet of the Great Lakes, the Saint Lawrence River. It was named in honor of the Oneida, the Iroquoian tribe that occupied the region.

We also found that crossing the lake was a relaxing change because we did not have to pass through any locks.

Reflection pulled into Winter Harbor Marina in the late morning. Our mail from home was delivered here, and because the weather was supposed to deteriorate the next day with heavy rain, wind, and chilly temperatures in the forecast, we planned to stay put for another day. Boat cleaning (inside and out) and repairing our broken anchor light were on our dockside agenda. Because the facility had two courtesy cars, we also took advantage of having transportation to take care of laundry and shopping.

June 19 — O, Canada — 100 miles to Picton, Ontario (Lock 23 on the Erie Canal, Locks 1-8 on the Oswego Canal)[17-19]

At 7 a.m., we left the dock at Brewerton in a heavy mist and headed for Oswego, New York, where we planned to stay for a day or two.

 The British established Oswego as a trading post in 1722, and after fortifications were built, they called it Fort Oswego. It was incorporated as a village in 1828, and the Oswego Canal, a branch of the Erie Canal, opened access to Lake Ontario there in 1829. Oswego later became famous for its "water cures" in the 1850s and for being a major railroad hub.

Our route would then take us through our last lock on the Erie Canal and then through seven more locks on the Oswego Canal. Two boats caught up with us in the first lock, and we were told by the lock tender to stay together so that we could traverse the subsequent locks easily without a wait. So with *Reflection* in the lead, that is just what we did for 33 miles. As we were conversing in a lock with other boats who were local to the waters, we learned that they planned to cross Lake Ontario today because the weather was favorable with light winds, waves under a foot, and improving skies. We gave their logic some thought and then immediately decided that it might be a good idea for us to do the same thing because with the impending forecast of rain and possible wind on the nose, we could be stuck in Oswego for several days.

With that in mind, we canceled our marina reservation and at 1 p.m. headed out through the Oswego breakwater, cranked up the engines to cruising speed (about 15 knots), and ran across the lake. In our whole trip across, which was pleasant, albeit a bit chilly, we saw only one vessel — a ship headed east for the

---

17-19 See notes on pages 61-62

Saint Lawrence Seaway. The waters of the lake were pristine, and the sky above was amazing, especially when the clouds parted to form an arrow that pointed our way to Canada.

The clouds parted over Lake Ontario, and we were on our way to Canada.

After entering Canadian waters, we made our way past Amherst Island, one of the Thousand Islands in Lake Ontario near Kingston, Ontario, and through a protected waterway known as the Adolphus Reach all the way to Picton, Ontario. Picton is located in one of Ontario's most beautiful areas of forests, camping, and wine making and was a terrific entry point for us to Canada.

We arrived at 6 p.m. at Tip of the Bay Marina after traveling about 100 miles and through eight locks. I checked us in by phone with Canadian Customs, raised the Canadian flag on the radar arch near our newly repaired anchor light, and then we all celebrated our arrival with libations and food at the waterfront restaurant at our marina.

It was a wonderful day! We completed our transiting of the Erie Canal, crossed beautiful Lake Ontario under ideal conditions, and we were spending our first night in Canada. I love it when the plan, or "change" of plan, comes together.

June 21 — 39 miles to Trenton, Ontario[20]

We left Picton this morning after a rainy day spent at the dock the previous day. It was a convenient location for us to go shopping and to walk around, despite

---

[20] *See notes on page 62*

the less than favorable weather. Today also dawned somewhat overcast, but with breaks in the clouds, we made our way through the Bay of Quinte on our 39-mile trip to Trenton, Ontario, and the beginning of the Trent-Severn Waterway.

 Europeans first settled the area around the mouth of the Trent River in the 1780s. Assorted settlements and town plots in the area went under a number of names until the Village of Trenton was incorporated in 1853. Trenton grew, thanks to its port location and area's lumber industry, and when the wind is right (or perhaps wrong), you can still smell the pulp mill upriver. During World War I, the town was the location of a large munitions plant, which eventually blew up in an explosion, and an early film production studio.

The sign reads "Gateway to the Trent Severn Waterway."

When we arrived at Fraser Park Marina in Trenton, Craig, the hospitable and knowledgeable owner/dockmaster, met us and we were quickly tied up and docked close to town. Craig was a busy man because besides assisting boats into their slips, he also tended the fuel dock and the ice cream stand, which was conveniently located on the premises. In the evening, we went to a car show with beautiful restored vehicles of the 1950s and '60s, followed by a tasty Italian dinner at Tomasso's restaurant.

June 22 – Trenton, Ontario[21]

Reflection's crew split up in the morning to take care of boat chores. Al and I took a dinghy ride up the Trent River to Lock 1 to purchase our waterway pass and to observe the activities of the lock before we would pass through it tomorrow. My sister Pat, in the meantime, took an extensive walk on the waterway trail alongside the river and did some grocery shopping. Admiral Pat took advantage of everyone's absence and cleaned the inside of the vessel and did some advanced planning on locations we would visit along the rest of the Trent-Severn.

We reconvened for lunch and then took a taxi to the National Air Force Museum of Canada. The museum was well worth the visit, and we saw many types of aircraft displayed inside and out, along with many artifacts. We even met volunteers who were working on refurbishing planes from World War II. We were shocked, however, when they told us that no one under the age of 75 was allowed to enter their work area. It had been a long time since we felt like youngsters! It was amazing to see the caliber of work these men had done on the Mark II Halifax Bomber that is displayed there — a task that took more than 350,000 man-hours to complete.

Our plan was to enter the 240-mile long Trent-Severn Waterway the next day. One of the National Historic Sites of Canada, on this passage we would lift to a height of 840 feet above sea level and travel through 44 locks.

 The Trent-Severn Waterway had been formerly used for commercial purposes but was now used exclusively for pleasure boats, connecting Lake Ontario at Trenton to the Georgian Bay area of Lake Huron at Port Severn. Its construction began in the Kawartha Lakes region in 1833 with the building of the lock at Bobcaygeon. Originally the canal system was intended as a defense route but it soon became a major transportation pathway. It took more than 87 years to complete the waterway with two temporary marine railways installed at Big Chute and Swift Rapids. It was not until 1920 that a boat could finally travel the whole route. Some still argue that the canal is not finished. The intended conventional lock in 1965 replaced only the Swift Rapids Marine Railway, but the Big Chute Marine Railway is still in operation, having not been replaced by a conventional lock.

Notes:

(1)

If you are looking for an anchorage with a view of New York City, this is a good one. To enter the anchorage, turn to the northwest at buoy G"29" just south of Liberty Island, and follow the charted buoys past the island. A series of uncharted buoys will guide you through a deep and narrow channel to the protected deep anchorage just south of Liberty State Park.

If you wish to visit New York City, you might want to consider a marina on the New Jersey side. The rates are expensive compared to those in other parts of the country, but they are considerably better than those on the New York side. Check your boating guides for marina locations, and when contacting marinas, ask them how close they are to either the ferries or the PATH railroad. The ferries and the PATH can take you to midtown or downtown locations in Manhattan.

(2)

When we passed through the Troy Lock, the operating schedule was from 6 a.m. to 10 p.m. To request a lift, call the lock tender on channel 13 when you see the lock and have your boat registration or documentation available for the lock tender. Secure your vessel to the lock by loosely looping a line from an amidships cleat around one of the pipes recessed in the lock wall back to the same cleat.

(3)

The dock at the Waterford Visitor Center has water and electric (30- and 50-amp service) on the floating dock. The first two days were free with a minimal charge thereafter. Space is limited, so try to arrive early, and, if possible, avoid tying up under the bridge that crosses over part of the dock unless you like bird droppings on your boat.

(4)

A ten-day pass will give you more than enough time to travel from the Hudson River to Lake Ontario. The pass covers the Erie and Oswego Canals. When transiting the locks, keep the pass handy because the lock tender might ask to see it. Call the lock tender on channel 13 for an opening.

(5)

On the Erie and Oswego Canals and the Trent-Severn Waterway, 50-amp electrical service is rare. Depending on your circumstances, you might want to carry a double 30-amp "Y" to 50-amp adapter. Dockage along the way was either free or had reasonable rates. All had water and electric except where noted.

(6)

Some of the locks have cables around which you can loop a line, while others have ropes hanging on weights that you loop over your cleats while letting the line in or out as necessary, and some have both. If you use the hanging lines and have a choice, use the longest ones available. In addition, if the weights are rusty, use gloves and have rust remover on board to clean your deck.

(7)

The Schenectady Yacht Club has 30- and 50-amp electric and is a friendly, basic facility that gives a discount for large fuel purchases.

(8)
Near Amsterdam's Riverlink Park's dock are a hardware store and a Chinese takeout restaurant.

(9)
At Canajoharie's River Front Park, there is room for three to four boats at the floating dock. However, there is water, but no power at the power pedestals (we were told that they were under repair). Nearby, there is a library with free Wi-Fi and an art museum, a meat market with some groceries, and a few restaurants. Across the canal on the Palatine side is a pharmacy and a hardware store.

(10)
Lock 17 before Little Falls — Secure your boat to the south lock wall. Extreme turbulence can push you to the side during the lift.

(11)
The town of Little Falls with shops, ice cream, and restaurants is about a 15-minute walk from the Little Falls Canal Harbor Marina.

(12)
Before starting the trip, I contacted the New York State Canal System to check the bridge heights on the Erie Canal. I was informed that at normal pool, the minimum clearance of all bridges should be 21 feet 6 inches. Before the start of the journey, I contacted the Canal System again to check on the pool. I was told that it was about normal. Unlike coastal waters, there are no tides on the canal; however, the pool height can change due to greater or lesser amounts of rain. It is always wise to check. What we found was that at normal pool you must be able to clear 20 feet, not the 21 feet 6 inches that we had been quoted.

(13)
The restaurant at Utica Harbor Marina is good and the dockage was reasonably priced. It is a short cab ride from the marina to town and the Matt Brewery. A local pizzeria, O'Squinnizo's, delivers to the boat.

(14)
Mariner's Landing Marina has 30- and 50-amp electric.

(15)
When crossing Oneida Lake, be aware of the "No-Wake" zones. The local residents will not hesitate to call the local authorities if you are going too fast.

(16)
The fuel prices at Winter Harbor Marina were unbelievably low compared to every place we had traveled since leaving New Jersey. Come in here as low on fuel as you

feel comfortable, and fill her up. It also has a 24-hour self-service pump. The phone number is (315) 676-9276. Call them ahead for current fuel prices. They are an America's Great Loop Cruisers' Association sponsor.

The marina has two courtesy cars, and shopping, a laundry facility, supermarkets, an auto parts store, a liquor store, a West Marine, and a post office are all within a short drive.

(17)
There is free dockage with water and electric along the Oswego Canal at Henley Park in Phoenix, New York, and at Canalview Marina in Fulton, New York.

(18)
The captain of a vessel entering Canada must contact the Canadian Border Services Agency as soon as he lands in Canada using a landline phone at (888) 226-7277. You cannot use your cell phone.

The master is required to follow these steps:
- *Give the full name, date of birth, and citizenship for every person on the boat.*
- *Give the destination, purpose of trip, and length of stay in Canada for each passenger who is a nonresident of Canada.*
- *Give the length of absence for each passenger who is a returning resident of Canada.*
- *Give the passport and visa information of passengers, if applicable;*
- *Make sure all passengers have photo identification and proof of citizenship documents.*
- *Declare all goods being imported, including firearms and weapons.*
- *Report all currency and monetary instruments of a value equal to or greater than CAN$10,000.*
- *For a returning resident of Canada, declare all repairs or modifications made to goods, including the boat, while outside Canada.*
- *Give true and complete information.*

As proof of presentation, the border services officer will give the master a report number for their records. The master must give this number to a border services officer on request. Record this number and keep it with your vessel's papers while in Canada.

For complete information, call (888) 226-7277 or visit the CBSA website at **www.cbsa-asfc.gc.ca/publications/pub/bsf5061-eng.html#s.**

This information was taken from the Canada Border Services Area website.

(19)

Picton Municipal Marina is only open on weekends in June. If you see an opening along the wall, you may tie up (if the marina is open, you pay, if not, you do not).

Tip of the Bay Marina is basic with floating docks, 30-amp electric, water, and the Funky Carp restaurant/bar (busy on weekends, live band, loud partying), but it is also close to restaurants, groceries, a bank, and shopping.

(20)

Fraser Park Marina is exposed to the Trent River, but wakes are minimal, and helpful marina staff will supply information about the waterway. Ice cream is available at the dock with banks, shopping, Tomasso's restaurant (Italian food), and an auto parts store close by.

(21)

If possible, purchase your lock permit for the Trent-Severn Waterway in advance. It will speed up your passage through the first lock. The permit can be purchased at the first lock, which is a short dinghy ride from Fraser Park Marina.

When beginning your trip, ask the dockmaster to call Lock 1 to let them know you are coming. If possible, do not schedule your trip to begin on a weekend or a Monday because this is the time with the most boat traffic. The locks are small, frequently only taking two boats at a time, so it is best if you are the first boat at the lock in the morning when it opens. To request an opening, tie up at the blue line or float along the blue line and wait. The lock tender will see you and open as soon as possible.

Listen for instructions. The lock tender will tell you on which side of the lock to secure your boat. Once in the lock, we secured our vessel with a line passing from an amidships cleat loosely around a cable and back to the same cleat. We secured the same way with an aft cleat. The lock tender at the first lock you enter for the day will ask how far you are going and will call the next lock ahead to let them know that you are coming.

Chapter 5

The Trent-Severn Waterway, Eh!

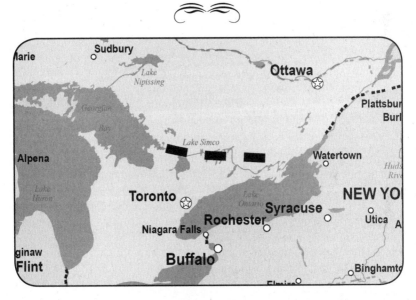

June 23 — 7 miles to Frankford, Ontario (Locks 1-6)[1-2]

We began our journey up the Trent-Severn Waterway by proceeding through six locks in close succession over a distance of only 7 miles. The Canadian locks were much smaller than the ones in the Erie Canal, but they seemed to be in better shape with rubber-coated cables to which we tied up for the lift.

Most locks along the waterway are located in park-like settings with groomed lawns and an abundance of beautiful flowers, picnic areas with grills, and lavatory facilities for boaters. At each lock, friendly lock tenders greeted us and were eager to give us information about their locale. They distributed wildlife cards about the animals, fish, reptiles, and birds indigenous to the specific area of the Province through which we were traveling, and they also graciously called ahead to notify the next lock tender that we would be coming.

[1-2] *See notes on page 88*

Entering the first lock on the Trent-Severn Waterway

Things went smoothly in the morning because we were the only boat traveling through the locks. After processing through 36 locks on the Erie Canal, we were rather proficient as a team in bringing the boat close to the lock wall and tying up quickly. We also appreciated the value of the six fenders that hung over the sides to be used as needed and the two boat hooks that were easily accessible to keep *Reflection* damage-free.

By noon, we were tied up to the lock wall above Frankford.

 This community was first settled by Europeans in the 1820s and incorporated as a village in 1920. The settlement went under a number of names, including Scott's Mills, Cold Creek, and Manchester, but it was eventually named Frankford after Sir Francis Bond Head, the Lieutenant-Governor of Upper Canada.

While settling in at the wall, the lock tender asked me if I would like hydro, to which I answered that we already had plenty on board. However, I did not understand what he really had asked me. At almost every lock, there was a hydroelectric plant, and he wanted to know if I wanted to have electric service. Note to self: The term "hydro" means electricity in Canada. I thanked him and hooked up. Later that afternoon, we walked into the small town for dinner at the Chinese Buffet, which the locals touted as a good place to eat. We thought the food was just all right at the restaurant, but we enjoyed the pleasant stroll alongside the beautiful and serene canal leading into town.

June 24 – 24 miles to Campbellford, Ontario (Locks 7-12) [3-4] (aka "The Tomb")

It was massively intimidating (at least at this stage of the journey) to enter the Ranney Falls Flight Lock (two locks connected to each other) on our way to Campbellford, Ontario. It felt like we were in a 4 million-gallon huge boat tomb, and what sounded like an unseen deity blared instructions for securing to the lock on a loud speaker. We were the only boat in this lock, and when the gates closed behind us, it was eerie being surrounded by massive walls of concrete and steel with our words echoing off those walls. When we looked around, we could not find the lock tender but could only hear her voice. In front and high above us was the second lock in the flight, and behind its blue steel gates were millions of gallons of water. Knowing this, we hoped and prayed that the design engineers knew what they were doing. It was an amazingly impressive sight because the distance from the water below us to the top of the gate was nearly 50 feet.

Ranney Falls Flight Lock

After *Reflection* rose to the top of the lock, the blue steel doors opened, and in what felt like a moment of déjà vu, we saw yet another set of blue steel doors at the end of the double lock. Once again, we received instructions on securing the boat. As we completed the final lift, we finally met the voice that echoed over the locks. She turned out to be a lovely young woman who suggested places to visit while we were in the area.

[3-4] *See notes on page 88*

After our amazing lock experience, we then traveled a short distance up the Trent River to dock at Campbellford's Old Mill Park. The park, which is located in the downtown area, is a welcoming destination for boaters traveling the Trent-Severn Waterway. A 20-foot replica of the Two Dollar Canadian Toonie is on display there because it was a local artist, Brent Townsend, who designed the coin's bear motif.

The waterway leading to Campbellford

 Campbellford was named after brothers Lieutenant-Colonel Robert Campbell and Major David Campbell, who received land from the British government in the 1800s to settle in the area. The Trent River passed through their land and was shallow enough that it could be forded there; hence, it acquired the name Campbellford and became a town in 1906. Today, it is the location of the Church-Key Brewing Company, the Blommer Chocolate Company, a local cheese factory, Empire Cheese, and the Dart Cup Factory.

Before returning to the boat, we visited a local brewpub and stocked up on wine and delicious, locally made Empire cheese. The icing on the cake that evening was a concert that a group of Irish fiddlers put on at the bandstand on the dock, and we could hear and see all the festivities from the comfort of our aft deck.

June 25 — 20 miles to Hastings, Ontario (Locks 13-18)[5]

We transited six more locks today, and were starting to sound like our Canadian lock tenders, who seemed to end every statement with "eh!"

Looking back after a double lift at the Healey Falls Flight Lock raised us up a total of 48 feet.

The waterway was made up of countless slow speed zones where boat speeds were regulated at 10 kilometers per hour (or about 6 miles per hour for the metrically challenged among us). As we slowly traveled through one of the areas, we came around a bend and saw an elderly man sitting on a porch overlooking the waterway. The Admiral was at the helm and gave the man a smile and a friendly wave. To her surprise, he returned her gesture with the middle figure salute! We wondered if this was an example of "road rage" on the Trent-Severn and were not exactly sure what we did to push his buttons — but push them we did. As laughable as this was, we took no offense because it simply made us feel a little homesick for New Jersey, where this kind of response can be fairly commonplace.

As we entered the last lock of the day, it had the usual park-like setting on the lower end. Rising to the top, we discovered that we were right inside the village of Hastings.

---

[5] *See notes on page 88*

Hastings is a village of about 1,200 residents on the Trent River that acquired its present name in 1852 and was incorporated as a village in 1874. Hastings has often been labeled as "The Hub of the Trent" because it serves as a center for fishermen, boaters, and tourists.

We tied up to the lock wall in the village, which was small, but it had all the essentials we needed, including a close-by laundry facility and a little Italian restaurant, La Gondola. Behind us was a boat from Montreal, whose owner played the guitar. After hearing Pat's voice, he offered to follow us so that he could accompany the Admiral's singing from port to port as we traversed Georgian Bay and the North Channel over the next few weeks, but we never took him up on the offer.

June 26 – 38 miles to Peterborough, Ontario (Lock 19)[6-8]

We traveled 38 miles to the city of Peterborough.

Peterborough has a population of about 75,000 and is known as the gateway to the Kawartha Lakes, otherwise known as "cottage country," a large recreational region in that part of Ontario. Named after Peter Robinson, a Canadian politician who oversaw the first major immigration to the area, the city has been the seat of Peterborough County since 1983. Located there is Artspace, one of Canada's oldest art centers run by the artists themselves and the Peterborough Museum & Archives, which is home to a diverse collection of local artifacts. Several large companies, including General Electric and Quaker Oats, also maintain large operations in the area.

On our way there, we crossed a good portion of beautiful Rice Lake, one of the largest of the Kawartha Lakes. The lake is fairly shallow and was named for the wild rice that grew there and that native people of the area harvested. Our route then proceeded up the Otonabee River (a continuation of the Trent River), which wound through many marsh areas and the Hiawatha Indian Preserve. The scenery changed dramatically from a wide-open lake to a narrow, winding river, and having to lift up in only one lock made today's entire trip seem like a breeze.

As we approached Peterborough Marina, we passed by a fountain right smack in the middle of Little Lake. It was lit at night, and we were looking forward to seeing the Festival of Lights Concert with fireworks the following night. Alas, to our dismay, when we arrived, we found out that the city had to cancel the scheduled fireworks due to budget cuts. We lessened the disappointment by having a fun, Cajun dinner at Hot Belly Mama's, a restaurant about a half-mile away.

June 27 — Peterborough, Ontario

On my early morning walk, I scouted out a substantial farmers' market located a few blocks from our marina, and I returned again later in the day with the Admiral and crew. We were all amazed at the huge size and the wide variety of the fruits and vegetables grown in the area, and we learned that this was due to the long hours of sunlight at this time of the year.

Farmers' market at Peterborough

The baked goods and butcher products also caught our eyes, and holding true to our family's Polish/Slovak heritage, we made purchases of kielbasa, golumbki, and veal franks. We also bought meat loaves. To our surprise, when we baked one meat loaf that evening, we found out that it was also made of kielbasa-type pork and veal and garlic — not beef, as we had expected. It was "different," and Al and I found it to be particularly enjoyable.

June 28 — 10 miles to Lakefield, Ontario (Locks 20-26)[9]

We received word before we left our slip that the huge Peterborough Lift Lock, one of the seven locks we would pass through that day, was not working. In essence, we could not go anywhere until it was fixed. My sister Pat and Al had hiked a few miles to see the lock yesterday, and a similar closing had occurred. This did not bode well for a departure today, and the weather was beginning to deteriorate. I phoned the lock tender before noon, and he told me that the lock was repaired again, so we decided to proceed, despite the weather forecast of rain and wind.

This particular lift-lock was the largest and highest in the world. We were lifted 65 feet by entering a 1,300-ton lower pan (in a sense, a giant bathtub filled with water), while 130 additional tons of water were allowed to enter the upper pan on the other side. The extra weight pushed the upper pan down and raised our pan to the top level. The view going up was stunning, and we were amazed at how quickly we rose. It felt just like going up in an elevator!

Approaching the Peterborough Lift Lock

Near the lock — notice the rectangular structure at the top. It is a gate that holds back a countless amount of water.

Inside the lifting pan, Pat secured Reflection *for the ride up.*

This is our view looking back from the top of the lock.

This is the scene ahead as we wait for the gate to be lowered after the lift.

The gate is now nearly fully submerged as we prepare to get under way.

We did all our locking today decked out in full storm gear because it was pouring buckets. When we arrived at Lock 22, another boat in front of the lock door was waiting to enter, and when the doors opened, we locked together. The captain of the other vessel was an older gentleman who put on a good show by bouncing his boat off the lock walls while he frantically ran around the deck and tried to secure his craft to the cables by himself. However, he was not alone on his vessel. During this whole scene, the young lady who accompanied him onboard merely lifted her head up periodically from the book she was reading and did not assist him in any way. Thank goodness I had my dependable Admiral and crew!

Before exiting the lock, the lock tender asked us to stay together to the next lock so that we could go through that one at the same time. Because the locks in this part of the waterway were closely spaced to one another, it made sense for boats to stay together. As we exited the lock, however, the guy in the other boat took off. Yet when we got to the following lock, there he was for the second time, waiting in front of the doors.

We locked through together again, and he put on another "show" while attempting to tie his boat up, and the girl once again simply observed. This lock tender also made the same request for our boats to stay together, and again, the other guy took off like a shot. The scene was repeated a third time at the next lock, where he managed to get in front of two other boats that had arrived before him and were also waiting to lock through. The lock tender reprimanded "Mr. Speedy," however, and ordered him to play by the rules by sending him to the back of the line. Regardless of boating etiquette, some people just do not know how to play nice!

It took us almost five hours to go only 10 miles through the seven locks. As luck would have it, when we arrived at the lock wall where we tied up in Lakefield, the worst of the weather was over.

June 29 — 14 miles to Mount Julian/Stoney Lake, Ontario (Lock 27)[10]

On my walk in the morning, I discovered that the town of Lakefield was only a short distance from where we had spent the previous night at Lock 26. To our dismay, we missed exploring it because yesterday's rain and the dense foliage near the lock wall had hidden it from our view. If we had known then that the local ice cream parlor had 55 flavors, we would have made an effort to walk there!

Today, we only went through one lock and then headed to Stoney Lake. The scenery was completely breathtaking with many multicolored rock islands, some with homes built on them. Evidently, this was a small precursor to what we would eventually see in Georgian Bay.

 There are more than 1,000 islands of every size and shape in Stoney Lake, from red granite rock to rounded hills of dense green foliage. Stoney lake is touted as the best one for fishing in all the Kawarthas. Many species of fish abound, including walleye, bass, muskie, and perch. Like most lakes in Ontario, it was created during and after the last Ice Age, many Indian tribes eventually lived here, and during the 16th century, French explorer Samuel de Champlain passed through Stony Lake, just like he had done through almost every other lake and river along the Trent-Severn Waterway. Along the eastern seaboard of the U.S., a frequently used historical phrase is "George Washington slept here." However, in this part of Ontario, the phrase is "Champlain passed through here."

---

[10] *See notes on page 89*

Unfortunately, the whole crew did not get to enjoy the wonderful vista that surrounded us because my sister was in her cabin not feeling well and my brother-in-law, Al, was reading a book on the back deck or napping. I looked at Pat and said they were missing some of the most beautiful scenery on the trip. The area was so spectacular that Pat and I agreed it was one of the highlights of our trip thus far.

My trustworthy Admiral kept a close watch on the bridge with me as I maneuvered *Reflection* through the sometimes-narrow waterway. The area was well marked with plenty of buoys, some of them even on top of rocks, so we made sure to stay in the middle of the channel and safely made our way to Viamede Resort, our destination of the day.

The landmark resort had a marina, restaurant, pool, spa, beach, watercraft rentals, walking trails, and riding stables. Because of the cool temperatures and overcast skies, however, we were only able to take a walk around the grounds and have dinner at the resort, but it was still a day to relax in a lovely setting.

June 30 – 30 miles to Bobcaygeon, Ontario (Locks 28-31)[11-12]

Since leaving Peterborough a few days before, our route continued to take us through the Kawartha Lakes area of central Ontario Province, and that day, we motored through Stoney Lake, Lovesick Lake, Lower Buckhorn Lake, Buckhorn Lake, and Pigeon Lake, each with its own characteristics, on our way to Bobcaygeon.

 The name Bobcaygeon is derived from the Indian word "Bobcaygewanunk," which means "shallow rapids." Bobcaygeon is built on three islands that are joined by a series of seven bridges. It is strategically located at the crossing of Great Bobcaygeon Road and the Trent-Severn Waterway, so early business flourished here, and like most other towns in this part of Ontario, lumbering and farming were initially the basic industries in the area. Some farmers got creative and tried their hand at raising Cattalo or Beefalo, a mix of buffalo and cattle that were crossbred to theoretically be able to withstand the rigorous Canadian winters.

We did not see any Beefalo along the way, nor were they offered on any local menus. The Admiral admitted that she was not disappointed!

While researching the trip, Admiral Pat and my sister Pat had chosen this town as a prime location for us to experience Canada Day on July 1, and we were interested in seeing how the Canadian celebration compared to our American Independence Day.

Canada Day commemorates the day when the British North America Act created the Canadian federal government on July 1, 1867. The Act proclaimed "one Dominion under the name of Canada," thus the original holiday was called Dominion Day. Dominion Day was officially renamed Canada Day by an Act of Parliament on Oct. 27, 1982.

We pulled into Gordon's Yacht Harbor in the early afternoon and secured a prime location for, what we hoped, would be a good day. Gordon's was a small marina with limited space for a boat our size, so the dockmaster had to tie us up on the fuel dock just past the pumps. It was a good spot to watch the activity in the canal and at the marina, and some of the boaters knew how to "entertain" an audience. There were houseboat rentals in the area, and the folks maneuvering these often large and cumbersome vessels to the fuel dock were captains in name only because most had only an hour's training under their belts! They were a thrill to watch! We were lucky because despite several of them crashing into the fuel dock behind us, none of them hit *Reflection*.

July 1 — Bobcaygeon, Ontario

As of this morning, we had traveled 624 miles in 26 days, used about 300 gallons of fuel, visited 18 towns and villages, passed through 60 locks, and were currently sitting at an altitude of 807 feet above sea level. The next day, we would reach our highest point on the entire trip at 840 feet above sea level.

Canada Day in Bobcaygeon was overcast with occasional showers, and the temperature was around 62 degrees. Yuck! Fortunately, however, it eventually cleared up enough so that we could attend the town's parade. They had bagpipes, fife, and drum bands along with a drum and bugle corps, antique cars, children on decorated bikes, fire trucks, bikini-clad girls giving out red and white leis, and several floats.

Pat and I wore our full red storm gear (pants and jackets) to honor the red and white colors of the Canadian flag, and a member of Parliament stopped and commented on how good our outfits looked! After the parade, we toured the town and watched fireworks from the flybridge of our boat that evening. This was our first-ever observation of Canada Day, and it turned out to be a fun and memorable occasion.

July 2 — 62 miles to Orillia, Ontario (Locks 32-41)[13-20]

Today's weather was even worse than the previous day's with rain, wind, and chilly temperatures. It was not exactly what you would call "summer-like." The Admiral is a weather "junkie," and despite the fact that she does not have a degree in meteorology, she monitors weather forecasts several times a day so that we always know what to expect in the near term and for several days ahead. Though Pat always prefers to travel under the best conditions possible, despite today's gloomy forecast, she thought that it would be in our best interest to put some serious miles under the keel. Ordinarily, if we were by ourselves, we would have broken up the trip into multiple segments, but the upcoming wind forecast for the next few days was not the best, and we wanted to be sure that we would have my sister Pat and Al at Orillia in time to make their travel connections.

Once underway, the route was again scenic despite the clouds and occasional rain, and it also posed some unique challenges: the first being the narrow cut that connected Balsam Lake to Mitchell Lake. It was so tight that two vessels our size would not be able to pass each other safely. So before we entered the 2.5-mile land cut through the Canadian Shield, I called a security alert on the marine radio to notify any vessel entering from the other end that we were about to come through.

The cut between Balsam Lake and Mitchell Lake

I received a call back that three boats had just entered the cut from the other end, and because there was no place to pass in the canal, we waited for about 45

---

minutes for the boats to come out at our end so that we could enter. Once on our way, it was obvious that except for a small boat, no one would be able to pass us.

The channel was so narrow because of its sheer rock walls on both sides that we did not pass through the water as much as it was pushed around us. It felt like we were going through a long, thin water trough, forcing us to travel slowly at about 5 knots, and it seemed like it would take forever to get to the other end of the cut. When we got about three-quarters of the way through, suddenly a boat appeared coming the other way. I turned to Pat and shook my head in disbelief, saying that I was not going to give up the middle of the channel. He was just going to have to squeeze past us. Fortunately, the boat was able to slip between our boat and the rock ledge.

The next interesting spot along the way was the Kirkfield Lift Lock, located in the city of Kawartha Lakes, Ontario, near the village of Kirkfield.

 The Kirkfield Lift Lock is situated at the highest section of the waterway at 840 feet above sea level, and its construction took place between 1900 and 1907. A hydraulic lift lock had never been put into operation in the harsh Canadian climate before the building of this one and the Peterborough Lift Lock, and at the time, the successful completion of the locks was considered to be a major technological breakthrough.

This lock was similar to the Peterborough Lift lock except that the Peterborough structure was somewhat enclosed, but this was not. The pan in which the boat sat was wide open, and it provided us with an excellent view of the surrounding area. Because we entered at the top of the lock, we had an exciting vantage point from the bow, which allowed us to look over the edge of the pan and down a sheer drop of nearly five stories to the canal below. The Admiral was not as thrilled with the view as I was, and the expression on her face as she looked around was like one of panic.

Several years ago, a boat entered the pan too fast and struck the forward gate. The gate then opened, and the water, the boat, and all onboard fell to the water below. Since then, locking pins were installed in the gate that prevent it from opening, even if hit, which was a comforting thought. We eventually safely descended in the lock without incident, and within a short time, we were on our way again.

The next challenge was crossing Canal Lake. This was a manmade lake, and when the land was cleared to form the lake, trees stumps were left on the bottom. The only place where they were removed was in the channel. However, throughout the many decades that followed, the submerged waterlogged stumps, known as "deadheads," had been uprooted and tended to move about under the water. They even sometimes rolled into the channel, where they would bend the boat propeller of an unsuspecting captain. Luckily for us, the water that day was high, and the channel was clear of hazards.

Sitting in the pan at the Kirkfield Lift Lock,
we were waiting to be lowered to the waterway below.

At the end of the lake is the Hole in the Wall Bridge, an arch-shaped bridge built in the early 20th century. We were warned that the deadheads from the lake tend to collect at the bridge, so we kept a sharp lookout on our approach, and we cleared it without any problems. Feeling happy that we had successfully dodged another "bullet", we found the rest of the trip to Lake Simcoe to be easy and uneventful.

Our crossing of Lake Simcoe proved to be an interesting change from the narrow canals in which we had spent most of the day.

Lake Simcoe is 19 miles long and is the fourth-largest lake in Ontario province. It is a remnant of a much bigger, prehistoric lake known as Lake Algonquin. The melting of an ice dam at the close of the last Ice Age reduced water levels in the region, leaving the lake we saw, which the Huron natives originally named Ouentironk, or "beautiful water." Later, after the first European's settled here, it was called Lake Toronto until John Graves Simcoe, the first Lieutenant-Governor of Upper Canada, renamed it in memory of his father.

The lake was the widest and deepest body of water we had crossed since Lake Ontario, and by then it was getting late in the day. So not wanting to arrive in Orillia after dark, we cranked up the engines and got moving. Picking up the pace considerably also gave us an opportunity to clear the carbon out of the engines.

We finally ended our almost 11-hour, 62-mile day arriving at the Port of Orillia at 7:15 p.m. It always feels good to enter a safe harbor after a long day at sea or, in this case, lake and canal, and the drinks onboard and the pizza we had delivered that evening were just what our crew needed after a long, rainy day on the water.

July 3 — Orillia, Ontario

 No one seems to know how the city and port got their names, but the first recorded use of the name to describe the region was in 1820. Known as the "Sunshine City," Orillia's large waterfront attracts boaters traveling the Trent-Severn Waterway every year, as do annual festivals and other cultural attractions that are held here.

We spent the day touring the town, window shopping, and having lunch out. Pat and Al also treated us to a farewell dinner that evening at a lovely restaurant called Messa Luna, where we made several toasts to our trip. Pat and I were most grateful for their spirit of adventure and the enthusiasm they had displayed as they went through 68 locks and traveled almost 500 miles with us on the Erie Canal and Trent-Severn Waterway. That was certainly a cause for celebration!

July 4 — Orillia, Ontario

The Admiral and I took a walk in the morning to the local farmers' market held at the Opera House parking lot to see what goodies we could find. Despite its elegant location, there was not an aria to be heard! After walking around, I spotted a line of men. Even though I did not know what the line was for, I got into it anyway because I figured that the locals knew something that I did not. The fellow in front of me explained that at the end of the line was a local butcher grilling homemade sausages and making sandwiches on artisan bread. He also told me that he comes there every Saturday during the summer to have breakfast. That sounded good to me!

When I got to the front of the line, I faced the dilemma of choosing between breakfast sausage, spicy bratwurst, bratwurst with garlic, and Italian sausage. I went with my new friend's recommendation and bought an over-the-top spicy bratwurst sandwich that was wonderful!

Bratwurst for breakfast at the farmers' market as the Captain keeps up with his "see food and eat it" diet

The Opera House in Orillia

Pat and I continued to walk around the market picking up fruits and vegetables while I ate my high-fat, high-calorie, high-carbohydrate breakfast. We spotted the guy who had been in the line with me earlier with another huge sausage sandwich! As I stopped and stared at him for a moment, he looked at me and said, "I have two of these every Saturday, and I know that they are probably killing me, but what a way to go!" The Admiral muttered under her breath that the fellow's wife was probably at home making sure his life insurance was up to date.

After shopping at the farmers' market, we said our goodbyes to my sister Pat and Al, who were catching a bus to Toronto, followed by a flight home to Richmond, Virginia. The Admiral and I caught up on our chores — laundry, cleaning the boat, and food shopping. By the time we were done, we were exhausted but were looking forward to being on our own and moving on to Big Chute tomorrow.

July 5 — 34 miles to Big Chute Marine Railway (Locks 42-43)

Someone we met earlier in the trip told my sister Pat that the area beyond Orillia would be some of the loveliest we would see on the Trent-Severn, and this certainly seemed to be the case today. Beautiful small lakes, rocky islands, quaint cottages, and enormous homes with boathouses abounded in the area. We also encountered the largest amount of boats of the entire trip past the Hudson River.

One of the many homes in the area that perches on a small island

As we approached Lock 42, Pat had concerns about how she would secure *Reflection* to the lock wall without the help of our trusty crew. Her apprehension quickly dissolved because as we entered the lock, waiting for us was a lovely young lock tender who took the lines from Pat and secured *Reflection* for the descent. It could not have been easier.

By the time we reached Lock 43 with its 47-foot drop, the Admiral was feeling more confident. Once again, she was assisted in securing the boat to the lock, and we found that we were able to manage everything well, even though it was now just the two of us working the fenders and lines. By mid-afternoon, we pulled up to the public dock at Big Chute, where we planned to spend the night. Cameras in hand, we walked over to the Visitors' Center and its observation deck so that we could closely watch the workings of the marine railway lift that would carry our boat the next day.

Big Chute is a boat lift that works on an inclined plane to carry boats in a cradle over a change of height of 57 feet, and it is the only marine railway of its kind in North America that is still in use. The original Big Chute Marine Railway was completed in 1917, and it could only carry boats up to 35 feet long. It was built as a temporary measure until a conventional lock could be built. In 1923, the original railway was replaced with another carriage, which was able to carry boats up to 60 feet long. It was in use until the current carriage, which can carry a boat up to 100 feet long with a beam of 24 feet, was opened in 1978 — so much for temporary measures. The system of locking is still in use today to prevent Sea Lamprey, which had been devastating the fishing industry in the Great Lakes and had been found in Gloucester Pool — at the bottom of the railway — from entering Lake Couchiching and Lake Simcoe.

Seeing Big Chute in action was an amazing operation, and we observed boats, as many as five at a time, entering the enormous apparatus that looked like something out of "Star Wars" and then being transported over a road from one body of water to another. Some boats were going upstream while others were going downstream. They looked like they were going up and down on a slow-motion roller coaster. The action did not stop until sundown. While we watched, I had a chance to talk to one of the operators, and when I advised him of some of the nuances of our boat, he assured me that they would take good care of us the next day.

Another load of boats traveling through Big Chute

The Big Chute Marine Railway beginning to submerge itself

July 6 — 19 miles to Midland, Ontario (Georgian Bay) (Locks 44-45)[21-25]

On this chilly, overcast morning, we headed over from our nearby dock to Big Chute, where we waited to be called onto the railway. Luckily, we were the only boat there — what a difference it was from yesterday's madhouse!

When we were called, I moved the boat onto the submerged platform, where the expert railway personnel moved three large straps under *Reflection* in a crisscross pattern so that she sat on her keel but could not move from side to side. The aft section of the boat hung off the back of the car so that her rudder and props would not be damaged. We were amazed at the time and care we got, and when the lock tenders and I were satisfied that everything was safe, *Reflection* went on one of the best rides of her life!

Pat and I sat on the flybridge for the best view. The rail carriage in which we were riding rattled and clanked like some mechanical beast. As we passed over the rail joints, we could feel each one and hear the wheels clanking as we went along. The view from the top of the hill before we went down in slow motion was like being on the top of a roller coaster. In about seven minutes, we made it down back into the water, where we easily and quickly floated on our way again. Thanks to the finesse of the lock tenders, it was a good experience.

[21-25] *See notes on page 90*

Reflection *riding on the Big Chute Marine Railway,*
first up out of the water, then over the hill, and down

We motored through winding channels to Port Severn and the final lock on the Trent-Severn Waterway. The lock was the smallest we had encountered, and our boat seemed to fill up the entire chamber. When we left the lock, we could not believe the tight little channel we had to transit to get through our final bridge. However, that was only the beginning.

By then, the wind was blowing hard right on our nose, and we had to carefully make our way through another series of tight, shallow channels to reach the open waters of Georgian Bay. Once we were safely out of the area, we then scooted across the bay to Bay Port Yachting Centre in Midland.

 Midland was founded in 1871 when the Midland Railway of Canada selected it as the new terminus of the railway. The once small village thrived on the shipping, lumber, and grain trade and was incorporated as a town in 1890. Today, Midland is the economic center of the region and is the main town in the southern Georgian Bay area with a summer population of more than 100,000.

Overlooking the main harbor, painted on silos, is a massive mural painted by artist Fred Lenz. Among the many sites to visit in the Midland area are the Jesuit mission of Sainte-Marie among the Hurons, which is now a living museum, and the Martyrs' Shrine, a Roman Catholic church commemorating the Canadian Martyrs, five missionaries who were killed during the Huron-Iroquois wars, and the Huronia museum.

Because we had gone through Big Chute and then negotiated through several rocky and narrow channels that morning, our ride seemed to take forever, but the trip had only taken three and a half hours. At that point, we had traveled 740 miles and gone through 73 locks during a period of 31 days. However, having left the somewhat narrow waters of the lovely Trent-Severn Waterway, we now looked forward to experiencing the majestic grandeur of Georgian Bay and the North Channel.

A one-way rock cut passage, Little Chute, which can be a real thrill,
especially if another boat is coming the other way

Notes:

(1)
The waterway in the area can have a considerable amount of weeds growing in it, so it is advisable to check your water strainers on a regular basis to prevent the overheating of your engine.

(2)
Lock 6 at Frankford has water and power at the wall above the lock at a reasonable fee for dockage and electric. It is a 12-minute walk to the town, which has a hardware store, grocery, a bank, and a Chinese buffet, the Golden House Restaurant. Other eateries will also deliver to the boat (ask the lock tender).

(3)
Whether staying at Old Mill Park or across the waterway closer to town, register at the tourism office at the park. The park side has 30-amp electric service while the town side has 30- and 50-amp electric. Dockage was moderately priced.

(4)
Fuel in Canada is considerably more expensive than it is in the U.S., and fuel on the water in Canada is more expensive than highway fuel — with one exception. Across the waterway from Campbellford's Old Mill Park is Macmillan's Fuel, which sells on the highway and on the water. What is unique about the place is that it sells the fuel on the water for the same price as the highway fuel. It was the lowest price for diesel fuel that we paid in all our travels in Canada.

(5)
Near the wall above the lock at Hastings is a laundry facility, bank, convenience store, and the La Gondola Italian restaurant, just steps away.

(6)
Entering Peterborough, take the green buoy near the fountain widely because there is an obstruction in the channel.

(7)
The Peterborough Marina is close to town with stores, restaurants, and laundry facilities. If possible, arrive on Friday because there is a farmers' market on Saturday mornings, just a short walk from the marina. There are concerts on Saturday nights in a park near the marina, and you can hear the music from the boat.

(8)
Call the Peterborough Lift Lock at (705) 750-4953 before you leave the dock to be sure it is operating.

(9)
Tie up at the far end of the wall on the starboard side because it is the shortest walk to the town of Lakefield. Walk up the path to Bridge Street and turn left for a NAPA auto store or turn right for the town itself, which has two hardware stores, a large IGA supermarket, a pharmacy, several restaurants, an ice cream parlor, and another automotive store. The channel beyond the lock is narrow, so sound your horn before entering.

(10)
When traveling through Stoney Lake, keep a sharp watch, and stay in the middle of the channel away from the buoys because they might be sitting on rocks near the surface. During our stay, the Viamede Resort was charging a reasonable price per foot for dockage.

(11)
Be careful of the blue bridge in the Gannon Narrows between red marker C328 and C332 en route to Bobcaygeon. The clearance might be closer to 21 feet than the official posted height of 22 feet.

(12)
Gordon Yacht Harbor is convenient to town. Make reservations early, especially for weekends, holidays, and for boats more than 40 feet. It is not recommended to tie up at the nearby lock wall. It has been reported that teenagers like to untie boats in the middle of the night and set them adrift.

(13)
At Fenelon Falls Lock, the current is strong below the lock. The wall above the lock is an excellent place to tie up because it is right in the middle of town, but it might be crowded on weekends and holidays.

(14)
The land cut is extremely narrow. So, broadcast a security alert before entering. It is nearly impossible to have two boats larger than 40 feet pass each other.

(15)
At Mitchell Lake, stay in the center of the channel because it is a shallow lake with deadheads.

(16)
At Kirkfield Lift Lock, if you need assistance, tie up on the tower side of the pan to the horizontal rails that are at three levels along the side. Red and green markers change positions here.

(17)
Follow channel markers at Canal Lake and stay in the center through the Hole in the Wall Bridge.

(18)
The bridge at mile mark 175.3 is permanently open, the bridge at mile mark 176.7 opens on signal, and the bridge at mile mark 182.2 is permanently open.

(19)
Lake Simcoe is a wide open lake. Ask the last lock tender about conditions on the lake. If it is less than desirable, you can tie up at the wall behind the breakwater to wait for better weather. There are widely spaced center channel markers to Orillia, and the lake narrows at Atherley.

(20)
The Port of Orillia has easy access, helpful dock personnel, a deal to pay for two nights and get the third night free at the municipal marina, an excellent farmers' market on Saturdays at the Opera House, a good Chinese buffet restaurant, a laundry facility, supermarket, pharmacy, and banks nearby.

(21)
Swift Rapids Lock 43 is extremely busy on weekends.

(22)
Big Chute Lock 44 should be avoided on weekends, if possible. You might want to observe the operation at the Visitors' Center before you go through. There is a public dock close by, which is available for tie up. The best time to go through is at 8:30 a.m. on weekdays.

(23)
As a safety precaution, before entering any narrow channel, broadcast a security alert on channel 16 on your VHF radio to let other boaters know your intentions.

(24)
Little Chute Channel is a narrow passage located just after the Big Chute Lock.

(25)
Port Severn Lock 45 is extremely small. After leaving the lock, the channel becomes narrow through the bridge, so keep a sharp lookout. Potato Channel on the way to Midland, Ontario, is also narrow.

Chapter 6

Georgian Bay and the North Channel – You Gotta' Love Rocks

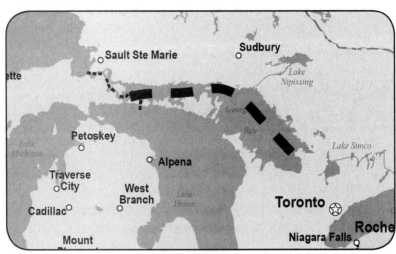

July 7 – Midland, Ontario[1]

Awakening to pouring rain and chilly temperatures, we decided that it would be a good day to stay put at Bay Port Yachting Centre. I walked up to the office with my Lake Huron chart book to see if anyone there could suggest some good anchorages and the best places to visit among Georgian Bay's 30,000 islands. By taking advantage of local knowledge, we fared much better than by merely relying on the information in guidebooks.

This was truly our lucky day! While in the marina office, I met Ken, the general manager of the 700-slip marina, and he was willing to come to our boat after closing time to review the charts with us. True to his word, Ken came aboard and spent more than an hour and a half mapping out the best routes and anchorages in the Canadian waters. He also provided us with two CDs of PowerPoint presentations he had given to boating groups, specifically about Georgian Bay and the North Channel. His knowledge was so extensive that we strongly suggested he write a guide for this area that he obviously loved so much. Ken is very personable and is a wonderful ambassador of Canadian hospitality who spent considerable time with us to ensure that our voyage would be a good one.

July 8 — Midland, Ontario

This is our 37th wedding anniversary and because we could not tour the area yesterday because of the weather, we decided to stay another day. During business hours, members of the marina's customer service staff were permitted to drive transient boaters to and from locations that they would like to visit in the local area, so we took advantage of the service and visited Discovery Harbor in the nearby port of Penetanguishene.

 As early as 800 A.D., the Huron Indians settled in the area, and the name Penetanguishene is believed to have come from one of several native languages and means "place of the white rolling sands." While visiting this area in 1793, John Graves Simcoe, the first lieutenant governor of Upper Canada, saw potential for a naval base to be built because he wanted to use the bay to station warships to protect British interests in the Great Lakes.

Discovery Harbor is an historical site that had its origins during the War of 1812 when the British Navy established a presence here to defend the Georgian Bay ports from a possible rear-flank attack by the American Navy. After the war, when Drummond Island in the North Channel was given to the U.S. by treaty, the British forces in the area were transferred to this fortification.

It is ironic that our two countries, once bitter enemies, are now the best of friends. We had an enjoyable time on our guided tour, and after returning to the boat, we enjoyed a lovely anniversary dinner in the town of Midland that evening. It had been 37 wonderful years — "and they said it wouldn't last!"

July 9 — 17 miles to Longuissa Bay, Ontario[2]

It felt good to be on the water, and although it was cool, it was also bright and sunny. There were many boats out with us in beautiful Georgian Bay, and we had

---

² See notes on page 109

to watch our GPS, charts, and visible buoys closely because the rocks were every-where! Occasionally, we would see white bottles tied in the water to mark another newly discovered rock.

The scenery was almost otherworldly with homes built on rock boulders in the middle of the water, and we speculated that these houses must be built in the winter when trucks would be able to drive across the ice with building materials. The water there was so clear that you could also see how close we sometimes came to the rock ledges along the channels.

Making the best of a "rocky" situation

We attempted to go into one anchorage, but though it was beautiful, the large amount of boats did not give us a safe feeling, so we traveled on to lovely Lon-guissa Bay, where we were sheltered and a little farther off the beaten track. Even in this spot, there were nine other boats with us, but at least they were well spread out.

After dinner we turned in, feeling secure in this quiet place, but around about midnight, I heard a buzzing sound in my ear. We had mosquitoes in our cabin! I can sleep through cold, heat, and even loud noises, but not mosquitoes. In a vain attempt to kill the little devils, I began swatting them in the dark around my head and eventually wound up slapping myself in the ear. Then, I had ringing in my ears in addition to mosquito bites. I decided to take the battle up a notch, got out of bed, and went into the head, where I turned on the light to lure them into my trap. My idea was that the light would attract them into the head where I could see them against the light-colored walls. The concept worked — sort of. I was able to kill a few of them by slapping them against the wall, but soon after, the Admiral woke up and asked me what I was doing. I said I was killing mosquitoes, and she said she had not heard a thing. I swear, that woman could sleep through a nuclear explosion!

After more kills, I felt that I had gotten them all and went back to bed. However, in just a few minutes, there they were again, buzzing in my ear. These things were going to drive me crazy! So I got up once more and went back to the head to see how many more I could find.

The stalking and killing went on for some time. The Admiral by then was immune to the pounding sounds coming from the head and stayed asleep (she says that's one of her secrets to our long marriage!). After several more successful swats, I once more felt victorious, but after a few minutes back in bed, I once again found out I was wrong. The battle between man and mosquito went on most of the night, and the next morning I was exhausted. Despite being sleep deprived, I inspected our window screens, looking for gaps in our defense, and found several places where the invaders got in. Repairs began immediately because I was determined not to go through another night like the previous one. Later, we found out that everyone in that area had experienced the same problem, and it did not matter if their boats were in a marina or at anchor. I guess it was just the "Night of the Mosquito," and it never happened again.

July 10 — 29 miles to Sans Souci, Ontario (Henry's Fish and Chips)[3]

In the morning, we heard a distress call from one unhappy boater who went on the wrong side of a buoy and tore the propeller shafts out of his boat. The Coast Guard was unable to render immediate assistance and advised the people onboard to put on life jackets and get into their dinghy. Other boaters came by to give whatever help they could; however, the boat sank in minutes. Luckily, there were no injuries. We later heard that the captain was doing about 30 knots and was unfamiliar with the area when he went on the wrong side of the buoy — not a good thing.

Environment Canada (similar to the National Oceanic and Atmospheric Association in the U.S.A.) kept announcing high-wind warnings and rain on the marine radio for that night, the next night, and Sunday, so we decided to journey to the famous tourist restaurant, Henry's Fish and Chips, where we could also dock overnight and evaluate conditions on Saturday.

---

[3] *See notes on pages 109-110*

Once *Reflection* was tied up, I decided to go for a walk to explore the small rocky island. I began heading up a marked trail over rocks and boulders toward a wooded area. As I went along, the walk became more of a climb than a stroll through the park. When I approached a wooded area, I heard something that sounded like an angry animal and decided that this might be a good time to return to the boat.

As I was on my way back, I met the dockmaster and asked if there were any bears on the island. "Sure," he said. "I see bears around here all the time." Then with a smile on his face, he said, "You should always walk with someone else around here, so if a bear comes along, all you have to do is outrun the other person." I thanked him for his words of wisdom and quickly continued back to the boat with this comforting thought in mind.

Shortly after I returned, we were happy to see *Maya Lisa*, with Hank and Ceci aboard, pull into the dock because we had not seen them since first meeting them in the Peterborough Lift Lock on June 28. We had cocktails together on their boat with dinner afterward at the restaurant. I then remembered that hike I wanted to take and thought I could probably outrun Hank. I wondered if he would like to go for a walk?

It was fun hearing about the places that Hank and Ceci had visited since we last saw them. They had lived all over the world because of Hank's career as a U.S. Foreign Aid official, and they now cruised on their boat about five months a year.

The four of us went to dinner at Henry's, where the food was served family-style with entrees of fresh pickerel, white fish, or perch, pan-fried or battered, along with tartar sauce and lemon slices, and side orders of French fries, brown beans, and coleslaw. We knew that the food here had to be good because on long weekends they serve more than 1,500 meals. Our fried pickerel dinner that evening at the restaurant was no exception, and afterward, we came back to our boat to discuss our mutual future planned stops.

July 11 — 7 miles to Kineras Bay, Ontario[4-5]

Despite early morning showers with continued high-wind warnings, conditions seemed fine enough for us to continue on our way. *Maya Lisa* had decided to head to a marina in Parry Sound, but we wanted to spend another night at anchor, so they headed out ahead of us and we hoped we would catch up to them. What was good about this trip was that we would see familiar looper boats on occasion, but everyone kept to their own particular schedule.

[4-5] *See notes on page 110*

That day we attempted to go into another designated Canadian public land overnight anchorage. Some of these even had small docks where you could go ashore and tie up to rings on the land or to moorings if the boat was less than 35 feet, but many boats also anchored Mediterranean-style by putting down a forward anchor and then tying a stern line to a tree. This kind of close anchorage was not a good idea for our 48-foot boat because on the weekends these spots were jammed, and we always liked to keep swinging room around *Reflection*. Instead, we again went a little farther afield and found beautiful Kineras Bay, where we were the only boat anchored amidst trees and cottages.

The view from Reflection *of our anchorage at Kineras Bay*

July 12 — 9 miles to Parry Sound, Ontario[6-7]

After a lovely evening at anchor, we made our way to Big Sound Marina in Parry Sound.

The body of water and the town of Parry Sound is named in honor of the Arctic explorer Sir William Edward Parry, and it is the location of the world's deepest natural freshwater port. This is also is the birthplace of hockey legend Bobby Orr, who is the namesake of the local community center and the Bobby Orr Hall of Fame. During the year, the town hosts several cultural festivals, including the Festival of the Sound classical music festival and an annual dragon boat race.

Several familiar boats were docked here and in the adjacent marina: *Adagio* from Ohio, *Maya Lisa* from Virginia, and *Houlegan* from Mississippi. We were all loopers and on relatively the same schedule.

Although it was a sunny day, the wind was howling, and many of the local Canadians were moaning about the fact that the weather had been about 20 degrees cooler than usual. Since their summer begins to wind down around August 15, every day counted for them, and we had to agree that it felt more like fall there than the middle of July.

Later that afternoon, we lost one of the most valued members of our *Reflection* family. Our faithful servant, the ice maker, passed away. For the past 18 months, it had served us well, producing thousands of ice cubes without asking anything in return. For the past week, it had not seemed itself, constantly running and hardly producing any ice. Then later in the afternoon, it stopped working altogether, and after valiant attempts, we were unable to resuscitate it. The problem was its compressor: After 22 loyal years of service on the boat, it had popped its last cube. I was in mourning because, as every one of my friends and acquaintances clearly knows, I love my ice!

The ice maker (1987-2009) — gone, but not forgotten
Notice the flowers out of respect for its passing.

July 13 — Parry Sound, Ontario

Because the wind was still blowing hard, we decided to stay another day and use our time to do chores around the boat, laundry, and food shopping. Food (and everything else) was expensive here compared to prices in the U.S. On top of it all, an additional 13 percent sales tax was added to just about everything with the exception of food, yet transient dockage prices at the marinas were reasonable compared to those at home.

We invited Pam and Dave from *Adagio* aboard for happy hour so we could share information we had about marinas in Florida. After they left, we went over to a local café for dinner and had a pleasant conversation with a Canadian couple from our marina that was seated at the table next to ours. As they watched me fumble around to pay the check with a combination of $1 coins known as "loonies" and $2 coins known as "toonies," plus a variety of colored paper currency, they asked us how we liked using their Canadian "Monopoly" money. Pat said that she had been having some issues with the loonies and the toonies and was sometimes not sure which was which. The couple told us that on their last trip to the U.S., because all our currency is the same green color, they nearly gave a taxi driver a $100 tip, thinking it was a $10 bill. We agreed that as long as it would still buy dinner, the color of the money did not matter.

July 14 — 29 miles to Hopewell Bay, Ontario[8-9]

Pat and I decided to get underway at 8:30 a.m. because the wind had finally lightened up. When we left, the marina looked like a ghost town because some of the boats that had waited out the weather here for as much as five days had made a run for it even earlier than we did this morning. It was only in the low 50s with a breeze when we started out, so we were dressed in our full storm gear with additional socks, gloves, hats, and hoods. Happily, there was no snow forecast! That was certainly the coldest July 14 we had ever experienced.

I carefully followed our GPS and the charts on this 29-mile trip that took place amidst rugged, yet beautiful scenery with pristine waters that had changed color to an almost ocean green. After we anchored in roomy Hopewell Bay, nine other boats joined us, with five of them forming a raft-up. A short time after our arrival, we heard a "Mayday" being called in our vicinity on the marine radio. One of a group of kayakers had experienced a serious breathing problem and needed emergency care, but she and her friends were located on one of the rocky islands. Boats were trying to come to the rescue but could not get close enough because of the rocks. The Coast Guard was on the line, and we did not hear the details, but the patient was eventually transported to shore where an ambulance was waiting.

8-9 *See notes on page 110*

Killbear Point Light on our way to Hopewell Bay

After the excitement, we enjoyed a quiet afternoon and evening. There was light in the sky until well after 10:30 p.m., and we believed it might have been the glow of the Aurora Borealis, otherwise known as the Northern Lights. Yes, we were that far north.

July 15 and 16 — 33 miles to Britt, Ontario[10-11]

We traveled about 33 miles in the company of *Adagio* to Byng Inlet and the village of Britt, Ontario. Thirteen of those miles were on the open waters of Georgian Bay, which we heard can be uncomfortable when the wind is in a westerly direction. Fortunately, that day it was coming from the southeast, somewhat on our stern, and we were safely into the inlet before things picked up.

 Britt is located on the north shore of the Magnetawan River, and it was originally a sawmill village known as Byng Inlet North when the mill was located here in 1880. Between 1903 and 1908, the community was established as a port for receiving coal, which was required for the Canadian Pacific Railway's steam locomotives. It was after this that Byng Inlet North was renamed Britt in honor of a CPR Superintendent.

Point au Baril Lighthouse along the way to Britt, Ontario

We stayed at Wright's Marina, which is a small, family-owned operation in existence for more than 35 years. They even offered us a courtesy car, but there was no actual town to visit. Although it was raining, we ventured out to meet Dave and Pam from *Adagio*, who were staying at another marina, for dinner at a restaurant called The Little Britt Inn. We had been advised not to miss it because it was on "The Best Places to Eat in Canada" list, and we were delighted to find out that the inn would send a car to take us to dinner.

The menu carried a varied selection of tasty items, including elk medallions and perchburgers among their other more conventional offerings. Those particular local dinner selections, our driver's account of the 35-degrees-below-zero winter temperatures often experienced here, and a tale of how he had often spotted bears along the road mere steps away from our boat reminded us that we were a long way from our lagoon in New Jersey!

We continued our stay at Wright's Marina for an additional day because the winds had increased and rain showers occurred all day. This brief respite, however, allowed us to catch up again on chores, make some phone calls, catch up on email, and cook an Italian dinner aboard. Weather delays can often be a blessing.

July 17 — 39 miles to Beaverstone Bay, Ontario[12]

Adagio called us from their marina this morning, and we initially decided to make the 33-mile journey to Beaverstone Bay together. The wind had calmed, but the skies were still overcast with cool temperatures. Our boat, however, was placed on an inside dock, which was perpendicular to the gas dock. So unfortunately, when a sailboat came in for fuel and a pump-out, it boxed us in and prevented us from leaving according to plan.

For our uninitiated readers, a "pump-out" is a process in which a vacuum pump hose is attached to a fitting on the boat's deck, and waste from a holding tank containing the boat's toilet deposits are vacuumed out into a sewer line. It is a simple procedure, but on this particular day, a 13-year-old dockhand was in charge.

Beaverstone Bay anchorage

The captain of the sailboat gave the boy his credit card for the fuel and pump-out, but for some unknown reason, the boy placed the credit card into his mouth. What happened next was a sight we will never forget. Trying to appear experienced, the boy quickly pumped out the tank, but then he inadvertently removed the hose too early. Suddenly, from deep within the bowels of the boat, a geyser of human feces erupted, shot several feet into the air, and sprayed the sailboat and the dockhand with all manner of human waste! Luckily, *Reflection* was clear of

---

[12] *See notes on page 110*

the "impact zone"! We felt so sorry for the boy, who was embarrassed and literally covered in crap. Not wanting to make him feel any worse than he already did, we turned away and cracked up laughing for the longest time. It had to be one of the funniest things I had ever seen, but I did have to admit that I admired the boy because, although he was filthy, he never did drop the credit card.

Amazingly, the boat owner kept his cool and cleaned up the mess on his deck, as the young dockhand quickly headed home for a shower and fresh clothes. I am sure his mother was glad to see him! Finally after cleaning up, the sailboat pulled out and we were able to leave.

By then, we were about an hour behind *Adagio*, but we called and asked them to find us a good anchorage. We operated our boat from the lower inside station to escape the chill as we crossed Georgian Bay, and eventually we tucked ourselves into a lovely anchorage among the rocky islands of Beaverstone Bay with *Adagio* nearby.

July 18 — 21 miles to Killarney, Ontario — The North Channel[13-14]

Adagio decided they would like another night at anchor, so we said goodbye to them in Beaverstone Bay at 7:30 a.m. because we wanted to move on and get to the Killarney Mountain Lodge early enough to enjoy a full day in the village. A good portion of the 21-mile trip took place through jagged Collins Inlet, a narrow, deep, high-walled fjord. It was breathtaking with its sheer, multicolored granite walls and trees that grow right out of the rocks. At the end of the Inlet, we crossed the last section of Georgian Bay to the village of Killarney, which marked our first port on the North Channel.

 For many years, Killarney was known as Shebahonaning, an Ojibwe name meaning "canoe passage." There seems to be no exact date when the community was established, and when and why the name was changed to Killarney (maybe because it is easier to say) is also unknown. Fur trading, logging, commercial fishing, mining, and tourism have all played a major role in Killarney's economy, yet before 1962 there was no road access to it. However, steamships that carried passengers and freight to locations around the area serviced the community.

Our slip was open when we arrived, and by 11:30 a.m. we had tied up the boat and scoped out the entire community, which was just a few blocks long. A town is small when it has only one gas station, and Killarney had none. However, we soon found ourselves on line at Mr. Perch, a fish restaurant located on the waterway in an old school bus that is attached to Herbert Fisheries and is famous for its fried whitefish and fries. Naturally, it began to shower just as we were about to order, but the rain did not last long. We procured seats at a picnic bench under a tent, where we enjoyed watching boats of all types passing by. The fish and fries lived up to their reputation!

Collins Inlet

The parking lot was filled with fish and chip seekers by the time we left. We followed up our low-cholesterol lunch with Farquhar's ice cream, a product made on Manitoulin Island, the enormous barrier island that is the breakwater for the North Channel from Lake Huron.

The weather fluctuated widely all day — sun, then clouds, then rain — almost every five minutes. We had a lovely dinner at the lodge and then headed for the Carousel Bar, which was also located on the premises, to hear Andy Lowe, a singer who had performed there for ten years. He put on a good show, acknowledged us as loopers from New Jersey, and noted Pat's trained singing voice that could obviously be heard on each sing-along.

Mr. Perch Fish and Chips — a fine dining establishment in Killarney

July 19 — 7 miles to Covered Portage Cove, Ontario[15]

Just as we thought the scenery could not get any more beautiful, we entered the magnificent North Channel. Though we had traveled only 7 miles out of Killarney to Covered Portage Cove, it was a wonder to behold. The mountains appeared to be covered in snow, but were made out of white limestone rock. Some of it reminded us of the British Virgin Islands, where the islands are built on coral. Instead, these were built on stone, but the water was equally blue-green and pristine.

As we entered the anchorage, we could see the Indian Chief, a stone outcropping in the cliffs that with little imagination looked like the head of a Native American. We decided to anchor in the outside anchorage of Covered Portage Cove, but we eventually put the dinghy in the water and explored also the inner cove, which we felt was too small for our boat. The areas turned out to be wonderful anchorage spots with at least eight more boats in the outer cove and another six in the inner cove that eventually joined us.

---

[15] *See notes on page 111*

Covered Portage Cove anchorage

July 20 — 21 miles to Little Current, Ontario[16]

After a quiet night, we traveled down the Landsdowne Channel past large limestone rock islands to the town of Little Current, where the waters of the North Channel were funneled into a 100-yard passage into Georgian Bay. The town is on the tip of large Manitoulin Island and is connected to Goat Island by a swing bridge that opens only on the hour for 15 minutes, so boats must time their arrival and jockey for position in front of the bridge in the often swift-moving current to make it through.

Luckily, there was little current when we arrived at the bridge, so we passed through smoothly and were tied up at the Town Docks by 11:30 a.m. This was a good place to get groceries and do our final banking and laundry before we returned to the U.S. We also found a Chinese restaurant that delivered dinner to our boat, and the meal provided us with authentic ambiance as we viewed one of our many "Charlie Chan" DVDs that evening.

---

[16] *See notes on page 111*

The harbor at Little Current

July 21 – 19 miles to The Benjamin Islands, Ontario[17]

We had an early breakfast at the Anchor Inn, which was an old hotel located one block from the docks. Upstairs, there was a room that is the broadcast studio of Roy Eaton, who is the host of "The Little Current Cruisers Network," which broadcasts every day in July and August at 9 a.m. on VHF channel 71.

Roy is a retired high school principal who began the service in 2004, and it has grown beyond his wildest dreams. He provides the latest marine weather, world news, sports scores, business reports, and North Channel events, and he also takes call-ins from boaters traveling in the area. Some have messages to transmit to other boats, but most just announce where they are located and what their next destination is. Roy's service is registered with the Coast Guard and Air Search and Rescue, and it has helped in finding many boaters. This morning, Pat and I were privileged to sit in at his broadcast with other boaters to see what goes on behind the scenes. On this one day we assisted him by writing down the names and information on 124 boats in the area, and during the previous summer, he had received 4,708 call-ins. We had a good time at the studio, and it was a pleasure to meet Roy, a wonderful man who volunteers his time and talent to help people.

We finally left the dock after the morning's events for the lovely Benjamin Islands, a favorite anchoring area in the North Channel. We rode around for a while among the pink granite rock formations to evaluate what would be the best location for *Reflection*, eventually finding a spot in a beautiful open area where we anchored in 41 feet of water. We were not alone, however, because 22 other smaller boats were also anchored in the shallower waters nearby.

The Benjamin Islands — You have just got to love rocks.
It is a quiet anchorage, but notice the leaning trees.

Many of the trees on the islands permanently leaned toward the southeast and had few branches on their northwest sides because of the fierce winter winds that blasted into them from that direction. We kept our eyes open for bears, which had been spotted on the shores in previous years eating blueberries, but we did not spot any that day. Speaking of wildlife, on our travels in Canada, the only wildlife we have seen was a bunch of partygoers on our first night in Picton. We have not seen a single bear, moose, or eagle since arriving in the country.

The forecast for the evening was an unusual one — clear skies — so I woke up at 2 a.m. to see if I could spot the Northern Lights. We were told it was visible at these latitudes, and there it was — the Aurora Borealis! At this latitude, it appeared as a false sunrise in the northern sky with a beautiful bright blue green glow. I woke up Pat so she would not miss this wondrous sight. She was somewhat less enthusiastic than I was about getting up at this early hour, yet we both stood there for a while staring at the marvel.

Pat returned to bed, and as I stayed up looking up at the heavens, I thought to myself about what an amazing journey it had been so far, despite the less-than-perfect weather. Together, we had traveled up the magnificent Hudson River, passed through the historic Erie Canal, crossed vast Lake Ontario, followed the beautiful Trent-Severn Waterway, cruised glorious Georgian Bay, and now we had seen the Aurora Borealis. I was one lucky man, and life was good.

July 22 — 15 miles to Gore Bay, Ontario[18]

After another peaceful night at anchor, we headed 15 miles across the North Channel to Gore Bay. Showers were expected for the next several days, so we decided to pull into the Gore Bay Marina for the night. Gore Bay is a small com-

---

[18] *See notes on page 111*

munity of about 1,000, but during the summer months, the population grows as boaters and tourists flock to the area. Yet it is not exactly known as a "party" town.

Shortly after we tied up, *Houlegan*, with loopers Ray and Caryl from Mississippi, pulled in. We had last seen them on Saturday in Killarney when they stopped by to chat, but because we never had gotten a chance to visit with them, we invited them aboard for happy hour. We had a delightful evening hearing about the experiences they'd had on their trip, which began in Gulfport, Mississippi, on Dec. 1, 2008. Ray, who is retired from the Navy, and Caryl, who is retired from the Air Force and is a registered nurse, expected to complete their Loop by Thanksgiving.

For days, I had been agonizing over the departed icemaker. Whether to buy a new ice maker — that was the question. You might remember that our icemaker gave up the ghost awhile back. Since then, I had been doing some figuring on whether it was practical to continue to buy bagged ice, or instead, to purchase a new ice-maker at the hefty price of about $1,100.

The calculation went like this: A 5-pound bag of ice cost about $2.25. If we used one bag of ice every day and a half, throughout the next year we would use about 240 bags because we would be on the boat almost all the time. So I figured the cost of bagged ice for the year would be about $540. However, after the year, we might only be on the boat about 30 days a year with an estimated ice cost of $45. The question was: How many years it would take to break even if we bought a new ice maker? I calculated about 13 years. Also added into the calculation was the fact that we might only keep the boat for another few years.

My heart overruled my head, and the answer became obvious. Definitely, I love my ice! Therefore, we ordered the ice maker with expected delivery and installation when we reach Holland, Michigan.

July 23 — 27 miles to Blind River, Ontario[19]

We left the dock under bleak skies with cool temperatures for Blind River.

 Blind River is a port 27 miles away from Gore Bay on the northern shore of the North Channel. The early settlers named the river, Blind River, because the mouth was not visible along the canoe route. Its name was also adopted by the settlement that grew at the mouth of the river area, which fur traders first settled in the late 1700s. Today the town's economy is based on tourism, fishing, logging, and uranium refining.

This location would be our last in Canada, but what we did not realize was that it is also the first stop in Canada for boats traveling from Lake Michigan and Lake Huron. After we tied up at Blind River Marine Park, and just as I thought we would leave the country without Canadian Customs boarding our boat, two officials made their way down the dock checking other boats and then headed to ours.

They came to our boat, because they thought that we were entering Canada, not leaving it, and were charming and gracious to us. All they did was check our boat papers, verify the customs number that we were given in Picton when we entered Canada, and stamp our passports. They did not even board us and stated that our boat was so beautiful that they did not want to come into our salon with dirty shoes. That is what I call good international relations!

We later took a cab into town to celebrate our last night in Canada with dinner at the Mustang Bar at the Iron Horse Restaurant. It was wing night, which always attracts me. Pat ordered a jumbo shrimp cocktail and a rib and wing combo platter that came with a salad. I ordered a platter of chicken wings, poutine (a Canadian dish of fries covered with yummy gravy and cheese), and an order of onion rings. You can imagine our surprise when this already over-the-top feast came out with a shrimp and fries platter — their version of a shrimp cocktail. Our table was filled, and it was a cardiologist's nightmare! We ended up taking most of the wings and ribs back to the boat and had lots of laughs on our last night in town. The Admiral and I fell asleep quickly, comfortable in the knowledge that by the next evening we would be back in the U.S.A.

Notes:

(1)
Bay Port Yachting Centre is a full-service marina that is a top facility in all respects and charges reasonable rates. The staff will drive you to stores and scenic attractions, and their customer service abounds. Go into the office with your charts, and help will be available to assist you in planning your route through Georgian Bay.

(2)
When traveling in Georgian Bay or in the North Channel, if you see what looks like a white jug or anything else white that is floating, it is probably marking a rock just below the surface. The deeper, safer water is clearly marked. If you are paying attention, you will have no problem transiting the area.

(3)
Henry's Fish Camp has a dock staff that is extremely helpful in tying up your boat on your arrival and untying on departure. Just call ahead on VHF channel 68

for information. Their dockage and the good food served at their restaurant are reasonably priced.

(4)
Anchorages are extremely crowded on the weekends, so it is wise to plan alternate anchorages.

(5)
Kineras Bay has room and is an excellent spot in all wind directions except southeast.

(6)
Parry Sound — The swing bridge leading to the harbor opens on the hour from 6 a.m. to 10 p.m.

(7)
Big Sound town dock has dockage that is reasonably priced, and several supermarkets are in the area, some even with shuttle service from the marina. A taxi service, restaurants, and an automotive store are available. All the marinas in the town have some exposure to wind and waves.

(8)
On the route to Hopewell Bay — If your boat is more than 40 feet, Canoe Channel should not be used. Instead, take the route around Squaw Island to the south.

(9)
Hopewell Bay has room and is an excellent anchorage in all but southeast winds.

(10)
Facilities at Point au Baril on the way to Byng are limited. Under no circumstances should you go through Hangdog Channel, which is dangerous in any weather.

(11)
Byng is an easy inlet to find and navigate because there are several sets of range markers to guide you in, and it is well marked with buoys. The marinas are friendly and The Little Britt Inn will send a car to bring you to and from dinner. There is limited provisioning in the area with not much of a town.

(12)
Beaverstone Bay has numerous anchorage possibilities. It is easy to navigate and is scenic, but choose your spot wisely based on wind direction.

(13)
Collins Inlet has a narrow low water area near the entrance about a half-mile long with the deepest water clearly marked by buoys. It is frequently deeper than is

indicated on the charts, but use caution. The fjord is scenic, deep, and somewhat narrow, but two boats have enough room to pass easily.

(14)
Killarney is a small village with several marinas, some limited provisioning, and no banks. It is home to the well-known Mr. Perch fish and chips eatery and has good breakfasts and home-baked bread at the Gateway Marina Restaurant. The Killarney Mountain Lodge offers traditional lodge dinners with entertainment nightly in its Carousel Bar.

(15)
It is an easy route to Covered Portage Cove with room for several boats on the inside anchorage and more on the outside anchorage, where the Indian in the Mountain rock formation is located.

(16)
On the trip to Little Current — Timing is important at the swing bridge (18-feet clearance) because it only opens for 15 minutes on the hour. The town docks are the most convenient to the town area with a nearby laundry facility, banks, a pharmacy, and a hospital. The grocery store will drive you back to the boat, and pizza and Chinese food can also be delivered. Just see the dockmaster.

(17)
The Benjamin Islands offers several anchorage choices. Some are completely protected, but they can be crowded in the summer even during the week, so get there early.

(18)
Gore Bay has a bank, supermarket, hardware store, pharmacy, several restaurants, and is an easy run from the Benjamins. Gore Bay Marina has long finger pier slips with plenty of room to maneuver. There is a fee for Wi-Fi at the marina and a small anchorage just outside.

(19)
Blind River has a pharmacy, bank, restaurants within a 15- to 20- minute walk to town, and a taxi service. The marina has a friendly staff and Wi-Fi. The local bank will also exchange Canadian money for U.S. at the current exchange rate.

Chapter 7

Back in the U. S. of A.

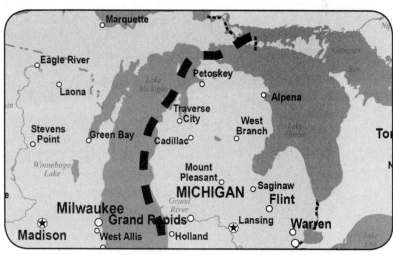

July 24 — 43 miles to Drummond Island, Michigan[1]

We spent our last bit of Canadian money at the Blind River fuel dock before we left in the morning on our 43-mile crossing to the U.S. After *Reflection* was about an hour out of the harbor, we headed into pea soup-thick fog, and it took us only a short while to decide that sitting up on the flybridge in cold and damp conditions was not that much fun, so we went below and ran the boat across from our cozy salon. With our running lights on, we slowed down our speed, turned on the radar, and listened closely to the many calls being made on the marine radio from boats trying to find out the fog conditions in various locations.

Once the fog lifted to visibility of about a quarter of a mile, we picked up a boat heading toward us on radar, so we quickly sized up the situation. It appeared that we would pass each other safely port-to-port with about 200 feet between us. As the other vessel came into view, I noticed one of the crew members looking at our boat through binoculars while gesturing to the other members on board to come look. We soon realized that we must have looked somewhat like a ghost ship because there was no one to be seen on our flybridge and, with our boat's tinted windows, they could not see that we were below. As our two vessels began passing each other, I gave a blast on the air horn just to let them know we were at the helm. It was amazing to watch them jump!

Eventually the fog cleared, and on our approach to Drummond Island, the sun came out. As we crossed into U.S. waters, Pat hummed "The Star-Spangled Banner." On entering the channel, we were delighted to see American flags flying on all the houses we passed. Even though our past five weeks in Canada had been great, we simply missed our own country for so many reasons: lower prices on just about everything, familiar currency, a broader variety of supermarket items and brands that were familiar to us, and fuel measurements in gallons, not liters. We were glad to be home.

 Drummond Island is a port of entry for U.S. vessels coming from Canada with a Customs and Immigration office located at Drummond Island Yacht Haven. The island was originally a part of Canada and was named after Lieutenant General Gordon Drummond, the commander of all British forces in Canada during the War of 1812, but after the war it was turned over to the US. Today, this island has a sparse population of about 1,000 people, and it is a gathering place for a birds and wildlife.

Within 15 minutes of docking, a U.S. Customs and Immigration official came onboard, checked us out, and charged us $27.50 for a Customs decal that would be sent to us to display on the boat. He asked if we had bought anything in Canada to bring back to the U.S., but when we jokingly told him we did not even buy a souvenir because of the exorbitant prices, he laughed understandably. It seemed that all he cared about was that we did not bring any lamb, goat, or citrus into the country. So, we told him that we had thrown all the lambs and goats overboard on our way in and that we would dispose of the one lime we had left on board (in our cocktails) that evening!

Houlegan arrived an hour later, and Ray and Caryl invited us to their boat to meet another couple, Dan and Mary Jo, who were traveling onboard their Island Packet 35 sailboat, *Dauntless*, from Michigan. After consuming adult beverages and swapping stories, we headed back to *Reflection* for a quiet dinner aboard. I could not help thinking about how much we had enjoyed our time in Canada, how good it felt to be back in the U.S., and how much I was looking forward to our next adventure in the Great Lakes.

July 25 — Drummond Island, Michigan

We awoke to heavy rain, so we decided to stay at Drummond Island Yacht Haven for another day to do chores, make phone calls, and plan the next segment of our trip on Lake Michigan. Dan and Mary Jo, whom we had met the previous evening, turned out to be a source of local knowledge for the best places to visit in the following few weeks, and we made changes to our itinerary based on their information. Afterward, we rented a car at the marina to do grocery shopping and returned back just in time to host Ray, Caryl, Dan, and Mary Jo on our boat for cocktails and more stories.

July 26 — 28 miles to Les Cheneaux Islands, Michigan[2]

With the skies still overcast and the temperatures in the low 60s, we traveled 28 miles through the DeTour Passage to the Les Cheneaux (The Channels) Islands.

De Tour Light

Located along a 12-mile stretch of the northwest shore of Lake Huron, Les Cheneaux are a group of 36 small islands, and only some of them are inhabited. The area is appropriately named for the many channels between the islands in the group, and it is also well known for hosting the world's largest antique wooden boat show each August.

The winds were fairly light, and we proceeded to Government Bay, one of the best places to anchor in this group of islands. Though the wind came up later in the day, we were in a protected spot and spent a calm night with occasional rain but with plenty of room around us.

July 27 — 23 miles to Saint Ignace, Michigan[3-5]

This morning, after winding our way carefully through the channels of the Les Cheneaux Islands and experiencing about 11 miles of its somewhat shallow depths and twisting turns, we finally entered the open waters of Lake Huron for the final 12 miles of our journey to Saint Ignace Municipal Marina.

 Saint Ignace is one of the oldest cities Europeans founded in Michigan. French explorer and priest Jacques Marquette built the Saint Ignace Mission, which he named for Saint Ignatius of Loyola, the superior of the Jesuit religious order, in 1671. In 1763, the British took over the territory after their victory over the French in the Seven Years War, and it became part of the US in 1783 after the pesky American revolutionaries won their fight with the English. After being kicked back and forth from country to country, it was finally incorporated as a Michigan city in 1833.

Saint Ignace is the location of one of the ferry crossings to Mackinac Island, and it stands on the northern side of the vast Mackinac Island Bridge over the Straits. A huge stone breakwater protects the marina, and we decided that this would be a better place to keep *Reflection* in light of the huge ferry wakes that are generated in the waters near Mackinac Island and in commercial Mackinaw City, which is another ferry crossing on the mainland side.

To our surprise, the waters of Lake Huron are as crystal clear and blue as those of the Caribbean, and they were certainly not what we expected. As we approached Saint Ignace, we came behind Mackinac Island and caught sight of the bridge as we made our turn toward the harbor. *Reflection* was tied up by 11:30 a.m., and we spent the rest of the day making plans for our visit to the famous island.

3-5 See notes on page 138

Boat houses along Les Cheneaux

Docked next to us was *Morningstar*, a Grand Banks 49, owned by Gerry and Jeanne, a couple from Livonia, Michigan. They had completed the Loop recently and had docked their boat in Marathon, Florida, last winter. They shared information with us about Lake Michigan and made other suggestions about good harbors for the rest of our trip. We really appreciated local knowledge!

July 28 — Saint Ignace (Mackinac Island), Michigan

Pat and I boarded the ferry to Mackinac Island at 9:30 a.m. for the 5-mile crossing.

 Europeans explored Mackinac Island during the 17th century, and natives lived there about 700 years prior to that. It was a strategic location for the Great Lakes fur trade, which led to the establishment of Fort Mackinac by the British during the American Revolutionary War. It was in the late 19th century that Mackinac Island became a popular tourist attraction, and much of the island had undergone such extensive historical preservation and restoration that the entire island was put on the National Historic Landmarks register. It is well known for its cultural events, the famous Grand Hotel, its fudge, and its ban on all motor vehicles except those for fire and police. Not to arouse suspicion by any wrongdoers, the single police car is unmarked!

As we approached the harbor on this beautiful, sunny day, the scene was extremely festive because about 100 sailboats that had just participated in the Port Huron-Mackinac Race filled the docks with their banners and flags flying. Because automobiles are not permitted on the island, the only methods of transportation are by horse-drawn vehicles, bicycles, or foot, so the downtown was crowded with animals and people.

Downtown Mackinac at rush hour

The first thing we noticed once ashore was the aroma of a combination of horse manure and fudge that filled the air. The island produces two main products: fudge (about 1,000 pounds a day) and horse manure (about 6,000 pounds a day), with horse manure being its chief export; they ship tons of it off the island as natural fertilizer.

We then joined our fellow tourists, and our first order of business was to take a carriage tour of the island. The tour made various stops, and we got to see the huge and lovely Grand Hotel. We also toured Fort Mackinac, where we took part in several reenactments of military life in the 1880s. We also enjoyed lunch that the Grand Hotel provided on a promontory of the Fort with a view of the town and harbor that was absolutely gorgeous. Following lunch, we visited several historic sites that were also part of the Fort tour and then returned to Saint Ignace by ferry. We also decided to come back to the island the next day for lunch, a tour of the Grand Hotel, and to do some shopping in this tourist "Mecca."

Fort Mackinac and the tea room deck (upper left)

Local transportation

July 29 — Saint Ignace (Mackinac Island), Michigan

Having finished our chores earlier in the morning, we took an 11:30 a.m. ferry back to Mackinac Island. The racing sailboats had completely evacuated the harbor, but a small American Caribbean cruise line ship, Grande Mariner, occupied some of the ferry dock space with about 100 passengers aboard.

The town was again bustling with bicyclers, riders on horseback, horse-drawn vehicles of various types, and many pedestrians. We surveyed the scene for a while and then summoned a horse-drawn taxi to take us up to the Grand Hotel. On entering, a concierge greeted us and advised us that the fee was $10 per person to tour the hotel and its grounds, but the fee could also be applied to the cost of lunch, which was $40 per person. Because this was our plan, we then made our way up to the enormous dining room that overlooked the hotel's porch, which was the size of a football field, with its stunning view of the water.

Limousine service at the Grand Hotel

The buffet lunch was lavish with choices of fruits, salads, shrimp, oysters, cold meats, breads, prime rib, fish, chicken, pasta entrees, potato and vegetable accompaniments, followed by sumptuous offerings on the dessert tables. Needless to say, we enjoyed a wonderful lunch in a delightful atmosphere and decided that, considering the price included tax and a tip, it was reasonable for the caliber of food, ambience, and service we received.

The Grand Hotel Dining Room (a grand lunch at the Grand Buffet)

We then ventured out onto the porch and sat in the sun on two of what looked like hundreds of rocking chairs that were out there and commented about our friends who would have enjoyed being there with us. Later, Pat and I returned to town via the elegant Grand Hotel carriage to shop, and then took the ferry back to Saint Ignace after having spent a very special day on Mackinac Island.

July 30 — 42 miles to Saint James Harbor, Beaver Island, Michigan[6-7]

We first filled up at Saint Ignace Marina with diesel fuel in the morning and then headed out for a 42-mile journey to Beaver Island, which is the largest island on Lake Michigan.

 Although Beaver Island today is known for its beaches, forests, and seclusion, at one time it was the site of a unique Mormon kingdom. After the death of Joseph Smith, founder of The Church of Jesus Christ of Latter-day Saints, most Mormons considered Brigham Young to be Smith's successor. Others followed James J. Strang, who founded The Church of Jesus Christ of Latter-day Saints (Strangite), which he claimed to be the only legitimate continuation of the church of Joseph Smith. Seeking refuge from persecution and isolation and to increase his control of the group, Strang moved his followers from Wisconsin to Beaver Island in 1848. He eventually declared himself king of his church; however, he tried to extend his rule to all the occupants of the island. Because not everyone was thrilled about the effort, clashes frequently broke out between his followers and the other residents.

One of his edicts declared how all the women on the island should dress, and when two women refused to go along with it, he had their husbands flogged. This was not a good idea because while the two men were recovering from their wounds, they were also plotting Strang's demise. On June 16, 1856, the U.S. naval gunboat U.S.S. Michigan pulled into the harbor and invited Strang to come aboard. Alas, he was being set up. As Strang walked down the dock, the men shot him and then ran onto the ship. The boat pulled out and dropped the men off at Mackinac Island. Neither was convicted of the crime, and they were not even arrested for it. "What goes around, comes around!" After Strang's death, mobs from Mackinac Island and Saint Helena Island drove the Strangites off Beaver Island and confiscated their property.

Conditions in the Straits of Mackinac as we traveled under the Mackinac Bridge were quite nice.

 The Straits is the strip of water that connects Lake Michigan and Lake Huron, and it is a shipping lane that provides passage for commercial vessels traveling between Lake Michigan and ports on the other Great Lakes and beyond. At its narrowest point, (5 miles) it is spanned by the Mackinac Bridge, which connects the upper and lower peninsulas of Michigan. Envisioned since the 1880s, the bridge was completed in 1957 and is the third longest in total suspension in the world.

As we left the Straits and made our turn into the lake, however, the wind and waves picked up on our nose. When the spray finally started hitting us up on the flybridge, we went down to the lower station in the salon to operate the boat. Pat and I were safe and thankful that we were in our fairly large vessel, but truthfully, the conditions were not that good — sort of like riding a bucking bronco! About 10 miles out from the island, some of the furniture in the salon was sliding about, and I looked at the Admiral and said, "Are we having fun yet?" She was less than enthusiastic, and then she gave me "the look."

Fortunately, although the seas made the trip rather uncomfortable, it was by no means a dangerous situation, and the wind and waves began to calm as we approached the island, but now it started to rain. When we finally arrived at Beaver Island Marina, the personnel were welcoming and friendly, and we were glad to get safely tied up. During the rest of the day, however, we kept watching for a sailboat we had seen in the Straits that we knew was also supposed to be coming into Beaver Island Marina, but it never showed up, and the crews of the boats that did come in arrived looking wet and weary.

I walked into town later to purchase groceries and found a fried chicken takeout restaurant that provided us with a tasty dinner while we watched cable TV for the first time since we had left home on June 6. After an hour of viewing, however, we decided that we had not missed a thing.

July 31 – 32 miles to Petoskey, Michigan[8]

Summer finally made an appearance. We had a lovely 32-mile trip across the lake to Petoskey with the wind at our stern for a change and calm seas with mild temperatures. What a difference a day makes! As we headed into Little Traverse Bay, the scenery was reminiscent of Chesapeake Bay with many small sailboats out on the water.

 Petoskey is a city and coastal resort of about 6,000 and is named after Chief Ignatius Petosega (1787-1885), who founded the community. The name Petoskey is thought to mean, "where the light shines through the clouds," and happily for us, that is just what it was doing. The city and the surrounding area were the setting of several of the Nick Adams stories by Ernest Hemingway, and it is also famous for its high concentration of Petoskey stones, the state stone of Michigan.

Petoskey Marina is a fairly new marina with nice facilities that is set behind a stone breakwater. The town is a close walk with many upscale stores and fun restaurants, and the marina adjoins a lovely museum and park.

We had dinner at Papa Joe's restaurant, and on our return to the dock, we were delighted to see that *Dauntless*, with Dan and Mary Jo aboard, had also come into port from Saint Ignace. We were all watching the weather as the winds were supposed to pick up from the southwest the next day, so we planned to make our decision to stay or leave in the morning.

---

[8] *See notes on page 139*

Aug. 1 — Petoskey, Michigan

The wind forecasts for Lake Michigan continued to deteriorate, and there were discussions on the dock about what to do. Dan and I traded Internet sites for wind and wave predictions, and being that he is a boater from the area, he even had a phone site to call for buoy reports on the lake. After reviewing our information, we agreed that we should stay put for another day.

The Admiral and I then made use of the day by catching up on our chores, did some advance planning on the Chicago, Illinois River, and Mississippi River legs of our journey, and emailed some of our Great Loop friends who had already traveled the areas for advice and suggestions. Mary Jo and Dan invited us over for dessert in the evening, and we enjoyed good conversation along with a delicious apple pie Mary Jo baked onboard. Boat ovens do work!

Aug. 2 — Petoskey, Michigan

That is right. We were stuck in port again, and it looked like we might not be able to leave here for another few days, if the weather predictions hold true. The marina had lots of early morning activity with antsy boaters anxiously walking up and down the docks trying to get a glimpse of the lake. However, the wind kept howling, and the boats were rocking in the slips, so no one ventured out despite the fact that it was a clear, sunny day.

Petoskey Falls (reminded me of Niagara Falls, just slightly smaller)

We walked into town in the early afternoon for lunch, ice cream, and some shopping, and then we even watched a girls' softball game at the park. On our return to the boat, we continued to monitor the marine weather Internet sites, made phone calls, and spent a quiet evening watching DVDs.

Aug. 3 — Petoskey, Michigan

The wind continued to blow out of the west today on Little Traverse Bay with waves on Lake Michigan predicted to be in the 3- to 5-foot range. I had hoped that we would have a window of opportunity to leave for Northport between 11 a.m. and 1 p.m., but that break did not happen. We still held out hope that we could leave the next day for Leland, a port farther down the coast, because we wanted to get to Manistee on August 6 to meet with our nephew, Chris, his wife, Angela, and their children, who were vacationing there with Angela's parents.

To see them and also get to Holland, where we had arranged to keep our boat while we make a return trip home during the following week, it seemed that we would have to skip some of the places we had planned to visit before the nasty weather cycle interfered. To cheer ourselves up, we entertained our new Michigan friends, Dan and Mary Jo, aboard our boat with a Bon Voyage party because they, too, were hoping to leave here the next day.

Aug. 4 — Petoskey, Michigan

It was the fifth day in Petoskey, and I was starting to get sick of the lovely town. We could not believe it, but the wind and waves would still not cooperate, necessitating our staying here yet another day. In our entire boating life of 36 years, we could not remember ever having to stay in one port for so many days.

By then, I had come down with a severe case of "channel fever," an affliction brought on by staying in one port for too long, and the only known cure was to get me back to sea. I issued a directive to Pat that we were leaving in the morning and that we would make a jump of 77 miles to Frankfort to get to Manistee on the following day.

The day's activities included making phone calls, cleaning, doing laundry, and planning where we would keep the boat in Florida from December until May. The Calusa Cove Yacht Club and Marina in Goodland, Florida (on the West coast near Naples and Marco Island), appeared to be our likely selection. We have many friends who spend the winters in that area, which is close to the Fort Myers Airport, and we could easily travel with our boat to the Florida Keys, the Dry Tortugas, and Sanibel Island as cruising destinations.

We had dinner in town at the Mitchell Street Pub and afterward went to a men's softball league game at the park adjacent to the marina. On our way back, we stopped by *Dauntless* to enjoy Mary Jo's wonderful, homemade chocolate chip cookies and said our goodbyes once again. They are a delightful couple that graciously shared their knowledge of the area with us, and we enjoyed spending time with them.

Aug. 5 — 77 miles to Frankfort, Michigan[9]

At 6:40 a.m., we finally left the dock in Petoskey! Conditions were still not the best with broken clouds and the wind between 10 and 15 knots, and we took waves and wind first across the bow and then on our starboard quarter as we turned to go south into Lake Michigan.

Another warm summer day on Lake Michigan

Shortly after turning into the lake, Pat looked at me and said, "I have had enough of this for a while. I will be back up when things get quieter (the Admiral's privilege)." So, I operated the boat from up on the flybridge, and Pat stayed down in the salon, monitoring our course, speed, and conditions at the lower station for several hours. The scenery along the way was beautiful, and as we approached Sleeping Bear Dunes National Lakeshore, the calming of the seas returned the

[9] *See notes on page 139*

Admiral to the bridge because she did not want to miss seeing the enormous sand dunes we were passing that rose hundreds of feet above Lake Michigan. They looked more like something you would expect to see in the Sahara Desert rather than along the lakeshore, and they were truly a magnificent sight with the sun shining off what looked like white sand mountains.

 The park, which covers a 35-mile stretch of Lake Michigan, was established in 1970 and is recognized for its outstanding natural features including forests, beaches, dune formations, and ancient glacial phenomena.

Sand dunes rising 480 feet above Lake Michigan

Dan called us on the boat radio to see how we were doing, and later we heard *Maya Lisa*, a boat we had not seen since Parry Sound on July 13, calling a marina in our vicinity. We were delighted to hear that Hank and Ceci were nearby, but they did not answer our radio call. Next we heard from *Houlegan*, which we had not seen since Saint Ignace on July 27. Ray and Caryl were also headed to Frankfort but unfortunately not to the same marina as we were. *Reflection* finally arrived safely at Jacobson's Marina at 2:15 p.m. after a 77-mile journey.

Frankfort was first settled in the late 1600s, and by 1873 it officially became a village. With steady growth throughout the years, it was eventually given city status in 1935. Today, the city of Frankfort has a population of about 1,500 residents, and its historic downtown is a good place for shopping and antiquing. The area provides recreational opportunities on and off the water, and it proudly proclaims itself to be a four-season destination. However, that could prove to be a tough sell in the dead of winter.

Aug. 6 — 23 miles to Manistee, Michigan[10]

Our trip to Manistee was a short and uneventful one of 23 miles, but boring is sometimes good. We came into the pretty inlet and eventually made our way up the narrow Manistee River that ran through the town, passing under several bridges including one at 22 feet in height. To do that, we had to take down our antennas — something we had not done since the Trent-Severn Waterway. Many eyes were watching as we went under the bridge and cleared it successfully by just a little more than a foot.

 In 1832, a group of traders from Massachusetts attempted to settle along the Manistee River, however, the Ottawa people living in the area did not think it was such a good idea and drove them off. In 1841, the first permanent Euro-American settlement was established here. By 1848, the settlers pushed the Ottawa out of the area, and so far, they have not made a comeback. Today Manistee, is a city of about 7,000 residents with its economy based on tourism and industry, with companies such as the Corporation of America, Morton Salt, and Martin Marietta.

We docked at Seng's Marina on Manistee Lake and made ready for our our visitors: Angela, the wife of our nephew, Chris, their three children: Charlie, Allie, and Anna, and Angela's mother, Linda. After snack-time aboard, we were invited to have dinner with Angela's parents at their lovely carriage house on their 14-acre property overlooking Lake Michigan. We could not believe they had built the house themselves, and the décor was perfect. As their family continued to expand with in-laws and grandchildren, we suspected that more buildings might be built on the property — a wonderful location for a family compound. They were warm and gracious hosts, the dinner was delicious, and we greatly enjoyed the time we spent with them.

[10] See notes on page 139

Aug. 7 – 21 miles to Ludington, Michigan[11]

We had company in the Manistee River as we made our way out in the morning. A Great Lakes ore carrier had stopped in the middle of the river and was apparently waiting for bridge tenders to arrive to open the bridges through which she would have to pass. In the small, narrow waterway, she was an imposing sight as we slowly and carefully maneuvered *Reflection* around her.

A Great Lakes ore carrier heading up the narrow Manistee River

After we left the inlet, we hugged the shore on our trip south along Lake Michigan. The wind was brisk, whipping out of the east off the shore, so we were able to avoid the higher waves farther out. Later, as the wind came up even stronger, the Admiral suggested we increase the boat's speed, which we did, so that we could arrive early in our next port, Ludington.

Within a few of miles of reaching the inlet, we heard an announcement over the marine radio that a small boat had capsized and that all boats in the area should keep a lookout for the vessel and give aid, if possible. On our approach to the inlet awhile later, we saw a Coast Guard boat towing the capsized boat. As it crossed in front of us, it was truly a sad picture. We eventually learned that the boat had been well offshore and that it had taken a wave over the stern that stalled the engine, followed by several more waves that began to flood the boat. Luckily, there was enough time for those onboard to call the Coast Guard and for everyone to don life vests before the boat rolled over. Unfortunately, the family dog that was with them did not make it. The Great Lakes can be tough on small boats, but traveling these waters can be done safely as long as the captain knows his or her boat's capability and is aware of changing weather conditions. There is simply no substitution for common sense.

 European explorers first arrived in the Ludington area as early as the late 1600s, and the first permanent residents didn't appear until 1847. The town was originally named Pere Marquette but was later renamed after industrialist James Ludington, who ran the logging operation there. It was incorporated as a city in 1873, and today, Ludington has more than 8,000 residents and is a center of tourism for boating, hunting, fishing, and camping interests. The downtown shopping area has several clothing stores, art galleries, jewelry stores, an ice cream parlor, and restaurants.

We were tied up at the Municipal Marina by 10 a.m., and within an hour, we were delighted that *Maya Lisa* joined us. We all had many stories to share about our adventures since we had last seen each other, so we invited them for cocktails on our boat followed by dinner at PM Steamers restaurant. The weather deteriorated considerably with high winds and rain as the evening wore on, but we had a good time anyway socializing with our boating friends.

Aug. 8 – Ludington, Michigan

After a night of heavy rain, the morning dawned dark and dreary with predictions of additional showers later in the day. Strong winds were blowing out of the southwest, so we decided to stay another day at the marina. *Maya Lisa* also opted to remain docked. I found a grocery/butcher store in town and an interesting pub-type restaurant where we stopped for some much-needed refreshment in the afternoon.

From our slip, we had several opportunities to see the *S.S. Badger*, the last coal-burning passenger/car ferry on Lake Michigan, as she came in and out of Ludington on her route from there to Manitowoc, Wisconsin.

 The *S.S. Badger* steamship that went into service in 1953 is an imposing 410-foot vessel which transports 620 passengers and 180 vehicles of all types including RV's, buses, cars, trucks, and motorcycles on a four-hour crossing of Lake Michigan. She was originally designed to carry railroad cars, automobiles, and passengers and was built with a reinforced hull for ice breaking for year-round service. As the last of her kind, she now makes the journey only between May and October.

S.S. Badger, *a floating dinosaur*

After a delicious Italian dinner on our boat, we were invited aboard *Maya Lisa* for a dessert of cherry pie with whipped cream topping accompanied by fascinating stories that Hank and Ceci shared with us about places they had lived abroad. However, when we returned to *Reflection*, we learned that the National Weather Service had issued a severe thunderstorm warning for our area with possible winds of 60 mph, and we saw many small fishing boats scrambling back into the harbor in the dark. I put additional lines on our boat, and with the lightning and thunder nearby, we were concerned about a small boat that had been briefly docked next to us earlier in the day but that had departed for the lake around 5:30 p.m. There were five men aboard who had apparently paid a long visit to a local saloon before boarding, and the only supplies they had brought on board were additional beer and potato chips. They had said they would be back, but so far, they had not returned.

Aug. 9 — Ludington, Michigan

Luckily, the previous night's storm had passed north of us, but true to form, the wind and seas did not back down — they increased. Once again, we decided to stay safely in port. The small boat alongside us the day before never returned to the slip, so we could only hope that they had found shelter elsewhere. *Maya Lisa* was still there at the marina, and we received email from *Houlegan* saying they were still stuck in Manistee.

Pat and I made the best of our stay by taking a tour of the town, having ice cream at Kilwin's, and an early dinner at The Grand Hotel, which reminded us of bars and restaurants from the 1950s, with knotty-pine walls and Formica and chrome tables and chairs. On our return to the boat, we then enjoyed viewing one of our William Powell/Myrna Loy DVDs. It was a fun day.

Ludington's Grand Hotel can be compared in some ways to Mackinac's. Each is called "Grand", and each serves good food and cocktails. Just the ambiance is different!

Aug. 10 — 57 miles to Grand Haven, Michigan[12]

Despite heavily overcast skies, we finally departed Ludington harbor at 7:30 a.m. for our 57-mile trip to Grand Haven, where we had a reservation at the Municipal Marina. Though the waters were somewhat choppy on our way south, the skies finally cleared, and conditions improved during the last few hours of our trip.

[12] *See notes on page 139*

Grand Haven originally was a fur trading post called Gabag-ouache, a Pottawattamie Indian name for the area. The city was first called Grand Haven in 1835 and was incorporated as a city in 1867. In the mid-to-late 19th century, Grand Haven's economy was centered on logging and shipbuilding, and by the early 20th century, the area was producing automobiles, furniture, lighting, and pianos. Today, Grand Haven is an active resort, boating, and fishing community with more than 100 miles of bike trails, a state beach, a boardwalk, and a large charter fishing fleet.

We docked by 1:00 p.m., and *Maya Lisa,* which expected guests to come aboard for a few days, was berthed three slips away from us. Unfortunately, all the boats were subject to rocking at this attractive marina, which is only a block from the town. We are not sure what caused the unusual turbulence, but it was rocky enough to cause novice boaters to get seasick right in the slip. Yet, we were fortunate that we were not there the day before. A storm with 60-mph winds had come through the area and caused damage to several boats at the marina and power outages across the river.

Grand Haven was a good place to shop, with many eateries in an attractive downtown area. We had a wonderful dinner at the Porto Bello restaurant, followed by ice cream cones at a store on the harbor walkway. For the finale of our grand evening in Grand Haven, we got to view, right across the river from our own back deck, the town's famous "Musical Fountain" performance, an impressive synchronized program with water, music, and a multicolored light show held each evening during the summer. It was truly spectacular, and well worth the visit.

Aug. 11 – 21 miles to Holland, Michigan[13]

We said goodbye to Hank before we left amid hopes that we would be able to travel with *Maya Lisa* down the Illinois River at a later point.

Pat and I finally had a beautiful 20-mile trip south on Lake Michigan to our boat's temporary two-week home at Crescent Shores Marina on Lake Macatawa in Holland. The Admiral particularly enjoyed the passage because when it comes to wave heights, her favorite word is "smooth," and it was.

---

[13] *See notes on page 139*

The entrance to Holland Harbor

 Holland is a city of about 35,000 residents that Dutch Calvinist separatists who were escaping from religious persecution in the Netherlands settled in 1847. Led by Dr. Albertus van Raalte, they might also have been motivated to emigrate for their opposition to certain scientific and social advances in the Netherlands, such as vaccination, insurance, and chemical fertilizers. I understand the vaccination reluctance because after all, no one likes to get poked with needles. That same year, Van Raalte established a congregation of the Reformed Church in America that would later be called the First Reformed Church of Holland. It is also known as the "City of Churches," named after the 170 churches that are located here, including the one that put Holland on the map when it started the trend of the "What Would Jesus Do?" bracelets in 1989.

The Dutch influence is still alive today with the annual Tulip Time Festival in May, Dutch-themed attractions along the nearby Lake Michigan shoreline, and the Holland Museum that contains exhibits about the city's history. It is also a college town (Hope College) with many reasonably priced eateries and watering holes.

On arriving at the marina, Eric, the owner/dockmaster, met us, helped us tie up, and assured us that he would take good care of our "baby," *Reflection,* while we returned home to New Jersey for ten days to check on things. Pat and I deliberately arrived there several days in advance of our scheduled departure for home to accomplish things that we want to do on the boat before we leave on Aug. 14. These items (minor repairs, cleaning the boat, and defrosting the refrigerator) would ready us for the next stage of our trip from there to Chicago, then down the Illinois, Mississippi, Ohio, Cumberland, and Tennessee Rivers to Alabama.

Aug. 12 — Holland, Michigan

In the midst of the preparations for our departure in two days, I contacted the manufacturer of the replacement ice maker we had on order to see when it would be delivered. To my delight, the representative said it would be delivered by noon. Sure enough, when I went up to the marina office, there it was! I had already removed the old unit in preparation for installation of the new one when we returned from New Jersey. I was able to do some of the work required to get it up and running before we left Holland. Because I love my ice, things were looking up!

When I thought things could not get much better, we received a personal delivery to the boat of 11 gallons of motor oil from the local NAPA store in Holland by Clark, the owner, who was also the uncle of our niece, Angela. He visited with us aboard for a short while, and we were grateful for his kindness in bringing us the order himself. It is good to have local relatives.

The view from our dock as the bulk carrier, the **Manitowac,** *passes by*

Later, while we were having dinner on our back deck, we looked up to see a huge ship, the *Manitowac*, going right past our bow. The commercial vessel was a surprising sight on the scenic lake, filled with beautiful homes, as it headed past the Heinz Company's modern plant farther up the lake to a power plant at the end.

The next day we would complete our final packing, load up our rental car, and leave at 4 a.m. for what we hoped would be a 12-hour drive to New Jersey. We had been aboard on this segment of the Loop for 70 days and had gone almost 1,400 miles since we left our home on June 6. A trip home was a good idea at this point, yet we were already looking forward to getting back onboard to continue the adventure.

Aug. 25 – Holland, Michigan

Our 12-day excursion/hiatus back to New Jersey allowed us to check on Pat's elderly mother and her health status, take care of small maintenance items at our home, celebrate my birthday, and catch up with family and friends. However, after our time back home, we found ourselves anxious to get back to our adventure and to our "second home," and happily we found *Reflection* waiting safely for us at the dock. We had a 13-hour drive back to Michigan, and the rental car was filled to capacity with items we brought back for the next leg of our Great Loop journey. Though tired from the drive, the unloading of the car, and the unpacking, we enjoyed a fun dinner at the New Holland Brewing Company, a restaurant that makes its own beer, wine, and spirits on the premises.

Aug. 26 and 27 – Holland, Michigan

The most important accomplishment of the last two days was my final installation of the new ice maker, and the sound of ice cubes being made and dropped into their bin was music to the Captain's ears.

My next big task was cleaning the outside of the boat. Ordinarily, washing the boat was time-consuming but not a particularly difficult chore. However, at this time of year, Holland, Michigan, seemed to be the gnat and spider capital of America. *Reflection* was covered with thousands of disgusting bugs. Cleaning them off the boat was work, and unfortunately that morning, after having washed all the bodies away from the day before, I discovered that the boat was once again covered with a few thousand more dead gnats. I wanted to get us out of there as soon as possible!

In addition to installing the ice maker and cleaning the boat from the massive spider invasion, we also did a major food shopping trip to stock the boat up for the upcoming few weeks. Pat and I then learned that there was a new development that could impact our trip coming up on the horizon. Asian Carp were discovered within 10 miles of the electrical water barrier in the Chicago Sanitary and Ship Canal just south of Chicago, a waterway through which we must pass to get from Lake Michigan to the Mississippi River. The barrier was built to keep the fish out of the Great Lakes, and the Army Corps of Engineers had just decided to increase the current load from one to two volts in the barrier in the hopes of keeping the fish away.

While they were in this testing and protocol phase, only large diesel-powered vessels with metal hulls would be allowed to cross the area. Despite the fact that the usual 30-day notice for an action like this was not given to mariners in advance and that no date was provided as to when future crossings would be allowed, the Coast Guard was holding fast on keeping the area closed. This was causing a huge problem for all recreational boaters in the Chicago area and especially for those of us doing the Great Loop.

There were close to 100 boats in our organization alone waiting in marinas all over Michigan who were prohibited from heading south because of the barrier voltage change. Marinas were filling up because boats were stacking up in areas close to Chicago. The press deemed us "Carp Captives," and we affected boaters were lobbying our congressmen and other government entities to get a plan together so that we could proceed through the barrier and then down the Illinois River to the Mississippi. This was a financial and a scheduling disaster for many people who had plans for guests, boat haul-outs, and jobs to which they had to return. As for me, now that I had enough ice, I was all right.

However, our friends Charlie and Helen had purchased airline tickets to meet us on Aug. 31 in Chicago, and they planned to spend ten days aboard before flying back to New Jersey on Sept. 10 out of St. Louis. We certainly did not want them to have to alter their plans. There was scuttlebutt on the Internet about an upcoming possible solution to the situation, but nothing was concrete. We sat tight that night, hoping to be able to make a decision in the morning about what to do.

Chicago, here we come, maybe.

Notes:

(1)

Drummond Island — Once you pass red buoy "8" on the port, follow the buoyed channel to Drummond Island Yacht Haven, where you will clear U.S. Customs. The U.S. Customs agent is on duty from noon to 8 p.m. daily (no citrus, goat, or lamb products are allowed to be brought into in the U.S.). If your boat is more than 30 feet and you did not get your Customs decal beforehand, the inspector will take care of it on-site.

(2)

If you are proceeding on to Mackinac Island, Mackinaw City, or Saint Ignace from Drummond Island, a good anchorage about halfway between is Government Bay in Les Cheneaux Islands.

(3)

If you are proceeding through Les Cheneaux to the Mackinac/Saint Ignace area, you will find that the route is, for the most part, well protected. Just follow the buoys.

(4)

We highly recommend not going into Mackinac Island harbor because it is exposed to the lake and has considerable ferry wakes. Saint Ignace is a better choice with a fairly new marina protected from the ferry wakes. Multiple ferry services and several reasonably priced restaurants are close to the marina, but liquor and grocery stores are at least a mile away.

(5)

Fuel — You might be tempted to purchase fuel in the first U.S. port (Drummond Island), however, if you can wait until Saint Ignace, you will be rewarded with fuel prices about 20 cents per gallon less. If you can hold out even longer, prices on the eastern shore of Lake Michigan might be even lower.

(6)

Before entering Lake Michigan, you might want to look at the following websites:
- *For wave height predictions in the Great Lakes — **www.windfinder.com/ forecasts/uswave_wave_height_direction_great_lakes_akt.htm***
- *For Great Lakes weather forecasts —**www.nws.noaa.gov/om/marine/ zone/gtlakes/glcstmz.htm***

(7)

Beaver Island — After you go through the Straits of Mackinac and start heading southbound in Lake Michigan, take Grays Reef Passage because it is said to be the safest route. The Municipal Marina in Beaver Island will not take reservations.

Beaver Island Marina will take reservations, and though it is an older facility with limited room for boats more than 40 feet, it has reasonable dockage rates that include electric, water, cable TV, and Wi-Fi. It has a friendly staff and is a short walk to the grocery store, liquor store, restaurants (some will pick you up), or good takeout.

(8)
Petoskey Municipal Marina has numerous reasonably priced transient slips and fuel that was 10 cents a gallon less than Saint Ignace. It is close to town with shopping and eateries, but it has only limited groceries nearby, and a liquor store is about a ten-minute walk. There is also a museum nearby, and its parks are good for walking and biking.

(9)
Frankfort — Jacobson's Marina has pricier transient rates and fuel that was 10 cents a gallon more than at Petoskey. The marina is close to town with numerous restaurants but limited groceries nearby. There is a pool and a hot tub at the marina, which is in a well-protected and easy-to-enter harbor.

(10)
Manistee River — The Municipal Marina is exposed to the river traffic. Seng's Marina is a newer facility and is easily accessible, but it has some exposure to the southwest on Lake Manistee. It is about a quarter-mile walk into town from the marina.

(11)
Ludington — The Municipal Marina's fuel was ten cents a gallon more than Petoskey's, but it has reasonably priced transient slips and is convenient to restaurants, a gourmet grocery, and town.

(12)
Grand Haven — The Municipal Marina was reasonably priced and is close to the town and restaurants. There is no fuel at the marina, but Crystal Flash Energy ((800) 875-4851, call well in advance) will deliver diesel fuel to your boat if you are in one of the western slips. They have a 200-gallon minimum with significant savings per gallon over marina prices. There is a fantastic light show every evening, and the best view is from the western slips. There is a surge from the lake felt in the slips, so you might be rocked to sleep.

(13)
Holland — The fuel at the first marina in the harbor was 25 cents per gallon higher than what we had found in Petoskey, and it is susceptible to surges from Lake Michigan.

Chapter 8

Chicago and the "Carp Captive" Caper

Aug. 28 – 85 miles to Chicago, Illinois[1]

Despite a weather forecast that called for 1 to 2 inches of heavy rain, northeast winds of 10 to 13 mph, and wave heights of 1 to 2 feet, we decided to leave Crescent Shores Marina at 6:50 a.m. for an 85-mile trip across Lake Michigan to the "Windy City." These were not the best conditions we would have chosen, but the next few days looked like they would be even worse with predictions of stronger winds and higher seas, so the Admiral and I agreed this was our best time to go.

"I put the pedal to the metal" as soon as we left the inlet and headed *Reflection* directly on course for Chicago. Everything was going terrifically for the first two hours, but as we approached the center of the lake, the sea heights increased and the wind came across our port beam, making it quite rocky onboard. The Admiral and I had made a deal before setting out that day. I would operate the boat at 15 knots from the flybridge to get us across as quickly as possible, but if it started to rain, causing poor visibility, I would come down below and pilot from the inside station at 10 knots. I stayed up top for the entire trip despite the rocky conditions because it never rained and I found it to be exciting up on the bridge! The Admiral, on the other hand, was a bit less enthusiastic (she never ever did like amusement rides) as she hung out below or, more accurately stated, "hung on" below. *Reflection* rolled through the high waves that occasionally rearranged the furniture in the salon as we rocked from side to side. Thankfully, conditions eventually calmed down the closer we got to Chicago, and we looked forward to reaching our destination.

Approaching Chicago's Monroe Harbor on a cloudy day

Originally, we had planned to visit a few other ports in Michigan before arriving in Chicago on Aug. 31 to meet up with our high school friend Charlie and his wife, Helen. However, because of our decision to cross the lake today, we were at our destination earlier than expected. Our reservation for Du Sable Harbor in Chicago was made for Aug. 31 through Sept. 2, but when we called to see if we could come in early, they told us there was no room for us at the heavily booked marina. Instead, we had to head out for Monroe Harbor, which had a massive mooring field. As we approached the field, a boat from the harbor office pulled alongside *Reflection*, and the operator took our lines and attached them to a mooring ball. Unfortunately, the area was exposed to Lake Michigan, and the constant rocking made us feel like we were in a washing machine. Neither of us was thrilled with this situation!

Realizing that we could not take three days of that kind of motion, I took the tender service in to see the dockmaster, and she kindly agreed to move us to an inside wall at a park in the heart of the city near the Chicago Yacht Club. After we tied up at the wall, we felt relieved to finally dock and were so tired from the day's activities that we decided not to do any sightseeing that evening. Pat and I settled instead for a nice dinner aboard with a movie, changed our watches and clocks back one hour to Central Standard Time, locked our doors, and went to sleep. Except for the occasional police patrol, there was no other security along the wall and the pedestrian path alongside it, but all seemed quiet.

At about 1 a.m. I woke up to the sound of footsteps on the deck above our cabin. "Somebody is on the boat!" I shouted to Pat. I jumped out of bed and ran out of the cabin wearing nothing but my skivvies. Flinging the door open to the aft deck, I started yelling, startling the two men on the deck. They quickly jumped overboard and ran down the path alongside the dock, but unfortunately, in my hurry to confront the intruders, I had left my eyeglasses on my night table, so there was no way I could identify them. We then called the Chicago police to report the incident, and to my dismay, they did not want to be bothered with what I perceived to be an attempted robbery because nothing was taken and I could not identify the culprits.

In light of this, Pat and I developed a deterrent plan to prevent a repeat performance. Suspecting that we were targeted because the boat was dark and perhaps looked unoccupied, we decided to change that perception. On the trip across the lake, we had rolled up our aft deck screens and had stacked and tied up the deck furniture for the crossing. So we set the screens up, arranged the furniture, and turned on our aft deck spotlights, which highly illuminated the area. The final part of the plan was that if uninvited guests ever boarded again, instead of confronting the intruders, I would continually blast *Reflection*'s air horn, a sound that could raise the dead! The plan seemed to work because we were not bothered again in Chicago or anywhere else when we were at an unsecured dock.

Aug. 29 — Chicago, Illinois

We played "tourists" and walked along Michigan Avenue, Grant Park, and through the fairly new Millennium Park, which is located in the Chicago Loop community area near Lake Michigan.

 Construction of Millennium Park began in October 1998, and it was opened on July 16, 2004, four years behind schedule. The park features the Jay Pritzker Pavilion, Cloud Gate (aka "The Bean"), the Crown Fountain, the Lurie Garden, and other attractions. Some consider the park to be the city's most important project since the World's Columbian Exposition of 1893.

After our tour, we had lunch at Giordano's, a restaurant famous for its stuffed pizza. Pat ordered a small, thin-crust pizza, but when it arrived, it turned out to be thicker than any pizza we have ever had in New Jersey. Although it was not what she had expected, it was excellent. I, on the other hand, went for the traditional Chicago- style pizza, and to say the least, it was a mouthful.

Famous Michigan Avenue in Downtown Chicago

On our return to the boat, it appeared that *Reflection* had become one of the tourist attractions at this tie-up. People stopped and took pictures while standing next to the boat, and many commented to us on how nice she looked. There was activity going on around us because the Chicago Triathlon was going to be held the next day, and we would have ringside seats. More than 9,500 people were expected to participate — swimming, bicycling, and then running the course. Excitement filled the air, and we looked forward to seeing the event from such a fabulous vantage point.

"The Bean" in Millennium Park

Aug. 30 – Chicago, Illinois

The Admiral was up well before dawn to check out all the action along the dock. I, on the other hand, conserved my energy and stayed in bed, asking her to wake me when something exciting happened. She watched the long line of triathletes with bikes and backpacks beginning to form around 4 a.m., and it did not stop until nearly 6 a.m. After placing their bikes in the stands at the nearby transition area, they walked down the path next to our boat on their way to the Lake Michigan shoreline. The air was electric with high expectations and positive energy around us.

There were also spectators and entourages of various participants convening in our vicinity. The air temperature was only 52 degrees, and we wondered what the lake temperature was. As we sat in the comfort of our warm salon, we wished the entrants luck as they walked past our open boat window. Noticing the New Jersey port displayed on our stern, several of them welcomed us to Chicago, and some jokingly asked us about what we would be serving them for breakfast after their swim. The average age of the athletes appeared to be between 30 and 35, but there were also a few much older and others who did not look in good enough shape to participate in a slow dance, much less a triathlon. There were even a few amputees with metal legs and another two in wheelchairs who were participants. We thought they should be given credit just for their amazing fortitude because missing a limb or two was not going to stop them.

The spectators and triathletes merge

The first wave of swimmers started to come past the boat headed for the bike leg about 6:15 a.m., and we cheered them on. With more than 56 waves of at least 150 participants each, this continued for hours as they completed the second bike leg and then ran past us on the walking track about 30 feet away during the last leg.

After the amateurs completed the course, the pros did the triathlon in record time. We truly had the best seats in the house, as we watched the action from our back deck and later from the flybridge. The crowds continued all day, and once again, we were a tourist attraction with people taking pictures next to *Reflection*. The entire day was delightful and entertaining, and things finally quieted down around 6 p.m. when the garbage trucks came around to pick up the litter. By 8 p.m., there was almost no one around, and we were able to get a quiet night's sleep.

Aug. 31 — Chicago, Illinois[2]

Our friends Charlie and Helen arrived by plane from New Jersey in the morning, and we were happy to welcome them aboard. After a light lunch, we then moved the boat from the wall in Monroe Harbor to our secure reserved slip at Du Sable Harbor. Once settled there, we walked to the Chicago River and boarded a sightseeing boat for an architectural river cruise the Chicago Architecture Foundation runs.

[2] *See notes on page 163*

The two pictures above are a small sample of the magnificent buildings we saw on the architectural river cruise.

The cruise was a fascinating and unique way to see and learn about the many buildings in the city. Afterward, we enjoyed walking along Michigan Avenue and studying pieces of stone from around the world and from ancient eras that were embedded in the outside walls of the *Chicago Tribune* building. Our group then took the elevator to the top of the John Hancock building and had drinks in the Signature Room Bar. That is a location from which to see the vast number of buildings and the Lake Michigan shoreline, and we even spotted *Reflection* in her slip space, but she only looked like a small dot from the 96th floor.

Sept. 1 — Chicago, Illinois

Our old friends Mike and Susan took the train from their home in Crete, Illinois, to meet us for lunch. Pat and Mike had been classmates since the second grade, and Pat, Mike, Charlie, and I were all classmates in high school. It was good catching up on one another's lives, and we particularly enjoyed sharing stories about our experiences in the unusual and remote places we all had the opportunities to visit throughout the years.

Our group had a lovely lunch together at the Park Grill in Millennium Park, and we were happy that Mike and Sue had made the effort to come into the city to see us. After taking pictures and saying goodbye to Mike and Susan, Charlie and Helen continued touring Chicago while Pat and I returned to the boat. That afternoon, she and I lowered *Reflection's* radar arch, which luckily is hinged for that purpose, in preparation for Thursday's journey down the Chicago Sanitary and Ship Canal when *Reflection* would have to travel under low bridges.

Sept. 2 — Chicago, Illinois

We spent a good portion of the day at the huge Field Museum.

 The Field Museum was founded on Sept. 16, 1893 as the Columbian Museum of Chicago and was housed in the World's Columbian Exposition's Palace of Fine Arts. The museum's name was changed to the Field Museum of Natural History in honor of Marshall Field, the museum's first major benefactor, and in 1921, the museum moved from its original location to its present site in the Chicago Park District near downtown. Only a small portion of the museum's collection of more than 21 million specimens is ever on display, and some of its prized exhibits include:

· "Sue," the largest and most complete Tyrannosaurus ever discovered

- artifacts from ancient Egypt, the Pacific Northwest, the Pacific Islands, and Tibet
- a large taxidermy collection, featuring large animals, including two African elephants
- a considerable assortment of dinosaurs
- an extensive collection of Native American artifacts

While there, we saw "Sue" and many other dinosaur skeletons and then enjoyed a special exhibition on pirates along with other comprehensive exhibitions on Polynesia and Egypt. We never saw so many mummies in one place!

"Sue," the largest and most complete Tyrannosaurus ever discovered

The four of us took a cab to Bockmueller's, a tiny but well-stocked grocery store that was hidden on the bottom floor of a beautiful high-rise apartment building near our marina. There was no sign outside to identify it, so you had to have local knowledge to know it was there. After doing our shopping, we returned to *Reflection* with our purchases, rested a bit, and then went out again to tour the Navy Pier, which was somewhat like a Chicago version of the New Jersey boardwalk. It was hard to believe, but the pier also housed huge stained glass collections by Tiffany, Frank Lloyd Wright, and other designers. We had an alfresco dinner there and then came back to our boat, where we had good seats for a fabulous fireworks display over the waters of Lake Michigan. We had not even scratched the surface of the many things we could have done in Chicago, but it would have taken us a lot more time than we had available on our schedule. So the next day, we would move on.

Sept. 3 — 57 miles to Joliet, Illinois[3-6]

We left Du Sable Harbor at 5:50 a.m. on a 57-mile trip that would take us through two locks and the electrical fish barrier to Joliet. Our journey began by our traveling across 11 miles of Lake Michigan to the industrial Calumet River, through the Chicago Sanitary and Ship Canal, and then into the Illinois River.

Along the way, *Reflection* transited under 56 bridges, including some that had to open for her to get under. But the biggest challenge by far proved to be the crossing of the electrical carp barrier, which I grumbled about in the previous chapter. To progress south on the Great Loop and to get Charlie and Helen to St. Louis in time for their scheduled flight home, we had to somehow cross the barrier. Our only choice was to contract with Artco Towing (which was mysteriously the only towing company allowed to do so out of the 16 in the city) to have our boat towed across the electrical barrier area for a fee of $600.

This was our view while waiting in the narrow Chicago Ship and Sanitary Canal for a long line of barges to pass. There is absolutely no room for error here.

We had applied for and received advanced clearance from the Coast Guard to proceed through, and *Reflection* was given an appointment to be towed across the barrier at noon. When we arrived early at the tow point, the towboat captain told us to be patient because he was in the process of taking a boat through the barrier but that he would return shortly to bring us across. Following his directive, we sat in the narrow waterway holding position with the engines running and waited. At about noon, we overheard a conversation between the towboat and its dispatcher, redirecting the boat from picking us up to escorting a commercial tow through the barrier instead. I immediately contacted the towboat, and the captain explained that as soon as he brought the tow through the barrier, we would be next. Because we knew commercial vessels always took precedence over private boats, we waited patiently for a while longer.

This is the lovely view looking astern of our tie-up alongside the coal barge.

Within a short time, three additional boats that also had appointments lined up behind us, and things got pretty crowded with us trying to maintain our spots while also trying to avoid blocking the barge traffic in this narrow, busy, commercial waterway. I was also getting tired of floating around in a holding position and wasting fuel for this long of a period of time, so I eventually decided to find a place to tie up our boat. It seemed that I only had two options from which to choose, and neither one was ideal. The first contender was a crumbling wall on the east side of the waterway, but I could not see any way of tying up there without damaging our vessel. My other option was to tie up alongside a partially empty coal barge, so I opted for the latter. As I maneuvered the boat in close, Charlie managed to get lines around the huge cleats on the barge, and with fenders in place, we safely tied up. The other three boats then followed our cue, and they tied up to another barge parked behind ours.

It was after 1 p.m. when the towboat reappeared. We naturally thought we would be the next to cross, but we were wrong. The captain told us he had to go back to escort yet another commercial tow through the barrier. On top of that bit of good news, he wanted us to move from the coal barge to the crumbling wall because he said the channel was so narrow in the area that he had experienced a hard time passing us with his previous tow. I told him, "No!" As the captain of my vessel, I was not going to jeopardize my boat or my crew by attempting to tie up to such a dilapidated, dangerous structure. It was truly disheartening that no one in charge seemed to be concerned with our safety or that of any of the other boats tied up to the barge behind us. The entire situation was extremely disorganized, and we could not figure out who was in charge.

While we were waiting, a few neighbors came by rather closely.

I just wanted to get out of there! What I found to be incredible was that the Army Corps of Engineers was concerned over the two volts of charge in the barrier. There are old marinas in New Jersey that have dock wiring so bad that they have considerably more than two volts of charge in the water at their slips. I just hated dealing with stupidity. That is exactly what the whole situation was, and to prove it, just a few weeks later, the Corps opened the barrier to all traffic with no tow escorts required, and they made no $600 refunds for the unneeded tows, either.

Because we had no alternative at that moment, we continued to wait. Finally, we could see the towboat coming toward us, escorting a series of barges through the barrier. Maybe we would finally get moving. I was wrong again! Once the tow cleared the barrier, the Coast Guard announced that the barrier area was being closed for the Army Corps of Engineers to conduct testing of the electrical current in the barrier area. We could not believe it!

Sometime before 4 p.m. the Army Corp of Engineers' boat finally emerged from the barrier, and they waved to us as they passed by. I was tempted to return their wave with the one-finger salute! The Carp Barrier was declared open again, however, not for us. The tow operator had to escort one more set of barges through the barrier, but he assured us that it would be our turn next.

Reflection being towed through the barrier

By this time I was seriously considering untying *Reflection* and taking my chances running her through the barrier in defiance of the Coast Guard regulations. It was not until nearly 5 p.m. when the last set of barges passed us, and we could finally approach the towboat. Once *Reflection* was secured to the tow, the operator told us that because he was running so late, he was going to raft up another of the waiting boats to our starboard side and take us both through at the same time.

Charlie and I helped the crew of the other boat secure their lines to us. The folks onboard were old, and the owner could barely walk. With some difficulty, we managed to get them off their boat, onto ours, and then onto the towboat.

For supposed safety concerns, I was told to disconnect all the batteries before we could be towed, but there was no way I was going to do that, so I compromised and turned off all the battery switches instead. We then all donned life vests, paid our $600 ransom to the towboat operator, boarded the towboat, sat inside the tow's galley, and eventually, at 5:23 p.m., were driven the three-quarters of a mile across the barrier.

Once on the other side, it took the boat that tied alongside us quite a while to get everybody onboard and to reconnect their batteries. Meanwhile, I just had to flip my battery switches, and we were ready to go, but we had to wait for them. By now, it was around 6 p.m. when the other boat untied from us and we were finally on our way — a mere six hours behind schedule!

Originally, we had planned to travel past Joliet to a marina farther downriver, but as I saw how the day's itinerary was unraveling, I called ahead to that marina and canceled our reservation. The marina owner was helpful, and he suggested that we stop at Joliet for the evening, which was the first safe place to tie up. With the sun setting at 7:15 p.m. and with about an additional 10 miles plus one lock for us to go, this could be a tight run, and this area of the waterway was not a place in which to be traveling at night.

As we approached the lock a few miles downstream, luck was finally with us. A tow was just coming out of the lock, and within a few minutes, we were allowed to enter. When we left the lock, the sun was hanging low in the sky, and as we approached a series of bridges just before Joliet, darkness set in.

The first bridge tender seemed somewhat hesitant to open his bridge for us, but once he did, we could see the next bridge getting ready to open for us. Each bridge in succession continued to open as we approached. When we got near the fourth bridge, the bridge tender called me and asked where we were going. I explained that we wanted to tie up along the wall in Joliet. He told me to pass through the next bridge and then immediately turn to starboard, tie up at the wall there, and stay there until morning. When a local gives me firm directions like that, I pay attention!

As we passed through the fifth bridge and headed to the wall at the Bicentennial Park, to our pleasant surprise, there were several other loopers who had already docked and were eagerly waiting to give us a hand with our lines. We finally got *Reflection* tied up at 7:45 p.m. after a long, exhausting, 14-hour day that tested our stamina and patience.

Our friends Ray and Caryl aboard *Houlegan* were even farther behind us because they were on the tow after us. They finally arrived about an hour later, and Charlie and I helped them tie up. We were all so tired that we just ended up eating Italian meatball and pasta leftovers accompanied by several cocktails. That day was a reminder that boating is truly an adventure, and that even our best-laid plans can often be subject to change. Flexibility is a virtue on the Loop.

Sept. 4 — 46 miles to Ottawa, Illinois[7]

Before leaving the dock, I wanted to look around Joliet.

 Joliet is the fastest growing city in Illinois with a population of more than 150,000 residents. Joliet's prison operated there from 1858 to 2002, and it was featured in the motion picture, "The Blues Brothers," as the prison from which Jake Blues was released at the beginning of the movie. During the Prohibition Era, mobsters from Chicago were sent there to do time, but the downtown area, which had once been downtrodden, was undergoing a total revitalization. Its main attractions included Harrah's Casino and Hotel, the Hollywood Casino, and the Rialto Square Theater, called one of the world's ten most beautiful theaters, also known as "The Jewel of Joliet."

I walked over the waterway, passing the Joliet municipal complex where a small farmers' market was held, and made a few purchases. The area was quiet for such a large city. There were no gangsters driving by with machine guns blazing, like in the movies, so I returned to the boat to get ready for the day's adventure.

Our plans were to travel 61 miles straight through to Starved Rock Marina, but the lock tenders' plans at the three locks through which we had to transit changed our schedule. A miscommunication with the Brandon Road lock tender at the first lock caused us to sit at the park wall in Joliet longer than we had intended. When we called him before our departure, he told us to hang back because he had commercial traffic coming through. Then he changed his mind and allowed some recreational boats through, but it was then too late for us to catch up and go with them. We later made our way to the lock with another boat that was tied up at the park, however, we ended up waiting at a wall near the lock until noon before we could enter.

The scenery past the lock was still highly industrial and not attractive, but after we transited to the Dresden Lock that followed it, the scenery changed and the river widened and became more rural with only an occasional factory, grain elevator, or barge dock.

When we arrived farther along at the Marseilles Lock, the lock tender told us there would be a 45-minute wait because a ten-barge tow was coming through the opposite way. The delay took about two hours, and we were less than thrilled about it, but there was nothing else we could do but wait and try to hold the boat's position in the waterway. This was not easy, and at one point we got into some shallow water, and just managed to avert going aground.

A six-barge tow, two barges wide by three barges long, was also waiting with us to be locked through and was headed in the same direction as we were. Because the lock could hold tows up to three barges wide, there would be room for us to fit alongside when the tow group was in the lock. So, I called the lock tender and asked if we could possibly lock through with the tow. The lock tender then called the tow captain to see if it was all right with him, and happily, it was. Fortunately, unless the barges were carrying explosives (benzene and gasoline), we were allowed to lock through with them, if we could fit.

Once the barges were moved into the lock and secured, we were told to enter the lock and tie our boat to the most forward floating bollard. *Reflection* was then followed in by the towboat, which had released itself from the barges it had been pushing; otherwise, it would have been too long to fit in the lock if it had stayed connected, and then it took up a position behind us.

During the locking operation, I contacted the lock tender to see who would be first to leave the lock once we were lowered. I did that merely as a courtesy, knowing that it would be common sense for us to leave the lock first, and he confirmed it. I did not want to be tied up within the confines of the lock walls as 600 feet of steel barges slipped alongside us just a few feet away. Once the gates opened, we maneuvered our way past the lead barge and were on our way again. Because of the multiple delays at the locks and the impending darkness, we scrapped our plans to reach Starved Rock and headed instead for Heritage Harbor Marina, which was only 2 miles past the lock.

Unfortunately, this had become another long day, the crew was tired, and the Admiral felt like she was coming down with some kind of "bug."

We finally arrived at the marina around 7:15 p.m., right at sunset, and received a warm welcome from Captain Moe, the dockmaster, at this beautiful new marina. Captain Moe is known among loopers as the "savior" of 26 boats that were caught for two weeks at Heritage Harbor during the Illinois River flooding in 2008. He had arranged transportation and field trips and made everyone as comfortable as he could during that terrible time. True to his reputation for hospitality, he could not do enough for us during our stay, and we were sorry our schedule did not permit us to remain here longer. Because we were all exhausted and Pat was not feeling well, we took the easy way out by buying dinner from the on-site restaurant and bringing it back to the boat. Afterward, a number of boaters in the marina entertained themselves by shining flashlights on the water to spot the infamous Asian Carp. The Admiral had no desire to participate because she had a grudge against the nasty, big-mouthed fish for costing us so much money in Chicago!

Sept. 5 — 75 miles to Peoria Heights, Illinois[8]

Reflection got underway at 6:50 a.m. for a 75-mile trip to the Illinois Valley Yacht Club (aka The IVY Club). We made sure to call the lock tender at the Starved Rock Lock ahead of time, and he told us the traffic was clear, so we were able to get in and out of that lock quickly. Our ride down the Illinois River was much more pleasant as the river widened, and we saw many people fishing who had set up campsites along the shores. The small boat traffic also increased because of Labor Day weekend, but it was nothing compared to a typical holiday weekend on Barnegat Bay back home in New Jersey.

The IVY Club (Illinois Valley Yacht Club)

Reflection arrived at The IVY Club at 3 p.m., and we received a warm welcome from the dockmaster and some of the club members. After taking on fuel, we were tied up at the wall right in front of the clubhouse. Their facilities were lovely and included a pool, dining room, bar, clean showers, and laundry facility. Once we were set up, our crew quickly scattered to do the laundry, to go to the bar to watch the football game, and to take showers. In the evening, we all had dinner in the club's dining room and were grateful for the relaxing day we had enjoyed, as compared to our previous two days of travel on the river.

Sept. 6 — 48 miles to Havana, Illinois[9]

It had rained overnight, and it was still overcast when we got up. I cooked a Sunday morning breakfast of scrambled eggs with onions, cheese, and bacon, accompanied by toasted cheddar cheese bread. This was our once-a-week big breakfast splurge.

At 9:45 a.m., we headed out into the river for a relaxing 48-mile trip to Tall Timbers Marina in Havana, Illinois. Again, we called ahead to the lock tender at the Peoria Lock, and he told us to come on ahead because he had no commercial traffic. Like the day before, the locking was effortless. We quickly entered and were given the option to float in the center of the lock because we were only being lowered eight feet. That was good because we did not even have to tie up.

As we headed down the river, we passed by the city of Peoria, home of the Caterpillar Corporation, the manufacturer of our two hard-working engines. Unfortunately, there was no adequate dockage at the city's slips for a boat of our size, so we were not able to visit.

As we continued along our route, the shoreline became rural with blue herons sitting along the banks and white pelicans floating in the river. We could see the damage that the previous autumn and spring flooding had taken on the trees along the river because many were completely uprooted or had their roots exposed. There were few houses in the flood-prone area, and those we did see were either built high on pilings or situated behind high levees. The boat traffic was also light, and small bass boats seemed to be the norm. The river was also quite shallow along its shores, so we stayed close to the center of the channel.

At 2:45 p.m., we arrived at Tall Timbers Marina, which was a small, tucked-away, private marina with an entrance that could hardly be seen from the river itself; you had to know that it was there. We entered through the narrow opening that was surrounded by rock walls into the marina's cove of about 35 boats, and *Reflection* was the biggest boat there. I carefully turned her around, and we slowly backed up to our assigned place at the fuel dock, an area that was quite snug.

[9] *See notes on page 164*

While we were backing into our spot, a number of Asian Carp (Pat's favorite fish) jumped out of the water and nearly landed on the swim platform.

Peoria, Illinois

Bob, the owner, warmly greeted us, as did other boaters who were sitting at the tropical bar area alongside our boat. Some even wanted to know when we would be giving them tours of our vessel! We were the talk of the marina, and during the late afternoon and early evening, people stopped by to chat and to ask questions about our Great Loop adventure. That evening, we finally had the steak dinner aboard that we had been promising Charlie and Helen for almost a week. This was a terrific stop!

Sept. 7 — 35 miles to Bar Island Anchorage[10]

Because we did not have many miles to travel to our anchorage location on the Illinois River, we did not leave beautiful Tall Timbers Marina until 10 a.m. The weather continued to be delightful, with temperatures in the high 70s and low 80s, light winds, and sunny skies. We only saw three barges with tugs along our 35-mile trip, and we entered a quiet spot (except for the carp jumping around) just outside the channel behind Bar Island at about 2 p.m. Despite the fact that the island was not large, we were sheltered from the barge wake, and *Reflection* remained steady at anchor. It was a wonderful, quiet Labor Day afternoon as each of us found

[10] *See notes on page 164*

our own spot aboard to read, nap, or watch a movie. After cocktails, I barbecued chicken on the grill for dinner, followed by a viewing of the classic movie, *From Here to Eternity* as our evening's entertainment. Life was tough here on the river!

A typical bend in the Illinois River — a far cry from the narrow conditions we encountered just a few days before that.

Sept. 8 — 65 miles to Hardin, Illinois[11]

As we were lifting anchor at 6:45 a.m., a large bolt in our anchor stem roller sheared off. That made raising the anchor difficult, but Charlie and I subsequently determined that we could find a replacement bolt for it in a few days. We called the lock tender at La Grange Lock, our last lock on the Illinois River, who told us to come on ahead, and again, after entering the lock, *Reflection* was allowed to float in the middle rather than having to tie up to a bollard. The scenery was lovely as we traveled south on the end of the river. We saw turtles sunning themselves on fallen tree stumps, blue herons, white pelicans, and even a bald eagle along the way.

Our days journey was a 65-mile trip to Mel's Illinois RiverDock Restaurant, a location that had a reputation for serving delicious food with an overnight dock right on the river. When we arrived, the dock wasn't quite what we had pictured, but it was adequate for us.

The simple-looking restaurant was on a hill behind the dock, and Charlie, Helen, and I decided to head up there to check out the menu and then report back to Admiral Pat. We were pleased with the menu and the atmosphere, and we even got to meet the famous owner, Mel, who also gave us samples of some of his cuisine.

---

[11] *See notes on page 164*

This could be a contender as our next boat. We were told we could get a good deal on it!

Mel's RiverDock (George's newest favorite place to eat)

Brisket was one of the specialties on the dinner menu that night, and though we enjoyed it, we ended up bringing much of the large portions back to the boat in doggie bags. The cooking was "down home" with ribs, fried chicken, potato salad, sweet potatoes, and cucumber salad being just some of the excellent dishes available. We finished dinner off with apple pie and ice cream, walked back to the dock, and watched *Farewell to Arms* as our evening's movie.

Sept. 9 — 20 miles to Grafton, Illinois (the Key West of the Midwest)[12]

We had enjoyed our dinner so much the previous night that we returned to Mel's for breakfast. This meal was also terrific, so I vowed that Pat and I would again return on Friday night for Mel's fried chicken special, one of my favorite meals. After all the good food we had consumed at this "find," our crew finally got *Reflection* underway at about 9 a.m. It was then only a short, 20-mile trip to Grafton Harbor Marina, dubbed "The Key West of the Midwest," which is located at mile marker zero on the Illinois River where it empties into the Mississippi River. The point where the Illinois and Mississippi Rivers come together is known as a "confluence."

 James Mason founded Grafton in 1832, and in 1834, it was described as "a post office, one store, one tavern, and a number of families." By 1850, Grafton's population reached its peak at about 10,000 because it supplied workers for the local stone quarries, boat building, and commercial fishing industries. Throughout the years, however, as companies closed, the population decreased to about 1,000 before the Great Flood of 1993. After that, the population slowly decreased to today's population of about 700 residents. Grafton's main industry is now tourism with restaurants, some antique, craft, and wine shops, and various other attractions.

We docked before noon at the lovely marina, bought some T-shirts in the ship's store to commemorate the spot, and then set out to explore the small town. Along Main Street, there were stores and eateries, a hotel that claimed to be haunted by a young girl, and even a winery. We made several stops along the way and later decided to split up, with Pat returning to the boat, and the others continuing to shop and going to the hardware store for a replacement bolt for the anchor.

On Pat's return to the dock, she was delighted to see *Houlegan* pulling in. We had not visited with Ray and Caryl since July, even though we had talked by phone, emailed each other, traversed the fish barrier on the same day, and been tied up at Joliet together. They came aboard, bringing my quick-release hose connection that I had left by accident back at Tall Timbers Marina and that Bob, the owner, had kindly asked them to return to us whenever they could. The people along the river were thoughtful that way.

We invited Ray and Caryl to come back later for cocktails so we could catch up with them on their activities. Everyone had a good get-together aboard in the early evening, and after our friends returned to their boat, our crew went to The Mississippi Half-Step for dinner. The restaurant is located in a charming historic home with dining available in various rooms inside and on the outside patio. Because three of us were already nursing mosquito bites on our legs from being outdoors at night, we chose to eat inside. The dinner was delicious, and we closed the place at 10 p.m. When I got into bed that night, I fell asleep looking forward to the next day's milestone: We would be entering "The Mighty Mississippi."

Notes:

(1)

Chicago — The Monroe Harbor mooring field can be unsettled, and waves can reach 4-plus feet in the harbor, so I do not advise staying onboard overnight at the moorings. You can tie up to a wall in a sheltered area for an additional fee, but there is no water, no electric, and no security, except for an occasional police patrol. If you tie to the wall, be sure to leave some outside lights on for security.

(2)

Chicago — Du Sable Harbor is expensive, but so is every other marina in Chicago. It is convenient to the Navy Pier and Bockmueller's grocery, which is located in the lower level of the building at 155 Harbor Drive. There is no sign outside for this store, which has good provisions.

(3)

Calumet is extremely industrial, and we found that the clearances at the drawbridges were less than the chart indicates. However, they open on signal. Also, there is a fixed bridge on the route that has a clearance of just 19 feet. The channel is narrow with much barge traffic, so be cautious. At the first lock, if you are the only boat, the lock tender will allow you to float in the center with no need to tie up. In any lock that is a lift/drop of 10 feet or less, the lock tender might allow you to float instead of tying up. If you wish to tie up to a floating bollard on the Illinois River system, ask the lock tender for permission. There are no floating bollards at the first lock. On all the other rivers, it is assumed that you will tie up to the floating bollards. Allow time at locks, and remember that military or commercial traffic always has the right-of-way over pleasure craft.

(4)

Call lock tenders ahead of time to find out the status of traffic at their individual locks. This might help you to avoid a multi-hour wait.

(5)
Joliet — Tie up to the Bicentennial Park wall (immediately after passing through the Jefferson Street bridge), which is across the river from the police headquarters. Do not tie up across from Harrah's Casino. There are many 30-amp electrical connections available, and water is also available, but at a distance. There is room for many boats, but use fenders (the top of the wall is in rough condition). There is no security, so leave some outside lights on. Walk across the bridge to the casino, delis, and restaurants, and a small farmers' market held on Fridays near the Municipal Building.

(6)
Fuel prices tended to be high on the Illinois River. We found the best price in Alton, Illinois, on the Mississippi River.

(7)
Heritage Harbor Marina gives a discount on dockage for America's Great Loop Cruisers' Association members and is a new, welcoming facility with a courtesy car and a small bar and café on the premises.

(8)
The Illinois Valley Yacht Club can take boats with a max draft of 4 feet. It has reasonably priced dockage, but the fuel is pricey. It has a nice restaurant, pool, showers, and laundry facility, but there is limited dockage for boats more than 45 feet (call ahead). It is a friendly place to stop.

(9)
Tall Timbers Marina has limited dockage for boats more than 45 feet, so call ahead for water depths and availability. It is a walk of four blocks to the Dollar General Store for moderate provisions and 1 mile to the drugstore, liquor store, IGA supermarket, and limited restaurants.

(10)
Bar Island Anchorage is easily accessible in 10 feet of water behind an island and is protected from river wakes with good holding.

(11)
Mel's Illinois RiverDock Restaurant — Look for the yellow floating dock to starboard just past the Route 16/100 Bridge. Dockage is inexpensive with no services available at the dock, but the food was inexpensive and good, and it was well worth the stop.

(12)
Grafton — Grafton Harbor Marina is a modern facility, reasonably priced, convenient to many restaurants, and has the lowest fuel prices on the Illinois River. There is no large grocery in town, but there is a hardware/general store 1 mile away and a winery nearby.

Chapter 9

Rollin' on the Rivers

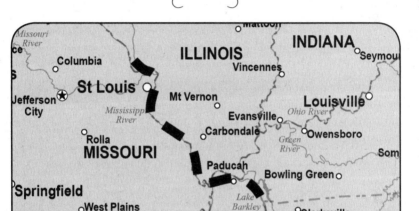

Sept. 10 — 17 miles to Alton, Illinois[1]

Charlie and Helen, who had been onboard with us for ten days, were booked on a 7 p.m. flight out of Lambert-St. Louis International Airport, so we got underway before 8 a.m. for a 17-mile trip to Alton Marina, our first stop on the Mississippi River. There, we would secure a rental car to take our friends to the airport.

When we entered the river, there was a certain "wow" factor because it truly looked like The Mighty Mississippi we had envisioned. At this point, it was wide, with high, light-colored, rock-layered cliffs on the eastern shoreline and a slow and gentle flow. I thought to myself, "We're here. We've made it to the Mississippi on our own boat! This is amazing!"

---

[1] See notes on page 182

The Mississippi deserves its characterization as "mighty" because it is 2,320 miles long, comprises the largest river system in North America, is the fourth longest river in the world, and is the tenth most powerful river in the world. Along with its tributaries, it drains all or parts of 31 states stretching from the Rocky Mountains in the west to the Appalachian Mountains in the east and runs from Canada in the north to the Gulf of Mexico in the south.

Confluence of the Illinois and Mississippi Rivers

We had a pleasant, easy-going ride on the river to Alton, Illinois, the day's destination.

 Alton has had its place in American History. It originally was developed as a river town in 1818 and eventually grew into an industrial and trading center. Within a few years, it also became an important location for abolitionists because Illinois was a free state located immediately across the river from the slave state of Missouri. Escaped slaves would cross the Mississippi to seek refuge in Alton and then would proceed to safe houses through stations of the Underground Railroad. Noting also its pre-Civil War's importance, there is a memorial site in Downtown Alton commemorating the seventh Lincoln-Douglas debate, which took place there on Oct. 15, 1858.

We made our way down the river to Alton Marina's entrance that is located under the magnificent Clark Bridge that spans the river, connecting Illinois to Missouri. Shortly after *Reflection* was settled in her slip, we rented a vehicle so that we could get in some sightseeing in St. Louis with Charlie and Helen and then be able to drop them off at the airport for their flight back to New Jersey.

We left the marina around 11:30 a.m. in search of a place to have lunch with our friends, and after riding around St. Louis for a while, we discovered Laclede's Landing, a small riverfront enclave of restaurants and historic buildings, and chose Hannigan's as the place where we would eat. After a pleasant meal there, we then spent several hours at the famous St. Louis Gateway Arch and took a tram ride to the top of the Arch for its amazing panoramic view of the city and the Mississippi River.

The Arch was built as a monument to the westward expansion of the U.S. and is the centerpiece of the Jefferson National Expansion Memorial. At 630 feet, it is the tallest manmade monument in the U.S. Although the Arch was originally designed in 1947, its construction did not begin until 1963, and it finally opened to the public on July 10, 1967.

We even found time to tour the Museum of Westward Expansion, which follows the lives of American explorers, such as Lewis and Clark, and notes their impact on the exploration of the American West. The wonderful facility is located beneath the Arch, and it provides an interesting and well-done educational experience. It was an enjoyable way to spend an afternoon.

View of the Mississippi River from the top of the Gateway Arch

It was then time to drive Charlie and Helen to the airport for their 7 p.m. flight. We were nostalgic when we said goodbye to our long-time friends, and we had truly enjoyed having them aboard with us to share in our adventure. On returning back to *Reflection*, we made phone calls to our neighbors back home to see what was happening there because we had heard there was a northeaster blowing with wind and rain on the New Jersey coast. Happily, our other home was all right.

The Gateway Arch

Sept. 11 — Alton, Illinois

This was a day of preparation for the next segment of our trip, which would take us almost 300 miles. We would pass through two locks and 201 miles on the Mississippi River, through two locks and 59 miles on the Ohio River, and through yet another lock and 32 miles on the Cumberland River to our next multi-day stay at the Green Turtle Bay Marina in Grand Rivers, Kentucky.

Our plan was to begin the segment on Sept. 13 and arrive in Kentucky on Sept. 18. We would tie up at only one marina during that time: Hoppie's Marina in Kimmswick, Missouri. During the rest of this portion of the trip, we could stop for the night only at anchorages or lock walls because no facilities were available. The upcoming week was going to be extremely interesting!

In the morning, Pat did the laundry, and I cleaned the outside of the boat. We rested in the afternoon and talked by phone to our friend Hank, aboard *Maya Lisa*. He and Ceci were supposed to stop at Mel's Illinois Riverdock for the night, but instead, they changed their plans and were in Grafton. We had planned to meet them at Mel's for dinner, and even though they were not there, we still decided to drive the 40 miles because I wanted to have the fried chicken special. We were not disappointed; the chicken was tasty and crunchy.

Sept. 12 — Alton, Illinois (home of Fast Eddie's)

It was our third and final day in Alton in preparation for our trip on the Mississippi, Ohio, and Cumberland Rivers. We left the boat at 8 a.m. and went to the local farmers' market, where we picked up fresh vegetables, homemade breads, cookies, and apple tarts. Knowing that we would not have access to a grocery store for at least five days, we stocked up with everything we would need for the refrigerator, freezer, and pantry at a small, local supermarket.

Pat spent the afternoon stowing away our purchases, cleaning the interior of the boat, and writing on our blog. Because I did not want to be in her way, I "volunteered" to visit a well-known bar/eatery in the area, Fast Eddie's Bon Air, to research its notoriety.

The desk agent at the car rental office in Alton first recommended the place to me. Folks at the marina also lauded it, so it became crystal clear that I, as the Captain, for the specific purpose of doing accurate research, should explore the wonders of Fast Eddie's!

I hailed a cab and was quickly on my way as the cab driver regaled me with stories about the glories of the landmark bar, where it sounded like I would experience the equivalent of bar "nirvana."

The exterior of Fast Eddie's was completely non-descript with the food menu and prices painted on the outside wall: half-pound burgers, homemade bratwursts, and a basket of French fries — each for $1. At these prices, I had to go in and sample things for myself!

On entering this unique establishment, I was struck by the immense size of the place and the number of people in it. It was huge and was a combination of Sloppy Joes in Key West, the old Jimmy Byrnes and Jerry Lynch bars I had occasionally frequented in my younger years at the Jersey shore, and the local tavern where your father might have hung out when you were a child. Only at Fast Eddie's, it was all done on a very grand scale!

There were literally hundreds of people in the place. The clientele ran the gamut from bikers to businessmen, blue collar, white collar, and no collar, and though most folks were in their 20s and 30s, there were also patrons who were well into their 80s. It was an quite interesting array of humanity!

I found a line and proceeded to the end of it. When I asked the guy in front of me what the line was for, he explained that it was the line to place food orders, and it wrapped half-way around a large, rectangular bar. He told me that I was in luck because when he had gotten on the line, it went all the way around the bar. It was convenient that the bar and food line were right next to each other because you could drink your way around the bar, and most people were doing just that. By the way, the beer was cheap, too.

My new food line/bar companion explained that Fast Eddie's' atmosphere had been quite an influence on him during his early 20s while he was in college because he sort of lived at the bar during that time. Even now, when he comes back home to visit his parents, he always stops by. The only difference is that these days he brings his folks along with him.

Eventually I drank my way to the front of the food line where I ordered a bratwurst and a Chick on a Stick (well-seasoned chicken wings on a skewer). When I paid, I was given a receipt and then stood on the side waiting for my food, but the nice young lady at the cash register told me to find a place to sit down to wait for my order because they were only calling No. 475 at that time. I looked down at my receipt. I held No. 2.

At the cashier's recommendation, I went over to one of the bars and found a stool next to a young couple. The guy had enough tattoos to be in the circus, and the woman sported a beautiful Harley Davidson logo on her forearm. Much to my hungry surprise, a half hour and 80 numbers later, my number came up. The quality of the food was far better than I had thought it would be and was not a reflection of the low prices. It was good!

After dining, I then took a stroll around the place to fully absorb the ambiance. Fast Eddie's was decorated in dark tones with splashes of neon. There were numerous rooms about the place, where patrons sat at tables eating and drinking while listening to the music that was playing throughout the large establishment. My friend from the food line told me that when the state of Illinois banned smoking in bars, Fast Eddie himself took quick action for his customers by "buying" the street adjacent to the bar from the city and then enclosed that area for the smokers. This I wanted to see, so I went out a side door into a whole "new" world!

Fast Eddie had built a high wall around the street. You could not see out, and no one could see in. The area was filled with tables and chairs, bars, a stage with two guys playing guitars, and hundreds of people eating, drinking, singing, and dancing.

When I asked one of the bartenders if it was always this busy, he explained that this was a relatively small crowd and that I should be there during mid-summer when it gets packed. By the way, this was only 4 p.m.

As I worked my way back to the main bar area and headed for the exit, I looked around at this true bar "heaven" and made a mental note to return here if I were to ever visit the area again.

When I arrived back at the boat, I followed up my excursion with a well-deserved nap. When I awoke, the Admiral (who had been working hard onboard all day while I did "research") announced that we would be having our dinner delivered by a local Chinese restaurant that evening. That was fine with me, and after our meal, we retired early because we were exhausted from our day's activities and anxious to get on our way at sunrise the next day.

Sept. 13 — 44 miles to Kimmswick, Missouri[2]

We left our slip at Alton Marina at 6:40 a.m. for a 44-mile trip down the Mississippi through two locks to Hoppie's Marine Service. The locks we encountered were enormous in length and width to accommodate the large sizes of the tows and barges we had seen as we traveled the river. The first lock we passed through was the Melvin Price Locks and Dam, a massive structure made up of two lock chambers side by side. One chamber was 1,200 by 110 feet; the other was 600 by 100 feet; and like falling down the rabbit hole in "Alice in Wonderland," entering the lock made us feel small.

The day's travels took us past St. Louis and gave us a different view of the Arch and its surroundings than when we had visited it on land a few days before. As we passed the Arch, the river current was moving at about 2 to 3 knots, and we were glad it was going our way. Water temperatures were in the low to mid 80s, and the river was somewhat brown in color but was not as muddy as the Illinois River.

Thanks to the current, we arrived at our destination earlier than expected, just before 11 a.m. Hoppie's was a famous stop for boaters on the Mississippi. Dockage consisted of three long barges tied to a cliff with cables, and it was also the only place to get fuel for the next 107 miles and the only marina for 249 miles. We were also fortunate to meet with the well-known owner, Fern Hopkins, who is a local expert on the rivers we would encounter as we headed south toward Mobile, Alabama. She was kind enough to review our charts with us, suggested good anchorages along the way, and pointed out potential trouble spots. Her sage advice was appreciated.

[2] *See notes on page 183*

The Melvin Price Locks — Its main chamber is 1,200 feet long.

Pat looped a line over a floating bollard and prepared to secure Reflection *in the lock chamber.*

Hoppie's Marine Services (any port you can find on the Mississippi is welcome)

Downtown in the city of Kimmswick, Illinois

I decided to take a walk into town just to look around. Kimmswick is a municipality that meets the definition of a city according to the U.S. Census Bureau, although it only has a population of about 100 residents. It barely seems big enough to be a small village. It is so small that if you ask for directions and someone tells you that it will take only a second to get there, he or she is telling the truth!

 In 1859, Theodore Kimms laid out the city, which he named for himself, on 160 acres. This made it big enough for a city designation, but most of it still remains vacant land. In the late 1800s, a spa and resort was built around the natural salt springs, and Kimmswick became a popular steamboat day trip from St. Louis. Today it is a tourist destination featuring numerous antique and craft stores where you can purchase everything from Christmas items to whips and saddles, plus there are two charming country-style restaurants.

When I returned from my city tour, Pat and I talked for a while with some of the other loopers on the dock about where each of us would be heading in the morning. After dinner, we retired for the evening (not much nightlife in Kimmswick, Missouri) in anticipation of our early start the next day.

Sept. 14 — 41 miles to Kaskaskia River Lock[3]

The places where we could safely tie up or anchor our boat on the Mississippi were few and far between. The gentle current of the river twisted and turned along muddy banks washed by its light brown water. The motion became almost mesmerizing, so we made sure to maintain our focus, paying close attention to what we were doing and always being on the lookout for the possible hazard that there might be a large towboat with a multitude of barges coming around a blind turn.

The towboat operators were friendly as we contacted them by radio to ask them about which side on which we should pass them.

After 41 miles, we pulled up to the Kaskaskia River Lock. We asked the lock tender whether we could tie up there for the night, even though it was only about 11 a.m. After providing him with information about *Reflection*, including how many people were aboard and our destination, he said that we could tie up. He then informed us that the Army Corps of Engineers was supposed to be bringing in a barge and equipment to work on the lock and dam, so we should be prepared for the possibility that we might be told to move if they needed our spot.

Imagine, then, a lovely summer afternoon with temperatures in the low 80s, little wind, and just the sound of cicadas — a perfect naptime! Just as Pat and I were

---

[3] *See notes on page 183*

lulled into a peaceful dream-like state, a loud voice on the marine radio interrupted everything: "Vessel *Reflection,* sorry to disturb you, but you're going to have to move." The towboat captain had arrived with a huge barge with major construction equipment aboard, and the dock wall where we were secured was exactly where he wanted to tie up, so we had to move to another section of the wall and out of his way. We did so quickly, and even though it was an annoyance, we were happy we were allowed to stay.

Rock formations along the Mississippi

Later, we heard another vessel, *Falkor,* call the lock tender and ask to also tie up. He granted them permission as long as we could make do together at the same space on the lock wall. We were glad to move our boat again to make room for them, and I jumped off *Reflection* to help them tie up. *Falkor* was a Grand Banks 36 with Allen and Gayle from Guelph, Ontario aboard, and this was their third time doing the Loop! When they joined us on our boat for cocktails, they shared some of the detailed logs of their previous trips, which became a wealth of information on what we would be encountering. The meeting proved to be fortuitous for us because they were headed to the Bahamas for the winter and we decided to travel together for some of our way south. We felt so fortunate to meet this charming couple!

Sept. 15 — 69 miles to Little Diversion Channel — Mississippi River[4]

Reflection and *Falkor* started out at 6:30 a.m. because we wanted to be out of the way of the Army Corps of Engineers before they started moving their barge equipment near our dock and because we had a 69-mile trip to reach our anchorage at Little Diversion Channel. The channel was merely a narrow cut in the west bank of the Mississippi River where a few boats could hide from the current and barge traffic of the river, and such safe stopping spots were rare.

We arrived at Little Diversion Channel about 1:30 p.m., and we purposely went past the entrance and turned our vessels into the current so we could maintain control of them as we entered the channel. It is ill advised to enter the narrow waterway from upstream because the swift waters of the Mississippi could easily push your vessel against the downstream bank of the entrance. *Falkor* led the way, pushing against the current and then turned into the channel, vanishing behind a wall of trees. Once inside the narrow cut, she turned around to face the entrance and set her anchor. We followed and went past her a short distance further into the channel and dropped our anchor. I then backed up to *Falkor*, and we tied our sterns together so our boats would not move during the night in such a tight situation. No other boats anchored, and outside of two bass fishing boats that motored by slightly rocking us, we had a quiet and peaceful night.

A towboat pushing 25 barges, but we saw some towboats pushing as many as 45 barges

Reflection and Falkor *at anchor-tied stern to stern in the narrow Little Diversion Channel with the Mississippi River in the background*

Sept. 16 — 81 miles to Little Chain Bar Anchorage — Ohio River[5]

We lifted our anchors at 6:30 a.m. for an 81-mile trip that would be our last on the Mississippi and would take us on to the Ohio River. We again encountered barge traffic and even saw some barges that had run aground outside the channel. That just proved that even professional tow captains had to be cautious on the turns in the waterway.

Toward the end of the Mississippi run, the scenery was almost surreal, with an overcast sky, muddy banks, swirling muddy waters, and incredible curves in the river. As we approached the confluence of the two rivers and then came around the final curve at Cairo, Illinois, into the Ohio River, the feeling and scenery completely changed. Even though Cairo was highly industrial, the riverbanks were made up of sandy shores and cliffs, and the color of water turned to a dark green. The scenery felt more familiar and comfortable to us because it was similar to what we had often seen on the East Coast of the U.S.

We experienced 1 to 2 knots of current running against us that slowed down our travel. We transited Lock 53 on the Ohio easily and then proceeded to an anchorage spot with which Al and Gayle were familiar from their past trip. It was about

[5] *See notes on page 183*

a mile and a half from a coal barge loading area, yet the anchorage was scenic with large stands of trees behind a sandy shore. The spot allowed us to stay far away from the coal carriers and to securely anchor behind a sand bar in the river in about 15 feet of water.

Reflection *at anchor on the Ohio River*

After dinner, as the sun was going down and I looked out across the great Ohio River, I had a moment to reflect on where we were and on our journey throughout the past few days. I could not help but feel grateful for how wonderful the adventure had been and how fortunate I was to be here living it.

Thanks to Al and Gayle's experience with the area, we again had a quiet night with the coal barge tows slipping quietly past us at a safe distance. It was a good spot right on the Ohio River.

Sept. 17 — 26 miles to Cumberland Island Towhead — Ohio River[6-7]

We lifted anchor at 6:30 a.m., but when we approached Lock 52 on the Ohio River at 7:45 a.m., we noticed tows and barges lined up on the shore before the lock. When I called the lock tender and asked him when we could come through, he told me, in about three to four hours! I then asked him if there were any places where we could tie up while we waited. He told us to anchor in the river behind a red buoy near the dam and then wait for him to call us.

We used the time to have a wonderful breakfast and grabbed a power nap. At about 10:15 a.m., we were told that the lock tender would fit our two boats in the lock with a tow with several small barges. It was a two-chamber lock, but the Army Corps of Engineers had closed down the larger lock chamber for repairs, thus causing a major backup on the Ohio River. Though we were lucky to be allowed through, it was a slow process because the lock was old and took a long time to empty and fill. One of the lock tenders who assisted in securing us to the lock told me the lock we were in was built in the early 1960s as a temporary measure and was only supposed to last a few years. No wonder it was falling apart!

We finally got through at about 11:15 a.m. Because of the lock delay and the current running against us, we amended our original plan to go to Grand Rivers, Kentucky, and decided to continue only 26 miles to the Cumberland Island Towhead anchorage on the Ohio River. If we had tried to proceed up the Cumberland River, it could have resulted in our being on the river in the dark.

Reflection *and* **Falkor** *at anchor in the Cumberland Towhead*
(a peaceful place to spend the night)

On the way, our boats passed the confluence of the Tennessee and Ohio Rivers at Paducah. Although we would eventually travel down the Tennessee River, we chose an alternate route that would take us through the Cumberland River, thus allowing us to bypass a lock on the Tennessee that was notorious for huge commercial backups.

We continued on the Ohio until we reached the Cumberland Towhead. Once again, Al and Gayle had visited the anchorage before, and it proved to be a terrific one. We were anchored by 2 p.m., saw some small deer on the island near sunset, and spent a quiet evening planning future stops on Kentucky Lake and the Tennessee River. We were so delighted to have met our new friends.

Sept. 18 — 32 miles to Grand Rivers, Kentucky[8]

Our two boats left late today — 7 a.m.! The Cumberland River was a narrow river that twisted and turned past small commercial areas and had tree-lined scenic areas along its banks. We saw vultures, blue herons, and our second bald eagle of the trip along the way. There were no other boats or barges on our journey, and the current was running against us at a speed of at least 2 knots.

After 30 miles, we finally faced the formidable Barkley Lock with its huge 800-foot lock chamber and a lift of 57 feet. The Army Corps of Engineers completed the Lock and the 10,180-foot-wide dam in 1966. We proceeded into the chamber quickly, tied up to a floating bollard, and were lifted speedily into beautiful Lake Barkley. Green Turtle Bay Marina was only a mile beyond the lock, and we were quickly tied up by 2 p.m. It was our first time in several days to be able to walk on land!

Al and Gayle invited us to *Falkor* for cocktails, and we decided that afterward, we would go to Patti's 1880s Settlement for dinner to celebrate our week of travel. Before our visit to *Falkor*, I called Hank and Ceci aboard *Maya Lisa* to see where they were at that point. To our surprise, Hank said they and ten other looper boats were in Barkley Lock, just around the corner from the marina, and would be coming in shortly.

A few minutes later, it was quite a sight to see! Eleven looper boats were lined up and came into the marina like a small parade. Most of the boats were members of the America's Great Loop Cruisers' Association, the organization to which we belonged, and all had begun their trips from various locations in the U.S. or Canada. We knew and understood some of the difficulties everyone had to surmount to arrive at this spot, whether they were "carp captives," "lock captives" (due to the delays on the Ohio River), or simply river travelers.

Everyone was happy to have arrived at the marina, with some appearing more tired than others, but all were ready to party. Aboard *Falkor*, Gayle had made delicious homemade scones and a chicken curry spread for hors d'oeuvres. Later, a restaurant van picked us up, and we had a wonderful dinner at Mr. Bill's, the partner restaurant of Patti's, a famous restaurant in the area. The restaurants had identical menus, including their famous 2-inch pork chops, and we enjoyed sharing a fascinating evening with this delightful couple.

Sept. 19 — Grand Rivers, Kentucky

Grand Rivers is a city with a population of about 400 residents. It originally was named Nickelville, however, because of the nearby iron ore deposits, it was renamed Grand Rivers in expectation of its establishment as a major steel-producing city. Unfortunately, the steel-producing enterprise died within a few years, but the name remained. Today, Grand Rivers is a small tourist village with antique shops, clothing stores, a playhouse, several restaurants, and a grocery store. Because the village is located in a dry county, there are no liquor stores or bars in the area.

We started the day with the usual chores — laundry, food shopping, and a stop at the local hardware store. Happily, the marina had golf carts and courtesy vans for rent so that boaters could make their way into town, which was about a mile away, or go to Paducah, which was 20 miles away.

We had rain showers in the afternoon, but the skies cleared and the crews of all 14 boats of loopers gathered later at a gazebo on the marina grounds for an impromptu party of cocktails and appetizers. The table was overflowing with wonderful treats that each boat brought, a true testimony to the fact that our band of travelers eats well underway. These were the boats present: *Reflection* — New Jersey; *Falkor* — Ontario; *Maya Lisa* — Virginia; *Still Busy* — South Carolina; *Early Out* — Florida; *Riff Raff* — Georgia; *Rick 'n' Roll* — North Carolina; *Perfect Remedy* — Florida; *Morningside* — Maryland; *Meander* — Florida; *Sterling Lady* — Florida; *Carolyn Ann* — Florida; *Pookie II* —Tennessee; and *Biddi and the Beast* — Kentucky. We all had a good time eating, drinking, telling stories, singing, and taking pictures. It was a fabulous get-together!

Afterward, we went out to dinner with Hank and Ceci from *Maya Lisa*, and Neil and Peggy from *Early Out*. Hank planned on moving *Maya Lisa* the next day at a fast pace to bring the boat to her winter haul-out location in Fulton, Mississippi. Our group headed to dinner at Patti's Restaurant, and in spite of the fact that it is a "dry" county, we were allowed to bring wine into the restaurant. However, the server was not allowed to touch the bottle. She could bring us wineglasses, a corkscrew, and an ice bucket if we wanted one, but she was not allowed by local ordinance to handle the bottle as long as there was wine in it. The waitstaff could also get rid of the empties for you, and we had several. After a terrific evening at Patti's, we said goodbye to our friends with the hope that we would see them again in Florida when they visited the Fort Myers area in the wintertime.

Sept. 20 – Grand Rivers, Kentucky

We awoke to rainy skies and were glad we decided to stay here before moving on to the Tennessee River. After breakfast aboard, we shopped at the Ship's Store, made phone calls, updated our blog, and enjoyed cable TV (a rarity). Later in the day, we were delighted to see *Houlegan* enter the marina and tie up right in front of us. They did a 293-mile push to get here in four days, which was quite an accomplishment.

Though exhausted, Ray and Caryl came over to our boat for cocktails, munchies, and conversation about our shared adventures throughout the past ten days. Later in the evening, I enjoyed watching a Giants football game on TV, especially since the Giants beat the Dallas Cowboys in an exciting finish. We turned in early, knowing that the next day we would continue on to Kentucky Lake and the Tennessee River.

Notes:

(1)
Alton Marina is a large modern marina that is reasonably priced, and it had the lowest price on fuel we had seen in a long time. Enterprise Rent-a-Car is located nearby for grocery shopping and visiting St. Louis. Fast Eddie's Bon Air is a not-to-be missed experience. Take a cab there. A casino is also located near the marina.

(2)

Hoppie's Marine Services is a unique experience, but use caution when docking into the current, and follow the dockmaster's instructions closely. Their fuel prices are considerably more than Alton Marina's, but there is a price break for a cash purchase. Fern, the dockmaster, holds court in the afternoon when she gives information on the rivers going south. The town of Kimmswick is about a quarter of a mile away with small shops and restaurants.

(3)

Kaskaskia Lock — Call the lock tender for permission to tie up. The tie up area is broken into three sections: The first section has two cleats, the second section has four cleats, and the third section has none.

(4)

Little Diversion Channel should be approached from downstream into the current. Set bow and stern anchors. It is narrow but is safe and sheltered.

(5)

Little Chain Bar Anchorage — Anchor close to shore and away from the channel. It has excellent holding and is out of the strong current, but it can be rough if the wind comes up.

(6)

Before Lock 52 — There is an anchorage on the left descending bank where you can anchor near to shore with good holding. However, the current can be strong.

(7)

Cumberland Towhead is an excellent anchorage with room for several boats.

(8)

Barkley Lock has light boat traffic. Green Turtle Bay Marina is an excellent spot to regroup. Local restaurants will pick you up here. If you stay three nights, you will also have access to the yacht club at the marina for dinner. It is located in a dry county with a small IGA supermarket 1 mile away. There are four courtesy cars (fee for use), but the marine fuel was pricey with prices going down as we traveled south.

Chapter 10

Lovin' the Land of Dixie

Sept. 21 — 14 miles to Sugar Bay Anchorage — Kentucky Lake[1]

Reflection and *Falkor* got underway at 10 a.m. for a 14-mile trip to Sugar Bay. It was only a brief time before we entered the Barkley Canal that connects Lake Barkley and Kentucky Lake, which is just a wide part of the Tennessee River.

Kentucky Lake is a major navigable reservoir along the Tennessee River that was created in 1944 by the Tennessee Valley Authority with the construction of Kentucky Dam's confining of the river. It is the largest artificial lake by surface area (160,309 acres) in the U.S. east of the Mississippi River. When the lake was created, farms, homes, towns, roads, and railroads had to be relocated, and other homes and buildings that were flooded still lie below the water surface today. Some of the roads that at one time crossed the valley where the lake now stands can be seen along the shore entering the water and serve today as public boat launch ramps.

The scenery was lush and beautiful and in some ways reminded us of Chesapeake Bay, with its many lovely coves for anchoring. We arrived at the sheltered and marvelously scenic location at noon. It felt good to have such a short way to travel after our seemingly epic journeys on the Mississippi, Ohio, and Cumberland Rivers.

Reflection *in the protected anchorage of Sugar Bay*

Later in the day, two more looper boats joined us, *Still Busy* and *Meander*. After lunch, all the boaters came out to play. Some went swimming in the 84-degree water, some washed their hulls, and everyone dropped their dinghies in to go for rides around the anchorage area. I grilled up some tasty spareribs for dinner, followed by a restful night in such a special place.

Sept. 22 — 29 miles to Buchanan, Tennessee[2]

We awoke to overcast skies and lifted anchor at 7 a.m. in the company of *Falkor*. Our destination was Paris Landing State Park Marina, which was 29 miles away.

---

[2] *See notes on pages 204-205*

The park offers a marina and has a variety of picnic areas, a par 72, 18-hole golf course, areas for playing softball, basketball, and tennis, fishing locations, an Olympic-sized swimming pool at the park's inn and conference center, and a good restaurant.

As we headed to the park, the wind blew against us at about 10 knots, causing a light chop on Kentucky Lake. It was quite reminiscent of the usual wind/wave conditions on our home waters of Barnegat Bay in New Jersey.

When we arrived, the marina had many available slips, and by late morning, the boats were comfortably tied up and we were in air-conditioned comfort because the temperature was in the mid-80s and the humidity was high.

Al, Gayle, and I went on exploratory walks around the park's grounds while Pat stayed aboard and used her energy to clean the inside of the boat. After naps and showers, we called the park's lodge where we all planned to have dinner. As a convenience to boaters, a ranger picked us up and transported us from the marina to the facility.

The lodge was a substantial hotel/conference center with large dining rooms where a chicken buffet was being served that particular evening. There were all kinds of chicken — fried chicken, barbecued chicken, fried chicken livers, chicken and dumplings, and chicken soup. I was a happy man because chicken in almost any form is on my list of favorite foods. The food was delicious, and we could return to the buffet as many times as we wanted. On top of that, when we went to pay for our dinner, we discovered we were also eligible for an "over 62" discount that brought the price down to only about $6.50 per person. That was reasonable beyond belief! After dinner, the front desk called the ranger, who graciously drove us back to the marina. It was a lovely night.

Sept. 23 — 30 miles to New Johnsonville, Tennessee[3]

Once again, the skies were gray as we cast off our dock lines at 7 a.m. for the day's 30-mile trip to Pebble Isle Marina. There was a slight mist as we got underway, so we broke out our storm gear jackets for the first time since crossing Lake Michigan in August.

For the past several weeks, we had experienced good weather with temperatures in the low 80s, light winds, and mostly sunny to partly cloudy skies since we left Chicago. Any rainy conditions had occurred overnight or when we had planned to stay in a marina.

---

[3] *See notes on page 205*

We encountered current against us as we made our way south because the Tennessee flows from south to north. The water levels on the Tennessee River and just about all the rivers in that part of the country were manipulated through the dams operated by the Tennessee Valley Authority; thus, they also controlled the current.

Because there had been substantial rain south of our location for several days, we began to see debris in the water, which had changed from a light green to a light brown color. *Reflection* arrived at Pebble Isle Marina at 11 a.m., followed by *Falkor* a short time later. After taking on fuel, we were assisted in tying up at the dock by other loopers, some of whom we had met before and others who were new to us.

A house perched high on rocks along the Tennessee River for flood protection

We had lunch at the dockside restaurant, and by 1:15 p.m., we were on our way in the marina courtesy car to the liquor store and the local grocery store in the company of Pookie and Evan from *Pookie II* and Al and Gayle from *Falkor*. On our return, Ray and Patsy of *PatsyRay* invited us to a happy hour. Whenever two or more looper boats meet, there is always potential for a party.

We also met up with Rick and Betsy of *Rick 'n' Roll*, Pia and Jack of *Still Busy*, and Dean and Marge of *Still Afloat*. That evening, 14 of us had dinner together at the dockside restaurant. We were treated like royalty, and we even shared an enormous dessert that was on the house. The food was delicious, the servings were huge, and the service was good. We again were privileged to experience southern hospitality at its best, and we felt that everyone we had met in Kentucky and Tennessee had gone out of his or her way to make sure we felt welcome.

Sept. 24 — 53 miles to Double Islands Anchorage — Tennessee River[4]

Unfortunately, we had to miss the warm cinnamon rolls and coffee that were being served gratis at the marina office at 8:30 a.m. because we wanted to be underway at 7 a.m. for the day's 53-mile trip to our evening anchorage at Double Island. *Falkor* had stayed there on one of their previous trips, so we were quite confident it would be a safe spot with good holding.

The current continued to run against us, and the river had narrowed considerably. We dodged tree and branch debris that had been dislodged from the rains farther south, and we passed many types of homes, some built close to the shoreline on pilings, some built high on rocky cliffs, and RV homes situated on the banks with metal sheds built over them.

The only boats we saw out on the water today were small bass boats. Whenever rain showers became too much on the flybridge, we ducked below to the main salon and ran the boat from the lower station. We were glad we had that option.

The rock layers along the Tennessee River are the remains of a prehistoric shallow sea.

Reflection lowered the anchor in 19 feet of water at 3 p.m., and *Falkor* arrived about a half-hour later. *Still Busy* then joined us around 5 p.m. The anchorage

[4] *See notes on page 205*

turned out to be a good spot, despite the fact that we were separated from the main body of the river only by the small island behind which we were tucked.

Sept. 25 — 67 miles to Counce, Tennessee[5-6]

Our original plans for the day called for us to travel to another anchorage only 37 miles away. However, after hearing weather reports that predicted a 70-percent chance of showers and a 90-percent chance of heavy rain overnight and into the next morning, we decided to push to Pickwick Landing State Park Marina, just beyond the Pickwick Lock and Dam. It would lengthen our trip by 12 miles, and we would also have to transit the Pickwick Lock with a lift of 59 feet — a procedure that could take time.

The current ran against us at a speed of 2 knots or more. Al and Gayle were not sure how fast *Falkor* could go with her single engine in that kind of current, so they told us to go on ahead and if they could make the lock in a timely fashion, they would.

Storm clouds finally clear at Grand Harbor Marina

The weather deteriorated steadily as the day progressed, and we could see the rain showers literally grow in front of us on our radar. Early in the afternoon, we received a phone call from our friend Caryl aboard *Houlegan* to tell us that she had just found out that Pickwick Landing was now closed to transient boats due to dock repairs. That was not the best news, so we quickly called Grand Harbor Marina, which was 9 miles farther than Pickwick, and they said that they would be able to give us slip space. We notified *Falkor* of the latest change to our plans, and they decided to head to Grand Harbor Marina also, saying they could probably make it there by 5:30 p.m.

As we approached the lock, we were dressed in full storm gear because it was pouring rain — just in time for Pat to take care of the outside line handling! The process took about an hour from start to finish, and by the time the lock doors opened for us to enter beautiful Pickwick Lake, the rain stopped long enough for me to have a quick celebratory refreshment.

We then swiftly made our way to Grand Harbor Marina, where we received a warm welcome and tie up from dockmaster Chip and his staff. They located us right behind *Rick 'n Roll*, who had arrived earlier, and sure enough, true to his word, at precisely 5:30 p.m., Al brought *Falkor* to the other side of the dock alongside us. I was impressed!

Sixty-seven miles, one lock, strong current against us, and rainy weather; we were happy to be here. We were so tired that our dinner aboard consisted of shrimp cocktail, pizza, and hot wing appetizers from our freezer.

Sept. 26 — Counce, Tennessee

Pat and I awoke to heavy rain and were thankful that we made the decision to move here. It was nice to have a leisurely breakfast, check email, and then check our calendar about when we might return home to check on Pat's mother, keep doctor and dentist appointments, and visit with family and friends.

I made phone calls to car rental agencies, and we decided we would move along to our prearranged slip at Joe Wheeler State Park Marina on Sept. 30. We would then rent a car and visit the U.S. Space and Rocket Center and other tourist sites in Huntsville, Alabama, and the huge Unclaimed Baggage Center in Scottsboro. Along with making repairs on the boat at the park, we planned to relax in the beautiful lake setting before packing up for our visit back to New Jersey on Oct. 8.

After a stay at home, we planned to return on Oct. 23 to *Reflection* at Joe Wheeler State Park Marina. That was the site of the upcoming America's Great Loop Cruisers' Association Rendezvous from Oct. 25 to 28, where activities, seminars, meetings, and get-togethers were planned for members who were in the planning stages, currently doing, or had completed The Loop. Having already met many of the expected attendees on our journey, we were looking forward to the event.

When the rendezvous was over, *Reflection* would then make her way down the Tennessee-Tombigbee Waterway to Mobile, Alabama, travel across the panhandle of Florida, and then move down the Gulf coast to her winter quarters in Goodland, Florida.

Boat chores and a visit to a marine store occupied our time today, and we took the marina's courtesy car in the evening to Pickwick Landing State Park's restaurant for the buffet dinner. The menu consisted of southern cooking, once again at a reasonable price. Rick and Betsey from *Rick 'n Roll* and Al and Gayle from *Falkor* accompanied us on the fun jaunt.

Sept. 27 — Counce, Tennessee

We awoke to a beautiful, sunny morning without a cloud in the sky. After a special breakfast, I drove Pat and Gayle in the marina's courtesy van to the Pickwick Market in the nearby town of Pickwick Dam.

Though the market was relatively small, we were pleasantly surprised at the variety of merchandise available. It was sort of a miniature Walmart with a more interesting atmosphere! Besides groceries and fresh meat, you could also purchase DVDs, clothes, hardware, and toys.

Later in the day, we went aboard *Falkor* for happy hour, where Lois and Mike from *Al di La*, a large powerboat from Memphis that was a slip holder at Grand Harbor, also joined us. It was another enjoyable evening after a quiet, restful day.

Sept. 28 — 14 miles to Rock Piles/Ross Branch — Anchorage on the Tennessee River[7]

Because we only had a 14-mile trip to our planned anchorage, we took our time getting started and left our slip at 10 a.m. It was a beautiful trip upriver with the wind blowing from the northeast behind us at 10 to 20 knots.

Our destination, Rock Piles, was named after three large rock formations that flanked the opening into the anchorage. Once we were anchored, *Reflection* and *Falkor* swung in various directions instead of heading into the wind. This happened because of the wind swirls in this bowl-shaped cove surrounded by high trees. Despite the effect, it was a beautiful spot that proved to be a safe and serene location for our vessels.

[7] *See notes on page 205*

*Falkor **sitting at the Rock Piles/Ross Branch anchorage along the** Tennessee River*

Sept. 29 — 26 miles to Florence, Alabama[8]

At 7:30 a.m., we pulled up anchor amidst fog that hovered low over the water. If it were the Atlantic Ocean, it would have been called "sea smoke," a phenomenon caused by the warm temperatures of the water (80 degrees) meeting the cold temperatures (50 degrees) of the air.

Within a half-hour, the visibility cleared, and we were surprised to see a considerable amount of bass boats out on the water. Because this was a weekday, I thought to myself that perhaps the folks around here did not work, they just fished — and that sounded good to me! The current continued against us at 1 to 2 knots on the 26-mile trip to Florence Harbor Marina, where we pulled in at 11:30 a.m.

 Florence is a city of more than 36,000 residents located in an area known as The Shoals. In 1818, it was surveyed by Italian surveyor Ferdinand Sannoner, who named Florence after the capital of Tuscany in Italy. Florence is known for its annual tourism events, including The W.C. Handy Music Festival and the Renaissance Fair. It is also the home of numerous museums, including:

---

[8] *See notes on page 205*

- The Kennedy-Douglass Center for the Arts that highlights artists from around the Southeast
- The Indian Mound and Museum that displays artifacts from the Mound and the surrounding area, dating back 10,000 years
- Pope's Tavern, one of Florence's oldest standing structures, which houses Civil War artifacts and antiques from the 18th and 19th centuries
- The W.C. Handy Home and Museum dedicated to "the father of the blues," which contains a collection of Handy's personal papers and artifacts
- The Rosenbaum House that was designed by famous architect Frank Lloyd Wright
- The Children's Museum of the Shoals built to promote education about the people and events that make up the Shoals' history

When we arrived at Florence, the dock mistress was friendly and informative, and she even took a picture of us standing near our boat's transom so our boat's name and homeport could be displayed in her marina's newsletter.

She also told us that the reason so many bass boats were out on the river was that Florence was hosting an invitational American Bass Anglers fishing tournament for the next three days. Many fishermen were expected to participate, and they would be vying for the first prize of a new boat with motor and trailer and $50,000.00. There would be $375,000.00 awarded in total prize money. We also learned that our marina was going to be "Bass Boat Central" the next morning because beginning at 3:30 a.m., it would be the launching site for all the participating boats before their anticipated start at 6:30 a.m. That would certainly make for an interesting wake-up!

Al and Gayle were looking forward to having old boating friends meet them in the evening for cocktails and dinner, and they were kind enough to invite us to join us for the festivities. They introduced us to their friends Jim and Sue, the owners of *Eagle I* from Mentor, Ohio, who brought along Joe and Joyce (whom we had seen briefly at Grand Harbor) aboard *Takitez II* from Goderich, Ontario. We had all either completed or were in the process of doing The Loop.

After cocktails and munchies aboard *Falkor*, we went to Ricatoni's Italian Restaurant to share a meal and a fun evening. On our return, we also phoned Pat's brother, Father Tony, who is an avid bass fisherman, to tell him about the fishing tournament on which we had stumbled. He was definitely envious!

Sept. 30 — 21 miles to Rogersville, Alabama[9]

Our morning began early. Pat got up and started looking out our boat's windows at 3:30 a.m. to see what was going on with the boat launching. The Admiral always likes to keep abreast of what is occurring dockside while I take care of on-board activities such as sleeping. Nearly 190 bass boats were being launched in three waves, and things were moving along by 5 a.m. SUVs and pickup trucks were quickly backing trailers with bass boats into the water in record speed. I was much more awake then, and by 5:20 a.m., we were dressed in our warmest clothes, and with portable chairs and cameras in hand, we walked to the adjacent park to get a prime spot for the kickoff of the tournament.

When we got to the kickoff location, we were pleased to make the acquaintance of Jim Bevis, a Florence/Lauderdale tourism board member, who went out of his way to make us feel comfortable and welcome at the event. He introduced us to Mayor Bobby Irons and his wife, who also were delighted that we were visiting their city. Mind you, all these conversations took place in the dark just before dawn, and we cannot say enough about the extraordinary warmth of these hospitable people, even at that early hour.

The formal tournament opening began at 6:30 a.m. with a parade of flags representing the U.S., Alabama, and various branches of the military, which were marched to the song, "God Bless the U.S.A." Following the moving piece (which brought tears to many eyes, including ours), the "The Star-Spangled Banner" was played.

During the ceremony, fishermen in 187 boats stood at attention holding their hats or helmets, and we later learned that about 80 percent of the participants were retired or active military personnel. Then, the president of the organization addressed the group and reviewed for the participants the stringent rules and return times. However, because of the sea-smoke condition that morning, he would not call the start until he felt conditions were safe.

Finally at 7:23 a.m., he finally began the organized start at which each vessel was called. This organization did not play games! Boats were stopped if they did not have proper running lights, etc. and he personally released each and every entrant. We were greatly impressed by the sights and sounds of this entire event!

Eventually, Pat and I walked back to our boat and called the lock tender at Wilson Lock about 3 miles above our marina. He told us not to get to the lock until about 10:30 a.m. because he had a tug with a long line of barges coming through southbound. Our timing was good, and when we arrived, we only had a short wait while the barge passed us, and we entered the lock for our 93-foot lift.

---

[9] *See notes on page 205*

The first boats of a fleet of 187 bass fishermen get underway for the tournament.

As we entered the lock, we were in awe at the size of this engineering marvel. Concrete walls almost nine stories high surrounded us, and as the massive steel doors closed behind us, we felt small, encased in this magnificent structure.

We live in a world where many words in the American lexicon have lost their meaning through exaggeration. However, in this case, the somewhat overused word "awesome" can be accurately used to describe the Wilson Lock and Dam. Towering in size and massive in scale, the lock chamber is 600 feet long, 110 feet wide, has a maximum lift of 100 feet, and on average, takes about 50 million gallons of water to fill.

Construction of the original double-lift lock and dam began in 1918 and was completed in 1927. In 1959, the main single-lift lock was completed. It is the highest lock east of the Rocky Mountains, and it stands today as the largest mass concrete lock and dam ever built in the U.S. It was the first project of its type attempted on the Tennessee River, and it revolutionized river transportation in the area and became the model for all future projects.

Falkor, *a 36-foot trawler, enters the Wilson Lock.*

The massive 100-foot high doors of the Wilson Lock closed behind us. We felt small.

The thought of the millions of gallons of water that it took to lift us was overwhelming. To our amazement, the lock filled rapidly, and in what seemed like no time, we were at the top. Passing through the lock was an experience that we will never forget.

We then traveled 15 additional miles to Joe Wheeler Lock; however, when we called the lock tender at 12:45 p.m., he told us that he would not be able to let us enter until 3:30 p.m. *Falkor* managed to tie off to the wall at the old side of the lock, and we were able to raft up to her.

The pool of foam, spray, and water is the outflow of the Joe Wheeler Lock as the water is let out of the lock chamber.

Our vessels remained tied up like that for several hours until a southbound tug with barges passed through, and we were finally notified to enter for our 48-foot lift. Although its size was not nearly on the scale of the Wilson Lock, it was impressive. Luckily, Joe Wheeler State Park Marina was only about 3 miles past the lock, and a short while later, we entered the slip where *Reflection* would stay for the next month. Our assigned location in front of the lodge was absolutely beautiful, and we were truly happy to be here.

The park is located on 2,550 acres along Wheeler Lake. It has a lodge with a pool, convention facilities, a restaurant, a campground, a marina, hiking and biking trails, and an 18-hole golf course, and it is an excellent place to spend time.

Oct. 1 — Rogersville, Alabama

My major task for the day was to install a new toilet pump in our aft head. I was back in my element again! When the installation did not completely accomplish what we wanted, I had the messy job of taking out hoses, examining, and cleaning them. It was such a joy to me! Finally after several hours, I removed the "Y" valve and discovered that it was partially clogged. It certainly was part of the problem with the flow. I cleared the clog and set the "Y" valve to the correct position, directing the flow to the holding tank. At last, after several hours, we had the powerful flushing action I wanted to achieve. I love working on the head!

In the afternoon, we continued cleaning the boat and then made special preparations for our evening meal because we had invited Gayle and Al to have dinner aboard with us. Our menu included shrimp cocktails, filet mignon wrapped with bacon, twice-baked potatoes, and Caesar salad. Gayle brought a delicious mandarin orange cake that she had baked for dessert, and we enjoyed the meal and the company of our boating friends and slip neighbors.

Oct. 2 — Rogersville, Alabama

This morning I was scheduled to be picked up by a local car rental company at the front desk of the hotel at 10 a.m. When the agent had still not arrived by 11 a. m., I explained my situation to the desk clerk and asked if there was any way I could get a ride to the rental agency. He replied, "Remember that you are in the South now, sir, where 10 o'clock doesn't necessarily mean 10 o'clock. It could be anytime today." I replied, "I understand that, sir, but I am from the North and you know that we Northerners have absolutely no patience!" He couldn't hold back his laughter, for I had openly stated what he was likely secretly thinking. A few minutes later, the rental agent arrived.

By 1 p.m., we were on our way with Al and Gayle to the Unclaimed Baggage Center in Scottsboro, Alabama. Their merchandise consisted of unclaimed cargo and the contents of unclaimed baggage, and a number of sources had told us that there were bargains to be had there. We did find a few items at good prices, but we would not go out of our way to shop there again.

On the way back we stopped at the Super Walmart in Athens for some light groceries and for engine oil for the boat. After dropping our purchases aboard, we then headed out for dinner at the local Chinese buffet restaurant right here in Rogersville.

Oct. 3 — Rogersville, Alabama

Our tourist destination in the morning was the Huntsville Depot and Museum. It included a collection of railroad cars, a multimedia presentation about railroad history, and a vintage fire truck exhibit.

The highlight for us was the personal tour the knowledgeable and interesting docent gave us. He was well informed about Civil War history and particularly on the details of this building, which had been captured by Union forces in 1862 and then served as a military prison. We also got to see the actual graffiti that Confederate and Union soldiers scratched into the walls. We often think that graffiti is a modern occurrence, yet there I was staring at graffiti from the 19th century. I wondered what the imprisoned solders were thinking and feeling as they drew the various images in the masonry walls.

After several hours there, we headed to Harrison Brothers Hardware Store in Downtown Huntsville. The store was established in 1879 but had operated at its current location since 1897. It was an old-fashioned hardware store with a collection of vintage tools and house wares that were sold alongside modern gift items and gourmet foods.

We then had lunch at Sam and Greg's, a nearby pizza restaurant. On returning to our boats, we saw that an outdoor wedding would shortly be starting on a terrace overlooking the docks, so Gayle and Pat went up to their respective flybridges to observe the proceedings through binoculars to get a closer look at the nuptials, while Al and I headed below to accomplish boat projects. We then spent a quiet evening watching TV accompanied by munchies in place of dinner because we had eaten a substantial amount of pizza for lunch.

Oct. 4 — Rogersville, Alabama

The final place we all wanted to visit in the area was the U.S. Space and Rocket Center in Huntsville. The facility displayed one of the world's largest collections of space and rocket hardware, the Saturn V moon rocket, a full-scale space shuttle, other interactive exhibits, simulators, and an IMAX movie theater.

NASA's Marshall Space Flight Center and the Redstone Arsenal were adjacent to the location, and it was easy to see how the important work done here at Huntsville, in testing and building, had influenced and continues to influence the U.S. Space and Defense programs. We could only wonder what future projects might already be housed or hidden in the mountains of Huntsville.

We truly enjoyed the day, but when we returned to our boats, the weather had deteriorated to a steady, chilly rain. Because we had not been able to connect to Wi-Fi at the boat slip, Pat spent time later that afternoon in the lodge's lobby checking email on our computer. Among our messages, we were delighted to receive word that our friends Caryl and Ray aboard *Houlegan* were making rapid progress south to their home in Gulfport, Mississippi. We had been following their journey and were looking forward to seeing them at the Looper Rendezvous on Oct. 25.

Rockets that are on display at the U.S. Space and Rocket Center in Huntsville, Alabama

The exhaust ports of a Saturn V rocket — the same one that took us to the moon

On each successive day since we had arrived here, we had seen more boats from our association take slip spaces in the marina, and we learned that all 58 transient slips would be filled for the upcoming event with 15 more boats on a waiting list. Additional vessels made plans to either raft up or anchor out across from Joe Wheeler State Park Marina, and other members had chosen to travel by car and stay at the lodge or in one of the guest cottages on the grounds. After Pat returned to the boat with the computer, we spent a cozy evening aboard watching football and movies while we were cooking, and later on enjoyed a delicious pork chop dinner.

Oct. 5 — Rogersville, Alabama

It was another overcast day with rain predicted for overnight, and Al and Gayle invited us to share a Bon Voyage dinner with them aboard *Falkor* that evening. They planned to move farther up the Tennessee River the next morning, while we would remain here at Joe Wheeler. The Italian dinner was fabulous with pasta and Bolognese sauce, salad, and homemade rolls followed by devil's food cake with chocolate chunks. Gayle is an excellent cook and baker!

The swimming pool and lodge at Joe Wheeler State Park

They also shared their pictures of *Parfait*, their canal boat, on the various trips they had taken in France aboard her. We shared a toast of champagne to celebrate the time we had traveled together (three weeks), and enjoyed a lovely evening with them.

Reflection **at dockside at Joe Wheeler State Park Marina**

Oct. 6 — Rogersville, Alabama

Our first order of business today was to say goodbye to Al and Gayle as they untied their lines at 7:30 a.m. After sharing wishes with each other for safe trips, hugs, and many waves as they left the marina, we returned to *Reflection* to begin the work of cleaning her from top to bottom and making her ready for a safe stay here while we returned home to New Jersey.

After working hard all morning, we slowed our pace in the afternoon as another weather-front started to make its way across us with rain showers. We organized our books and charts to take home, wrote substantial to-do lists for here and New Jersey, and had phone calls with our siblings to try to organize our activities in both places. After a chicken dinner, Pat got to watch one of her favorite shows, "Dancing with the Stars." I, on the other hand, was so thrilled that I fell asleep.

Oct. 7 — Rogersville, Alabama

The night brought heavy rain with lightening, but in the morning, we were up and working early. By 8:10 a.m., Pat was at the supermarket making ship store purchases so we would not have to deal with that chore on our return, and I finished my final exterior cleaning of the boat in my dedicated set of clothes that have a permanent bleach smell and stains for the task.

We then packed up and loaded the car with items we were taking home from the boat. Our 11-hour road trip the next day would begin at 6 a.m., and we planned to visit my sister, Pat, and our brother-in-law, Al, in Richmond, Virginia, for an overnight stop. On Friday morning, we would get back on the road to New Jersey and looked forward to seeing our family and friends. Then on Oct. 23, we would return to Alabama for the America's Great Loop Cruisers' Association Rendezvous and for our journey down the Tombigbee Waterway to Florida. Our mileage thus far since leaving our home on June 6, 2009 was 2,390 miles, and we had passed through 89 locks.

Oct. 8 — Heading Home

While driving home, we received a call from the dockmaster at Banana Bay Resort in Marathon, Florida, informing us that a slip had become available for a winter layover. The location was where we had initially wanted to stay in Florida; however, we had previously been told before our departure on the Loop that there was no open slip for us there. But now that we had the new opportunity, I asked the Admiral what she wanted to do. We could keep the boat in Goodland, Florida, near our friends or go farther south to Marathon in the Florida Keys. For years, we had dreamed of spending a winter in Marathon. We had spent many of Pat's school vacations there, and at one time had even owned two duplex homes there. The Keys were calling us back again, so we decided that we should fulfill our dream — the Keys option won.

Notes:

(1)
Sugar Bay Anchorage — The best spot was in the cove immediately to starboard with room for four to six boats, and Clay anchorage was also excellent.

(2)
Paris Landing State Park has a low dockage price, but its fuel prices were on the high side. At the lodge, good food is available at inexpensive prices with buffet

choices that change daily. The Park Ranger will transport you from your boat to the lodge and back again.

(3)
Pebble Isle Marina has a BoatUS discount with good fuel prices, reasonable slip fees, and a friendly staff. Its restaurant is open for breakfast, lunch, and dinner, and a courtesy car is available.

(4)
Double Island Anchorage has good holding in current with room to swing on one anchor.

(5)
Pickwick State Park Marina was rebuilt in 2009, and its slip fees are inexpensive.

(6)
Grand Harbor Marina has a good laundry facility on-site, and has several courtesy cars available. There is good shopping at the Pickwick Market and delicious food at the Rib Cage restaurant in town. The marina staff supplies river information for the Tenn-Tom and is helpful and friendly. Aqua Yacht Harbor is also nearby with a large ship store.

(7)
Rock Piles is a small, good anchorage with protection on three sides but is somewhat exposed to Pickwick Lake.

(8)
Florence Harbor Marina has a friendly staff, a courtesy car, and an on-site restaurant. There is also a traditional Italian restaurant in town, many historic sites, and a wide variety of shopping.

(9)
Joe Wheeler State Park Marina has reasonable transient rates with a restaurant and lodge on the premises. There is no courtesy car, but an Enterprise car rental agency is in the area. Rogersville is a small town with a supermarket, a laundry facility, small shops, and an inexpensive steak restaurant nearby.

Chapter 11

Heading Down the "Not" So Straight, and Narrow

Oct. 25-28 — Rogersville, Alabama

After returning from our trip back home to New Jersey, we spent four days here at the America's Great Loop Cruisers' Association Rendezvous. We attended a series of seminars on topics pertinent to our ongoing trip, met many other loopers at various meals and parties, went on a shopping excursion sponsored by the Rogersville Chamber of Commerce, and were guests at a wonderful concert given by local musicians at a beautiful bed and breakfast inn in the area.

There were several hundred attendees at the event, which was sold out, and everyone there graciously shared knowledge and information with one another about the incredible Great Loop journey as we made new friends. The attendees ran the gamut from those who had done the trip several times, to those who were in the process, to those who were still in the planning or dreaming-about stage. At any rate, we were happy we had come!

We also enjoyed making the acquaintance of Sallyann and Andrew, boaters from Illinois who were aboard *Freedom*, an American Tug 34. Pat had briefly met Sallyann at Green Turtle Bay Marina in Grand Rivers, Kentucky, when we were there in September. Sallyann was originally a "Jersey Girl," and after Andrew's recent retirement, they had put their house up for sale and started out on their Great Loop trip only a few weeks ago. They, too, were headed to Marathon, Florida, for the winter, so we decided it might be fun for us to be buddy boats on our trip south. We planned to begin the next segment early the next morning.

On the last evening of the rendezvous, we also opened our boat up for the "Looper Crawl," which is comparable to an open-house event. People toured *Reflection*, and we were thrilled with all their positive comments about our vessel.

Oct. 29 — 61 miles to Counce, Tennessee

We pulled away from the dock at 6:40 a.m. in the company of 12 other boats, and it looked like a conga line as we made our way out into Joe Wheeler Lake, and then entered first Wheeler Lock, and next Wilson Lock. We even had boats rafted together in the locks. It was a misty morning, and naturally, it rained the hardest when we had to monitor our tie-ups to the lock bollards. Then we had to go back to wearing our full storm gear. After traveling 61 miles and through two locks, we arrived at Grand Harbor Marina, where we had stayed a month earlier before our side trip up the Tennessee River. Andrew and Sallyann joined us for cocktails, and afterward, we enjoyed dinner aboard.

Oct. 30 — Counce, Tennessee

Pat was up before 6 a.m. to do laundry at the marina laundromat. When she arrived there, she found that Sallyann had gotten up even earlier than she had and was nearly finished with her laundry.

Later in the morning, Sallyann, Andrew, and we used the marina's courtesy car to go out for lunch at the Rib Cage, an eatery for local ribs and chicken, and to the Pickwick Market for groceries. On our return to the marina, we got together to plan our tentative itinerary to Mobile, Alabama. An expected cold front then arrived with heavy wind and rain — not exactly the best boating weather. Sallyann and Andrew returned to *Freedom*, and we relaxed on our boat with a movie and cable TV for the rest of the evening.

Oct. 31 — 36 miles to Five Fingers Anchorage, Mississippi — Tenn-Tombigbee Waterway[1]

The rain finally stopped early in the morning, and after a brief delay to look for our missing storm gear jackets we had inadvertently left in the marina's courtesy van, we made our way out of Grand Harbor at 9 a.m.

Our boats would be traveling down the Tennessee-Tombigbee Waterway for 234 miles to Demopolis, Alabama, and then we would go an additional 217 miles down the Black Warrior-Tombigbee Waterway to Mobile, Alabama, for the next two weeks.

 The connecting of the Tennessee River with the Tombigbee River, a 12-year, $2 billion Army Corps of Engineers earth-moving project, moved more soil than the building of the Panama Canal. It was the building this man-made waterway that has made the Great Loop journey around the Gulf coast, East Coast, and Canadian and Midwest waterways possible.

The Tennessee-Tombigbee Waterway, commonly known as the Tenn-Tom, was first proposed in America's Colonial period. However, it was not until 1875 that engineers surveyed a potential canal route, but they also issued a negative report at the time emphasizing that prohibitive cost estimates made the project economically unfeasible.

The construction of the Pickwick Lock and Dam on the Tennessee River under the Tennessee Valley Authority in 1938, however, helped decrease the Tenn-Tom's potential economic costs and increased awareness of its potential benefits. In 1971, President Nixon authorized $1 million for the Army Corps of Engineers to start construction of the Tenn-Tom. Funding shortages and legal challenges again delayed the start of construction until December 1972, and in 1984, the project was finally completed two years ahead of schedule.

Although many people at the time of its completion called its $2 billion price tag a pork barrel project, since 1996, the U.S. has realized a positive economic impact of more than $43 billion due to the existence and usage of the waterway, and it has directly created more than 29,000 jobs.

We cruised 36 miles that day down this lovely passage lined with autumn foliage that opened up into wide Bay Springs Lake, and then we turned into the Five Finger anchorage there, where we had a choice of beautiful locations at which to stop. We dropped our anchor, and *Freedom* rafted up to us for the evening. Pat and I were invited over for happy hour, and Sallyann made delicious bread that was topped with tomatoes, onions, and pepperoni and then expertly grilled outside. Their "boat cat," Tut, decided to take a tour of the outside decks of *Reflection* while we were eating and returned home an exhausted adventurer. Our night at anchor was quiet, cozy, spectacular with stars with an almost-full moon, and chilly temperatures in the low 40s. Autumn had arrived.

Heading south on a beautiful fall morning on the Tenn-Tombigbee Waterway

Nov. 1 — 21 miles to Fulton, Mississippi[2]

Pat and I left our anchorage at 7 a.m. after making a call to the Jamie Whitten lock tender to check on conditions at the lock. As we rounded the corner of one of the "fingers" of the Five Fingers anchorage area, other looper boats that had also been scattered in other anchorages overnight joined us.

Because the lock tenders were aware of the large amount of boats traveling south at this time, we were kept together as a group and transited the next two locks that way in quick succession. There was no use in anyone trying to speed up to the next lock because the lock tenders would wait until all the boats in the pack caught up and entered the lock before they would lock down. Just before the last lock was about to close its doors, we were surprised to have this particular lock tender hand us a holy card, which had never happened before on the trip. We were surprised by the gesture but chose to take it as a sign of God's blessing on us and on our journey.

We arrived early in the day at Midway Marina, one of the few marinas along the remote waterway. There the dockmaster greeted us, and we got quickly tied up to a long floating dock that would eventually be filled with loopers. Across the dock from us was an interesting vessel — an old motor cruiser more than 50 feet long — which was likely someone's project boat. It looked as though it had not seen soap and water in years, along with moss growing on the transom, plant life emerging from the deck, and all manner of debris strung over it. If you have ever traveled through rural America and seen an old junk car sitting in front of a house that was being fixed up, this boat was the marine version. We did not know it then, but the old boat was not the last one like it we would see along the river.

The fleet leaving Whitten Lock

Nov. 2 — 36 miles to Blue Bluff Anchorage — Aberdeen, Mississippi[3]

Despite leaving the marina at 7 a.m., the day turned out to be a long travel day. We transited three locks and went 36 miles, but we had long waits at the locks because our locking group included two sailboats that could only go about 6 knots. Because they could not travel any faster, the rest of the group had to wait for them to catch up with us at each subsequent lock.

The Tombigbee Waterway had now become littered with floating logs and foliage caused by the flooding of the upland rivers, and we had to dodge them constantly in the 2-knot current that was thankfully running with us. By 3:30 p.m., we made a sharp turn into the narrow, shallow channel leading into Blue Bluff Anchorage. Three boats were already tied up to the short "T" dock of the recreation area, so we dropped our anchor a little way off, and *Freedom* rafted up to us. By the time dark descended, there were 11 boats there, including the two sailboats we had previously mentioned and two other loopers who had run aground coming into the channel.

Nov. 3 — 23 miles to Columbus, Mississippi[4]

Coming from New Jersey (the most densely populated state in the country), we were amazed at how much nothingness was out here. We would travel for miles and see only water and trees. Back home, the prices of 50-by-100-foot waterfront lots start at about $200,000 and are hard to find, but along this waterway, there were vast amounts of beautiful waterfront acreage with no homes and no people. We were definitely in a different place!

The Tombigbee Waterway continued to flood with debris as we passed through one lock and motored 23 miles to Columbus Marina. After we pulled in at 11 a.m., other looper boats, including the two sailboats we had talked about earlier, joined us.

 Previously called Possum Town, Columbus was incorporated as a town in 1821. During the American Civil War, Columbus was the site of a Confederate hospital and arsenal. Many of the casualties from the Battle of Shiloh were treated here, and thousands were buried in the town's cemetery. Because of the arsenal, the Union army tried to invade Columbus more than once but was never successful. Thus, the beautiful antebellum homes located here were spared from being burned or destroyed, and the collection is second only to that of Natchez as the most extensive in Mississippi and is occasionally open for tours.

We borrowed the marina's courtesy car to check out the town and the antebellum area, but we returned quickly after just visiting the liquor store to pick up basic necessities with Sallyann and Andrew, since none of the houses were open that day for tourists. We were delighted, however, to join an impromptu looper get-together on the deck beneath the marina office at sunset. It turned out that the two sailboat captains were musicians headed to Florida. They came with their guitars and sound equipment to provide the evening's entertainment, and Pat also got up and sang at the microphone as the evening wore on.

Nov. 4 — 28 miles to Pickensville, Alabama[5]

The weather continued to be good with clear, chilly nights in the high 30s and low 40s and sunny days with temperatures in the low 70s. After one lock and 28 miles, we arrived by 11 a.m. at the quaint Pirate's Marina Cove, where the dockmaster and his assistant gave us a warm welcome.

The fleet entering the Aberdeen Lock — Note the debris in the water

After getting tied up, we, along with Sallyann and Andrew, borrowed the marina's courtesy car. Before starting out, we discovered that the vehicle had a flat tire, but the dockmaster quickly repaired it. However, we found out soon after that the flat tire was not the only problem with the car. As we began driving out of the marina, we passed over a few bumps and realized the car's suspension was completely shot. The vehicle pitched and rolled along the country roads, which made handling it a challenge. Luckily, we were a group of experienced boaters; otherwise, some of us might have gotten seasick from the motion!

We then made our way to the Down Yonder restaurant for local southern cooking. Our fried chicken lunches were delicious. So were our appetizers of fried macaroni and cheese and onion rings. Get out the cholesterol pills!

The women then went to do the laundry at the local laundromat while the men waited patiently at a picnic bench outside with beers purchased at the mini-mart next door. Afterward, we drove to the Tom Bevill Visitor Center that is a reconstruction of a southern mansion with interpretive exhibits on the history of the waterway. We also toured the *U.S. Snagboat Montgomery*, which was the last steam-powered sternwheeler used to keep seven of the south's rivers navigable and free of debris from 1926 through 1982. It was a fun-filled day.

Sign outside the mini-mart — Check out the last line (I was told it only applied to men.).

Nov. 5 – 32 miles to the Warsaw Cut Off — Warsaw, Alabama[6]

Just south of Pirate's Marina Cove was the Tom Bevill Lock and Dam. As we approached the lock, from atop the flybridge, I could see the water pouring swiftly over the dam. Due to flooding upriver, there was considerably more water coming downstream than usual. The river beyond the lock looked to me to be more like a thrill ride at a water park than a navigable waterway, and for quite a distance ahead, all I could see was white water and whirlpools. Pat was at her station below preparing for locking and could not see what was going on in the river, so I decided not to tell her what I saw because I figured she would find out soon enough — and she did!

Once we were lowered and the lock doors opened, there was nothing but white water in front of us. Sallyann and Andrew had tied *Freedom* up to the wall immediately ahead of our bow, and using proper lock protocol, I let them proceed out first. We were able to observe how the water pushed them around as they exited the lock, and I gave them room to get ahead of us. After Pat released us from the bollard, I told her to come right up to the flybridge and to hold on. Once we cleared the lock doors, I put the "pedal to the metal" to gain control of *Reflection* as we ran through the fast-moving water. It was quite a ride! Yet in less than a mile, things calmed down and we could once again enjoy the rest of the trip downriver.

Pat cannot see what awaits her on the other side of the lock wall.

Surprise, surprise! Yes, it was as bad as it looks!

The waterway continued to run quickly as we made our way through the winding route along the 33 miles to our next stop. Tom Blevill Lock also marked the 100th lock we had gone through on our journey thus far.

Marinas were few and far between as we continued south, and mariners must plan ahead carefully to find anchorages. Luckily, the spot we had chosen in the Warsaw Cut Off proved to be lovely and safe, and we dropped anchor in more than 30 feet of water with *Freedom* tied next to us. The crews got together for cocktails, and we toasted our 100th locking while enjoying shrimp cocktails and Sallyann and Andrew's homemade grilled bread. They even brought us presents: wine from Andrew, tea from Sallyann, and kitty treats from Tut, their cat, who had made several visits to our boat and was using up our supply for him.

Nov. 6 – 59 miles to Demopolis, Alabama[7]

For the past few nights, fog had settled in on us, but it usually cleared shortly after sunrise. Our boats left the anchorage at 6 a.m. in what appeared to be a lifting fog, but that morning it did not dissipate as quickly as we had hoped. We made our way slowly and carefully into the waterway, but even with radar, the situation was tenuous, and before long what seemed to be a lifting fog became a settled-in dense fog. It turned into "pea soup," and at times we could hardly see *Freedom* only a few hundred feet to our stern. We pulled over to the side of the channel once, and then the fog lifted so we could continue, but then it filled in again. So much for the early start to our day.

We pulled out of the channel a second time to again wait for the fog to clear, but unfortunately, this time *Freedom* ran aground in an area where the depths went from 46 to less than 4 feet in an instant! We managed to get *Reflection* close enough to have Andrew throw a towline to Pat, but the current was dragging us sideways into the shallows, so it took two more passes before we finally got the line secured to their boat. We then were able to tow them safely to deeper water without going aground ourselves.

After this "adventure," the fog finally lifted for good, and I was relieved that it did. Fog is the worst thing you can encounter on a narrow waterway, where not being able to see what is ahead, behind, or close around you is a dangerous situation. We then made our way to the Howell Heflin Lock. There, the lock tender informed us that we would have at least an hour wait because he had a southbound and northbound tow he had to lock through before us. His next comment was "Hang around behind the bridge, and count the pigeons!" That was easy for him to say! The wait then turned out to be more like two hours because one of the lock

---

[7] *See notes on page 228*

gates got stuck and needed repair. Because of the delay, 12 more boats managed to catch up to us, and we eventually locked through as a group of 14. After we left the lock, we still had 50 more miles to travel, so we upped our usual cruising speed so we could get to Demopolis Yacht Basin before dark.

A total of 14 boats were locked down at one time through the Heflin Lock, and some had to raft-up so they could all fit.

The white cliffs of Epes, ancient rock formations along the Tenn-Tom

Demopolis (Greek for "city of people") was founded in 1817 by a group of French expatriates fleeing a slave rebellion on the sugar plantations of Haiti. They came to the area believing that the climate would be ideal for the growing of grapes and olive trees, but within a year, things went bust, and most of them were forced to move. Thus, in reality, Demopolis became the city of no people.

There are several historic sites in Demopolis including: Gaineswood, an antebellum historic house museum built between 1843 and 1861; Bluff Hall, another antebellum historic house museum built in 1832; the Laird Cottage/Geneva Mercer Museum, a restored 1870 residence built in the Greek revival and Italianate style; the Demopolis Historic Business District; the Demopolis Town Square; and Lyon Hall.

We ended up arriving by 3:30 p.m. and found the marina almost completely filled with looper boats. There was some concern on the docks about Tropical Depression Ida's forecast to head up the Gulf of Mexico and what its possible impact might be on Mobile Bay and the Florida Panhandle because this was the area to which most of us were headed within the next few days. Rumors abounded about the waterway being closed shortly, and we decided it would be wise for us to stay here and monitor the weather before we headed any further south.

Later in the evening, Sallyann and Andrew joined us for cocktails, and then we had dinner at the marina's restaurant, the New Orleans Bar and Grill, where shrimp and catfish were a house specialty, and the "people-watching" was a real show in itself!

Nov. 7-9 — Demopolis, Alabama

We remained in a watchful, waiting mode throughout the last three days because we were keeping a "weather eye" on what path Tropical Storm/Hurricane Ida would take as she headed north over the Gulf of Mexico toward Mobile, Alabama, our final destination on the Tombigbee Waterway before heading into the Florida Panhandle and the Gulf. Thankfully, we were still safely docked in the only marina for the next 230 miles between here and Mobile, and *Freedom* and *Reflection* were lucky to be among the last few boats to get a slip here pre-hurricane. There were many boats backed up the entire waterway south and north of us who had been warned by various sources to stay put until the storm had passed, and we had taken advantage of our respite time on the past three days to clean the boat, shop for groceries, do laundry, and have several happy hours. We enjoyed eggplant lasagna and carrot cake made aboard *Freedom* and learned a dice game called "456," which

Sallyann and Andrew seemed to have taught us as a means of making laundry money. The Admiral and I used our time well during the layover because we were able to completely sketch out a tentative plan for our trip to Marathon, Florida.

Ida was forecast to hit the Gulf Coast in the morning, but we expected to feel her effects overnight. If all went well, we were cautiously optimistic that we would be able to finally leave here in two days before "channel fever" kicks in. I knew it was already too late for me because I had already contracted a severe case of the condition, and its only known cure was for us to get moving again.

Nov. 10 — Demopolis, Alabama

We felt the effects of Tropical Storm Ida beginning around midnight with heavy rain that lasted until about 4 p.m. The wind blew at a steady 25 mph with occasional gusts to around 40. We were safely tied up in our slip, but we could see the water level on the Tombigbee River steadily rising. Rumors were again rampant on the docks, and those of us in the America's Great Loop Cruisers' Association received email informing us that the locks might close down and that the water level would rise with so much debris coming downriver that we might not be able to make it out onto the waterway for a few more days. Needless to say, that did not make us happy, but we decided to see what the situation would be in the morning. If we could not move, we would get the courtesy car and try to do some touring in the area to make the best of the situation.

Nov. 11 — 117 miles to Silas, Alabama[8]

The morning dawned bright and beautiful with much lighter winds than the 15 to 25 mph that was forecast. At 6 a.m., we received an email from our association that still advised us to stay put where we were because of the flooding on the river and to not try moving down the river for possibly another five days. "I'll go stir crazy in five days!", I muttered to myself, but we could see for ourselves that the river was rising, so we decided to take the warning seriously and to take the advice. Pat then began working at the computer, and I went for an early morning walk to assuage my dim mood over not being able to finally leave Demopolis that day.

I eventually made my way to the dockmaster's office to get the latest local scuttlebutt on the river conditions, and while I was there, I had the good fortune of meeting Richard, an experienced boater who was heading downriver on his boat, *Holiday VII*. Richard was a veteran of about 27 trips on the Tombigbee Waterway and was highly recommended by the marina staff and other loopers as an expert on the river. He told me that in his opinion, today was the day for us to leave

---

[8] *See notes on page 228*

before the situation got worse. He explained that the real flood was still coming and that if we did not leave almost immediately, we would probably be stuck there for a number of days.

Richard, himself, was about to leave (operating his beautiful 54 Jefferson solo) within a half-hour. He knew the best anchorages along the way and said he would be glad to lead *Reflection* and *Freedom* downriver. When someone with Richard's experience said it was time to go, it was time to go! To my delight, God had sent us our guardian angel!

As I rushed back to our boat, I could feel the "channel fever" leaving my body. I stopped by *Freedom* and told them that Pat and I (although Pat did not know it yet) were leaving in a half-hour.

It was just about 7 a.m. when I returned to our boat, threw open the door, and said to Pat, "Come on, we're leaving now." Sometimes the Admiral is wise enough not to ask me too many questions, and this was one of those times. Pat quickly finished the email she was writing, changed out of her nightgown, and got into her clothes. As I started getting ready to cast off, the folks in the boat next to us asked me what I was doing. I did not want to be rude, but I did not even look up from loosening the lines and said, "I'm getting out of here. If you want to leave, you have to go now!" They probably thought that I was deranged, but opportunity had knocked, and within 30 minutes, we pulled away from the dock with *Holiday VII* in the lead and *Freedom* close behind us.

Right after leaving the marina, we entered Demopolis Lock and were quickly lowered. As we exited the lock, we followed *Holiday VII* through whitewater, whirlpools, and light debris and headed downriver. The flood was coming! The current on the river was going our way at a rate of about 3 knots, and there were tree branches and other floating garbage that we had to avoid, but it was not nearly as bad as it could have been on the winding river.

We had more than 100 miles to go to get to the Coffeeville Lock and a safe anchorage beyond it. Because of our late start and the distance we had to travel, we knew that any delay at the next lock would bring us to the anchorage after dark, which was something we wanted to avoid on a normal basis and even more especially in these flood conditions.

Throughout the day, Richard was in contact with the towboat operators along the route to check with them about which side of them was safest for us to pass, and to ask if they knew of any additional commercial traffic ahead of us. Within a few miles of the Coffeeville Lock, we came across a southbound tow. Knowing that the commercial tow would be allowed to go through the lock first and with darkness coming on us soon, Richard asked the tow captain if we could possibly proceed ahead of him through the lock. To our delight, he said, "Yes!"

We eventually reached the lock with the sun hanging low in the sky. Richard called the lock tender, and after he verified with the tow captain that he was willing to allow us to go first, we thankfully were locked through.

Holiday VII — *The leader of the great escape from Demopolis in the Coffeeville Lock*

Pat at her post at the last lock (for now)

By that time, the river had risen so much that no land was visible. All you could see were water and trees in areas where the riverbanks used to be. Within a few miles of leaving the lock, Richard carefully guided us into the narrow channel leading to the Old Lock One anchorage. Normally there was about 5 feet of water in the opening, but today, the depth was *25* feet. The flood was here.

The flooded waterway into the Old Lock One anchorage —
Notice you can see trees and no land.

We had traveled 117 miles in eight and a half hours and through our last two locks on the waterway. It was hard to believe, but we had locked through 103 locks so far on our trip.

Pat and I anchored in this wide, protected cove just before dark in about 30 feet of water with *Freedom* rafting up alongside and *Holiday VII* anchored in front of us. After a few celebratory cocktails and dinner, we sat outside looking up at the sky. There was a slight chill in the air with virtually no wind, and the sky was clear with the stars of the Milky Way clearly visible. It felt good to be in the quiet anchorage after a long day, knowing that tomorrow, we would be in Mobile and out of the floodwaters.

Nov. 12 – 115 miles to Mobile, Alabama[9]

Overnight, the river rose another 5 feet. We were anxious to see how strong the current would be and how much debris would join us going downriver. By 7 a.m., we had lifted anchor and began the final 115-mile leg of our journey down the Tombigbee River to Mobile with *Holiday VII* again in the lead. The current was still running at about 3 knots with small debris floating along and only an occasional large limb to dodge.

The flooding continues. Overnight, the water rose an additional 5 feet.

Freedom *heading south through the flood*

Unfortunately, due to the extremely high water, with rare exception, all the buoys on the river were submerged. Rather than being aids to navigation, they became hazards. As we approached an area where buoys were charted, we kept a sharp eye for small whirlpools that marked where the buoys laid below the water. We saw only a few pleasure craft out, and, unfortunately for them, the ones we saw were all headed northbound into the onslaught of the flood current that carried us downstream.

We were now days ahead of the pack of other boats that, like us, were also headed south, but they were bottled up in the marinas and anchorages behind us because of the flooding situation. As we listened to the radio, we heard that the flooding would only get worse over the next three to five days. I was so glad that I had listened to Richard and that we had left when we did! Because we had moved so quickly, we were able to get back on our original schedule, despite our extended stay in Demopolis.

At about 3 p.m., the Mobile skyline rose in the distance.

 Mobile is the largest municipality on the Gulf Coast between New Orleans, Louisiana, and Saint Petersburg, Florida. It began as the first capital of colonial French Louisiana in 1702, and for the first 100 years of its existence, it was a colony of France, Britain, and then finally Spain. Mobile first became a part of the US in 1810 with the annexation of West Florida. In 1861, it left the Union when Alabama joined the Confederate States of America and came back in again in 1865 after the end of the Civil War.

Mobile is the only seaport in Alabama and the ninth largest port in the US. The port has always played a major role in the economic health of the city since its beginning as a key trading center between the French and Native Americans. The city has several art museums, a symphony orchestra, a professional opera, a ballet company, and a large concentration of historic architecture. It is also known for having the oldest organized carnival celebrations in the U.S., which began in the 18th century and pre-date the New Orleans Mardi Gras.

As we made our way through its busy harbor, we passed by barges and tows, large ships, ships in dry dock, and even an experimental ship recently commissioned by the government to combat pirates.

Reflection also cruised past the waterfront convention center, a new maritime center, and the Carnival Cruise Lines ship terminal. About a mile further, we finally entered the open waters of Mobile Bay. There was saltwater at last; I could smell the sea! After spending five months on inland waters, we felt that we were now in more familiar territory, even though we were almost 3,000 miles away from our starting point at home in Barnegat Bay.

Reflection *gets back to sea level and is in seawater again, after more than five months and nearly 3,000 miles as we enter Mobile Bay.*

We journeyed a few more miles down Mobile Bay and then turned into the Dog River on the west side of the bay. Our three vessels all had reservations at Dog River Marina for that night and the next night, but we noticed that the marina was jammed with boats that had previously sought refuge here from Tropical Storm Ida and had not yet left. Despite the crowded conditions, we found space and finally got tied up just before dark.

Instead of going out for dinner as we all had planned, we instead decided to have pizza delivered to our boat. So Pat and I welcomed Richard, Sallyann, and Andrew aboard for cocktails to celebrate our successful journey together. Richard turned out to be a fantastic conversationalist. He lives in Memphis, Tennessee, but travels south to Marathon, Florida, for the winter months. He and his wife had owned a travel company from which he had recently retired, but in which his wife is still involved. She joins him when her schedule permits, but he often moves the boat himself and seems to enjoy it. Because he had done the trip to the Keys so many times, he had advice for us, and we were thankful to have met him and for his sharing of his Tombigbee and Gulf waters expertise.

Nov. 13 — Mobile, Alabama

We reserved the marina's courtesy car for four hours today with Sallyann and Andrew so that we could do some sightseeing, shopping, and laundry. Our first stop was Battleship Park, where we spent two hours touring the Battleship Alabama. Next, we did laundry while having lunch from a Chinese restaurant next door and then did some grocery shopping.

We returned to our boat to have short naps, worked on the computer, and then awaited our friends Ray and Caryl, who were driving from their home in Gulfport, Mississippi, to meet us here. They recently completed the Loop in October aboard their boat, *Houlegan*, and we were delighted that they were coming for a visit.

When they arrived, we had a terrific time catching up with them on what had been going on since they had returned home and filled them in on our adventures. Sallyann and Andrew also joined us for happy hour aboard, and then we all had dinner together at the Mobile Yacht Club. It was a good evening, and we were looking forward to exploring the Alabama and Florida coasts.

"Used boat for sale — some minor smoke damage." This picture was taken at Dog River Marina. It looks like "Kate's Dream" turned out to be a nightmare!

Notes:

(1)

Bay Springs Lake — The Army Corps of Engineers charts are useless here because no depths are given; nor are the areas off the main waterway included on the charts. The Five Fingers area, however, has many good anchorages with good depths and holding.

(2)

Midway Marina has fixed docks, a courtesy car, good fuel prices, and good shopping.

(3)

Blue Bluff Anchorage — Look for a small sign on the starboard side of the waterway designating its entrance. Although the channel is marked with red and green sticks, go in carefully because the channel is shallow (5 feet) and winding. Once inside, the anchoring is good for several boats, or pull into the "T" dock, if available.

(4)

Columbus Marina is a newer marina with a courtesy car, and shopping and a post office are available in the town that has a number of historic homes.

(5)

Pirate's Marina Cove is a basic marina with a few transient slips. It has a friendly staff, a courtesy car, and a small laundry facility. In the area, there is also the Down Yonder restaurant for local, inexpensive dining and a larger laundromat with a general store adjacent. Tour the Tom Bevill Visitors Center nearby with the U.S. Snag Boat Montgomery on the premises. At the Tom Bevill Lock, if the water is high, there is a strong current when leaving the lock that will push your boat to port.

(6)

Warsaw Cut Off — Enter through its downstream entrance, then come one-half to three-fourths of the way behind the island, and anchor in the widest opening in 30 feet of water. There is little current here with good holding on one anchor and with room for a few boats. Do not attempt to enter the nearby creek unless your draft is less than 3 feet. Always check current conditions because things constantly change.

(7)

Demopolis Yacht Basin is a basic marina with a laundry facility, a restaurant on-site, a courtesy car, and a repair facility, and it can be busy with transient boats. There is shopping on the main highway where there is a large laundromat and a number of chain food restaurants.

(8)

Bashi Creek is narrow for anchoring, and Okatuppa Creek is much wider. For the Lock 1 Cut Off anchorage, check with the Coffeeville lock tender for water heights. Then approach the opening from downstream, and follow its narrow entrance into a wide anchorage with room for several boats with good holding and protection from all sides. The Alabama River Cut Off looked good, but you might need two anchors. Bates Lake is a good anchorage if the water is high.

(9)

Mobile — Travel through the harbor at "No Wake" speed. Watch for debris and tows through the entire Tenn-Tom. Call ahead on VHF channel 13 before entering a blind turn, and if there is an oncoming tow, the tow captain will help you get through. Dog River Marina offers good fuel prices, a repair facility, a courtesy car, and has a West Marine on-site. A laundromat, supermarket, and Chinese restaurant are only a few miles away. Many historic sites and restaurants are in and around the city.

Chapter 12

On Our Way to "Kokomo"

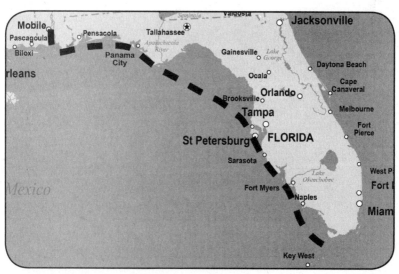

Nov. 14 – 11 miles to Fairhope, Alabama[1]

After filling our boats with fuel, we left Dog River Marina on a short trip across Mobile Bay to the town of Fairhope.

 The Fairhope Industrial Association, a group of 28 followers of economist Henry George, founded Fairhope in 1894 as a utopian single tax colony. They combined their funds to purchase land and then divided it into leaseholds. The corporation paid all taxes from rents paid by the lessees, thus replicating a single tax. It might have been a single tax, but, in reality, lessees still paid taxes. The purpose of the single tax colony was to encourage productive use of land, which would thereby retain the value of the land for all.

The Fairhope Single Tax Corporation still operates, with 1,800 leaseholds covering several thousand acres in the area. Today, Fairhope is a resort community and a suburb of Mobile, and although it might not exactly be a tax-free Utopia, it is still a nice place to visit.

The bay was almost flat calm for our crossing, and we traveled at a leisurely pace for the first time in days and tied up at the Fairhope Yacht Club by around 10 a.m. Because Sallyann and Andrew were members of another recognized yacht club, they received reciprocal privileges here, and the benefit was also graciously extended to us as their guests. It turned out to be a lovely location, and the dockage price was free.

We then called a cab to take us into the town that had many quaint and high-end shops and restaurants. I also took the opportunity to get a haircut, while Sallyann, Andrew, and Pat spent time browsing in the stores and doing some "people watching" from the rocking chairs on the porch of the town hall.

Sunset at the Fairhope Yacht Club

When I emerged from the barbershop all trimmed and well groomed, we went for a late lunch of seafood at a local eatery. The area is known for its fresh shrimp, catfish, grouper, and Apalachicola oysters, and we never liked to miss a chance to try local food specialties. The oysters were large and had shells as thick as my head. Then we topped the meal off with ice cream cones from the local ice cream shop.

When we returned to the boats in the late afternoon, we had a happy hour on the back deck of *Reflection*. Even Tut, the cat, joined in. It was a beautiful evening, and the view of the golden sun setting over Mobile Bay was magnificent.

Nov. 15 — 41 miles to Roberts Bayou, Alabama[2]

With the early morning fog lifting, we headed out into Mobile Bay at 7 a.m. for our trip south. The 30-mile bay can often be a treacherous body of water because it is quite shallow, and steep waves at short intervals can build up easily. However, on this beautiful morning, the water was completely smooth. We then entered the Gulf Intracoastal Waterway that would take us across coastal Alabama and the Florida Panhandle to Carrabelle.

Reflection and **Freedom** *at anchor in Roberts Bayou, Alabama*

Our destination today was Roberts Bayou, where we could anchor and have lunch at the Pirate's Cove Bistro, a local beach bar famous for its burgers, beer, and pizzas. We entered the cove through a narrow opening around a sand spit and then anchored in the small hurricane hole that was surrounded by sailboats either intentionally or, in many cases, not intentionally grounded. Many of them were on their sides and tied up to trees, and we speculated that some of the vessels had moved there to avoid Tropical Storm Ida, but a lot also looked like they had been there for a while.

There was a new songwriters event going on at Pirate's Cove, and we could have paid extra to sit on the porch of the restaurant if we wanted to hear the live music. We decided to decline all the generous offers, opting to wait until these musicians hit the "big time." After listening to some of the tunes we could hear emanating from the beach, Admiral Pat (a retired music teacher) said she hoped that most of them still had their day jobs.

Finally our names were called, so Andrew and I went to pick up our orders. Unfortunately, as is often the case, in our opinion the burgers, fries, and onion rings did not live up to the hype. An order of onion rings consisted of four pieces, the French fry order was minimal, and the burgers were just all right. Sallyann's food was cold. We figured we paid the price for the ambiance, not the food quality.

After we returned to the boat, six people from a large Morgan sailboat dinghied over to us and were thrilled to hear that we were doing the Loop. They had some suggestions for places for us to stop along the Panhandle, and to prove what a small world it is, one of them was from New Jersey.

Nov. 16 — 65 miles to Destin, Florida[3]

We left our last anchorage in Alabama at 7 a.m. and crossed over into Florida about an hour later. The morning temperatures, however, were still not Florida-like. It was in the upper 40s, so we still wore our storm gear, hoods over our heads, and gloves when we started out.

Now that it was mid-November, Pat was anxious about the weather. Since we left Chicago, we had been running ahead of the cold and toward the warm, yet we still had nearly 700 miles more to travel to reach our winter destination of Marathon, Florida, in the warm, sunny Florida Keys. Her biggest concern was our upcoming 175-mile crossing of the open Gulf, since each day as winter approaches, there are fewer windows of opportunity for good weather to make the trip. Her apprehension about having a smooth crossing was evident, plus, except for two trips home and the hurricane delay in Demopolis, we had been almost constantly moving since early June. The Admiral made it clear that she was looking forward to staying in one place for a while. With that in mind, as long as the weather was good, we decided to continue to keep up the pace so that she would reach her "nirvana"

---

[3] *See notes on page 253*

in the sun as soon as possible, and the prospect of having a tropical drink while relaxing on a beach chair under a palm tree definitely appealed to me!

Our destination for this day was Destin, Florida.

 Destin is known for its white beaches and emerald green waters, and though once it was only a small fishing village, it is now a popular tourist destination with about 4.5 million visitors each year staying there. It boasts that it is "The World's Luckiest Fishing Village" and claims to have the largest fishing fleet in the state of Florida, plus vacation condos that seem to go on forever. Destin is named after Captain Leonard Destin, a fishing master who settled in the area in the mid-1800s. The first condominiums were built in the 1970s, and it appears that they never stopped building them.

Shops, condos, and restaurants — this must be Destin.

After a 65-mile trip we pulled into the narrow opening of Destin's harbor at about 3 p.m. with the temperature finally hitting about 70 degrees, and we then knew from the view that we were in Florida. We passed a large high-rise resort and marina and countless other marinas of all sizes with outdoor seafood restaurants and bars alongside. There were hundreds of private fishing boats rigged for deep-sea fishing that were docked all around the harbor, along with many tall condominiums that ringed our anchorage. The close access of the harbor to the Gulf made it a popular destination for boaters and other visitors to its white, sandy beaches.

Once we were anchored, *Freedom* rafted alongside *Reflection*, and we had all settled in for a quiet afternoon when Sallyann soon appeared on deck with barber clippers in her hand. I said to myself, "I'm not sure what is going to happen here, but I am sure it will be entertaining!" — and it was. Next out of the cabin came Andrew, who looked like he was going to the gallows instead of being the recipient (or victim) of Sallyann's hair-styling expertise. Seizing the opportunity for fun, I was more than willing to suggest how she should proceed because Sallyann had never given a haircut before!

First, there was the problem of Andrew's hair clippings getting all over him, so I suggested that he get a trash bag, put a hole in the bottom that would be big enough for his head to fit through, and then turn it upside down and slip the bag over his head and down his arms. The idea worked except that he could not move his arms in the bag. He kind of looked like a human sausage!

Sallyann gives Andrew a custom haircut.

Andrew then sat down on a chair and the clipping began. While that was going on, I encouraged Sallyann to clip more hair off Andrew. "I think you should take more off the left side to even it out, now more off the right, maybe a little more off the left." I just loved egging her on. The haircut finally came to a conclusion when Sallyann clipped a little too much from the back of Andrew's head, and a bald spot appeared.

By that time Andrew, had had enough and tore out of his sausage casing. We all told him how good the haircut looked and that the bald spot was hardly noticeable. It was a fun afternoon — for some of us!

When we sat out on the deck that evening and looked around, we were completely surrounded by high-rise hotels and condominiums that were all lit up. This was a stark contrast from the dark anchorages on the Tenn-Tom. The location reminded us in a small way of New Jersey's Atlantic City with the lights of the buildings reflecting colorfully on the water.

Nov. 17 — 53 miles to Burnt Mill Creek, Florida[4]

Even though we would have liked to take the dinghy in to visit the sights of Destin, we made a decision that we should move on today to a quieter anchorage 53 miles farther along the Panhandle. The weather was windy and overcast with an occasional light drizzle, so we operated the boat from the lower inside station for quite a bit of the trip.

Our journey took us past sand dunes known as Florida's Grand Canyon.

We talked to *Morningside*, a boat from Annapolis that we had met along the way down the Tennessee River, and found out that they, too, were in the area. Unfortunately, we would miss each other because they were proceeding on to Panama City that day, and that was our destination for the next day. When *Freedom* and *Reflection* reached the anchorage, the weather cleared, and we had the place to ourselves except for the occasional dolphins that jumped and dove around our boats and the local fishermen who dragged their nets nearby. We were back in solitude again, and it felt peaceful.

Nov. 18 – 15 miles to Panama City, Florida[5]

It was another chilly, but sunny morning when we pulled up anchor at 7 a.m., and by 8:40 a.m., we were docked at Panama City's Municipal Marina, which was only 15 miles away.

 Panama City was incorporated in 1909, and the developer of the town, George W. West, came up with its name because it was on a direct line between Chicago and Panama City, Panama. It claims that its nearby beach is one of the best-known and most beloved resorts in the world, with white, sandy beaches and every imaginable water sport, including scuba diving and fishing.

After settling in, Pat did the laundry, and then we all headed out to one of the town's trolley stops because we heard there was a good Chinese buffet in town for lunch. The trolley took us on a 20-minute ride quite a distance beyond the downtown area out to the highway, so we also got an interesting tour of the area. The restaurant turned out to be good, and we had a fabulous lunch for only $5.49 per person. When we returned again by trolley to the boats, we rested and had only a snack for dinner because our lunch had been a big enough meal for the entire day.

Nov. 19 – 44 miles to Port Saint Joe, Florida[6]

We continued 44 miles east across the Panhandle to Port Saint Joe Marina after making a quick stop at Pier 98 Marina on Pitt Bayou for fuel. Our trip included wide expanses of water, but it also took us through miles of narrow canals reminiscent of the low country areas in North and South Carolina, bounded by pine and cypress trees. Traveling along that part of the Gulf Intracoastal Waterway looked like another scene from the "African Queen."

Once a bustling port, Port Saint Joe is now a tourist destination with a soft, white sand dune beach, snorkeling, fishing, and a variety of dining options.

We tied up at around 3 p.m. and had dinner at the Dockside Restaurant right at the marina.

That day we also moved our clocks forward an hour because Port Saint Joe and its nearby town, White City, had put us back into the Eastern Standard Time Zone.

Nov. 20 — Port Saint Joe, Florida

We closely monitored the weather today from the marina because we were trying to time our journey to Carrabelle. That would be the point from where we would make the about 175-mile trip across the Big Bend of Florida through the Gulf of Mexico to Clearwater. The ideal trip would be in seas of less than 2 feet with winds of less than 10 knots, and we were hoping that a window of opportunity with those conditions might open up for us early in the coming week.

I perused all my Internet weather sites and sources and even spoke to a meteorologist in Tallahassee to examine the impending conditions for the passage.

We also made our purchases today for the Thanksgiving Day dinner that we would have aboard with Andrew and Sallyann wherever we were on that day. I purchased a perfect 12-pound turkey that would fit in our oven, and for the time being, it was housed in our ice maker.

Pat and I, at least, had fun during the day, since our modes of transportation were via a marina bicycle and a tricycle. We first used them to go out to lunch at Joe Pappas for wood-fired pizza and caprese salad and then to pick up grocery purchases that Pat got the chance to carry in the loaded baskets on the tricycle, while I playfully rode around her in circles as she pedaled slowly back to the boat. The Admiral does deserve to drive the bigger vehicle, and I am a generous guy!

Nov. 21-22 — Port Saint Joe, Florida

We continued to be in watching and waiting mode for our Big Bend Crossing from Carrabelle. The weather was windy and rainy at times, and we decided that it would be better for us to pass the time waiting for a good weather opportunity here at Port Saint Joe Marina with its good facilities, close shopping, and Internet and telephone access, rather than to move farther on to Apalachicola or to Carrabelle itself, which has dockage that can be questionable in strong river currents.

Throughout the past few days, we had completed all necessary chores aboard our boat, and we were ready to go when the time was right.

On Saturday evening, we planned to have a Chinese delivery dinner aboard with Sallyann and Andrew, but when we placed our order, we were a little surprised when the person taking our order did not seem to know where the marina was located, even though it was only a few blocks away from the restaurant. That did not give me a warm feeling.

When I finally got a call from the deliveryman that he was on his way, I went to the front of the marina office to wait for him. Pat then got another phone call from the deliveryman in broken English about where he was to go. She tried to explain what I was wearing, and where I was waiting, but all she got back from him was a garbled reply.

Finally, I spotted someone who I suspected was the deliveryman walking across a field in front of the marina, but he was going the wrong way. I then ran toward him, flailing my arms and shouting to get his attention. I later learned that this deliveryman, who was bringing us our order on foot, had walked to the Piggly Wiggly supermarket that was two blocks away in the opposite direction. I am not sure how you can mistake a Piggly Wiggly for a marina, but when he arrived at the supermarket, he commandeered an English-speaking customer into phoning me to find out where I was. He again got directions to the marina, but when I finally saw him, he still was not headed the right way until I flagged him down. All the group back at the boat could see from their vantage point was me running back and forth up and down the street waving my arms and yelling — and they thought the sight was hysterical! What we had there was a major failure to communicate, but to some of us the delay was well worth the laughs!

Sunday was another day of rest and planning for our crossing. We finally decided that we would head straight to Carrabelle the next day, bypass the marina there, and go to an anchorage near the East Pass from which we would tentatively leave at 2 a.m. on Tuesday morning. Having consulted with meteorologists, weather prognosticators, sea buoy sites, and NOAA wind and wave sites, I determined that our weather window would open from Monday afternoon into Wednesday morning. Our boats could make the crossing in about 15 hours, so for some of the time, we would have to travel in the dark. With a 2 a.m. departure, we would only have about four and a half hours of full darkness and could safely make the journey across the Gulf before dark the next day to Clearwater on the other side. This was at least our current plan.

While discussing things, Sallyann asked what we were doing about seasickness prevention. Pat and I were not overly concerned about it because of our experience in sailing in the North Atlantic for more than 30 years, where we had gotten used to being in lumpy seas. However, we did carry Scopolamine patches (which we highly recommend) onboard in case things got bad. Knowing that Sallyann and Andrew's boating experience was mostly on rivers and lakes, when they asked if we could spare any, we gave them two patches to be used on the crossing, and then we all made last-minute preparations for our day at sea.

Before any departure, I always check the engines. On checking the transmission oil on the starboard engine, I noticed a large bolt in the bilge. That was not a good sign, and I tried to find out its point of origin. While I was looking around, another bolt, then another, then large nuts, and washers began to appear in the bilge. A total of three bolts, four nuts, and four washers were found. We had a problem. Finding a collection of hardware rolling around the bilge could scare any captain.

What I eventually found was that the propeller shaft coupling was parting from the transmission coupling. The remaining bolts were only hanging on by a few threads, and the shaft coupling had parted from the transmission, opening a gap of about 1 inch between it and the propeller shaft. It would have only taken a few more turns of the engine, and the whole thing would have come apart!

The fun part was putting it back together. Good fortune smiled on us because after rummaging through the bilge, I was able to find all the missing hardware, got all the bolts and nuts in place, forced the propeller shaft back into position, and secured everything in less than an hour.

It is good to be lucky and blessed.

Nov. 23-24 — 55 miles to Carrabelle Beach Anchorage[7] then 175 miles to Clearwater, Florida (Big Bend Crossing)[8]

We left Port Saint Joe Marina for our 55-mile trip to the anchorage off Carrabelle Beach at 7 a.m. The winds were still coming out of the northeast, but for some reason, when we anchored in the spot where the charts showed that we should have been somewhat protected, we were still bouncing around. Because of that, for the safety of the boats, *Freedom* anchored separately away from us instead of rafting up as we had been doing since we first started traveling together.

Conditions continued to calm as late afternoon approached, so Pat and I had a simple early dinner, showered, went to bed in our clothes (so as not to waste time later getting dressed), and attempted to get some sleep before our departure time, which we had bumped up to midnight.

[7, 8] *See notes on page 253-254*

Our boats left our marine radios on, and I told Andrew that if they could not sleep, they could call us and we would leave even earlier. At 10 p.m. they called us, and we decided to get underway. Andrew asked if we had put on our Scopolamine patches yet, and I said that we had not. We were not concerned for ourselves because we did not think that with the wind and wave forecast which was predicted, that it would be a problem. I then signed off and went about getting the boat ready to go. What Pat and I did not know was that because we were not putting on our patches, Andrew and Sallyann decided not to put on their patches — something they might possibly regret.

I asked the Admiral if she was ready to go, and she said that she was, although I suspected with some trepidation. The Admiral and I said a prayer for our safe passage, and with that, we were prepared to get going, and so was the boat — or so we thought. I started up the engines, and the port engine started right up, but from the starboard engine, all I could get was a clicking sound. After about a dozen attempts, the starter finally engaged, and the engine fired up. One good thing about diesel engines is that once you get them to start, they keep on running. I was counting on that (and the bottle of holy water that Pat kept onboard), and by 10:20 p.m., we lifted anchor and were on our way.

A fixer-upper houseboat on the Gulf Intracoastal Waterway

It was surreal to be headed out the inlet in the dark, first passing lighted buoys "13" and "12," picking up unlighted buoy "11" on the radar, and then moving between it and lighted buoy "10." We finally passed Dog Island, which was the last piece of land that we would see for the next 12 to 15 hours. Now there was little to see — just two lit buoys in the distance that we could spot and two unlit buoys that we had to avoid hitting. Luckily, I had previous experience doing this in many offshore sailing trips because beyond the last buoy, all that was visible was a black void. There was no moon, no stars, and no horizon that appeared. It was so dark that if we had turned off all the lights on the boat, we literally would not have been able to see our hands in front of our faces.

Passing through the inlet went smoothly, but as we headed farther out, the wind and seas started to pick up directly on our port beam, causing *Reflection* to rock from side to side. The motion was not what we had hoped for, nor what we had expected.

Earlier in the evening I had phoned a meteorologist in Tallahassee to check the wind and seas forecast for the Gulf. The official forecast was for winds of 10 knots or less and seas of 2 feet or less, which sounded excellent. However, he also said that because the wind had been out of the northeast for several days, we could possibly experience a phenomenon on the Gulf known as a wind burst, where winds and waves could be considerably higher. If that should happen, he explained, it would start after 10 p.m. and continue through the night. Well, that was exactly what was happening!

Pat and I decided to leave the flybridge where the motion was greatest and went below to operate the boat from our lower station in the salon. We did not have a fixed helm seat at the lower station, and we were rolling too much to chance moving one of the barstools that was secured to the salon counter to sit on. However, we did not want to stand all night either, so we placed our recliner so it would face the wheel and took turns standing (actually sitting) watch on the lower instruments and occasionally getting up to look around at the darkness surrounding us — not that there was anything to see out of the windows anyway. In that part of the Gulf, there are no buoys, no day markers, no towers, and no oil platforms. There is nothing — just wind and waves. With the aid of our radar, GPS, depth finder, and autopilot, there was not much to do but hold on tight.

When one of us was in the recliner, the other attempted to lie down and get some rest on the couch that slid back and forth across the cabin, depending on the height of the waves on our port beam. It was quite a ride! Luckily, everything else on the boat but the couch and recliner was battened down, including our outside deck furniture. We felt like we were on the bridge in "Star Wars" with the darkened cabin dimly lit by only our instrument and low-voltage valence lights. It was going to be a long night. The Admiral was less than thrilled about the conditions, but we knew that the situation was by no means dangerous, just uncomfortable.

Aboard *Reflection*, however, we were faring better than *Freedom*. Within a short time, we got a call from Andrew that Sallyann and Tut were seasick. They had not put on the Scopolamine patches! Stalwart Andrew then had to man the helm for 15 hours of our 16-hour passage by himself on the little sleep he had gotten since the day before. As a safety precaution, however, we spoke to him frequently over the radio, watched their boat on our radar, and left our back deck lights on so that he could follow us more easily on the passage. During the whole crossing, the only vessel we spotted in the dark was a shrimp boat some distance away from us.

The 7:00 a.m. sunrise was a welcome sight, although we could not see the sun because of the overcast skies. At about 10 a.m., things calmed down somewhat, and after avoiding a number of crab pots on our way in, we finally completed our 175-mile trip at 2:20 p.m. when we entered Clearwater's harbor.

Clearwater had its beginnings around 1835 when the U.S. Army began construction of Fort Harrison on a bluff overlooking Clearwater Harbor as an outpost during the Seminole Wars. The area slowly grew and eventually took the name "Clear Water" after a freshwater spring that flowed in the area. The town began developing in the late 19th century after the completion of the first passenger railroad line into the city in 1888. By 1897, a nearby Victorian resort hotel named the Belleview Biltmore made Clearwater a popular vacation spot. In the early 1900s, the town was booming with 400 year-round residents, a number that rose to about 1,000 residents in the winter. Today, Clearwater is still a resort destination with all the usual Florida attractions, including white sand beaches, fishing, and water sports of all types, plus annual festivals including, the Imagine International Film Festival, Fun 'N Sun Festival, and the Clearwater Jazz Holiday.

We headed for the Clearwater Yacht Club where the harbormaster was waiting for us as we arrived, and he was helpful in tying us up in our slips and supplying us with information about Clearwater Beach. We were all tired and decided to take short naps once we were settled. We planned that we would later have celebratory cocktails on *Reflection* at 5 p.m., followed by dinner at the Yacht Club. Around 4:30 p.m., I woke up, but since Pat was still sound asleep, and seeing no signs of life on *Freedom*, I decided not to disturb anyone. Sometime after 5 p.m., Pat woke up, but *Freedom* was still dark, and knowing that Sallyann and Andrew had experienced a much rougher crossing than we had and that they were exhausted, we decided not to wake them.

At 6:30 p.m., Pat and I went for dinner alone because there was still no movement on *Freedom*. As it eventually turned out, Andrew, Sallyann, and Tut slept through the rest of that evening and into the next morning once they had put their heads down on their pillows.

Shortly after dawn Freedom *makes her way through choppy seas*

Looking back on the past 24 hours, the Admiral and I were happy to have safely arrived here. The Big Bend crossing was now behind us, and we could rest up for a few days before moving on. We then had less than 300 miles to travel to our destination of Banana Bay Resort and Marina in Marathon, so we were almost in the final stretch of getting to our winter home.

Nov. 25 — Clearwater, Florida

Andrew on *Freedom* woke up in the morning at 5 a.m. thinking that it was still yesterday afternoon and was afraid that he was missing happy hour on our boat. It took a bit of convincing from Sallyann that it was 5 a.m. on Wednesday morning, not 5 p.m. on Tuesday, and that yes, they had missed happy hour!

The day was fairly quiet after our adventures of the past two days. Pat opted to stay aboard our boat to clean up, catch up on email, and rest, while Sallyann, Andrew, and I took the Jolly Trolley and toured around Clearwater Beach, had lunch out, and purchased some groceries. The weather continued to deteriorate, and by evening, it was still raining quite heavily when we all went to dinner at the Yacht Club and toasted our crossing of the Big Bend. However, Sallyann's stomach still had not fully recovered from the experience.

Nov. 26 – Thanksgiving Day – Clearwater, Florida

Thanksgiving morning dawned bright and sunny, but the temperatures were in the 40s and the wind was still blowing strongly out of the north. Nonetheless, the crews of both boats prepared to have an elaborate Thanksgiving feast aboard *Reflection* at 3 p.m., when we were hoping that it would be around 70 degrees with lighter winds. Our vessels were humming with activity to the accompaniment of The Macy's Thanksgiving Day Parade on our cable TVs.

The table was set on our back deck, and what a wonderful dinner it was! It is simply amazing what a vast amount and variety of food can come out of two small galleys. Pat and I prepared the roast turkey with sausage stuffing and gravy, baked sweet potatoes, and dinner rolls, and Sallyann and Andrew brought the jellied cranberry sauce, mashed potatoes, string bean casserole, and homemade apple pie. Knowing the precision of the captains, everything was timed to a "T", and after our blessing in which we thanked God for all the wonderful gifts he had bestowed on us, all the food was ready to eat exactly on time.

The table is set for Thanksgiving dinner aboard Reflection.

After our delicious meal, we toasted again with champagne and chocolates, but how we could have ever eaten another thing was a mystery. Tut, the cat even joined us aboard for turkey bits. We had received a Thanksgiving card from him earlier in the day mentioning that he would like to have some white meat, lightly basted, with no bones, and not dried out. Though he is a picky gourmand, we complied with his request. After we divided the leftovers between the crews, Sallyann and Andrew returned to their boat, Pat did the dishes and cleaned up our galley (She did not want my help.), and then we retired early after our wonderful celebration.

Nov. 27 – 38 miles to Bradenton, Florida[9]

Although Sallyann was still not feeling completely up to par as a result of the Big Bend crossing, the captains decided that we would still slip our dock lines before 7:30 a.m. to continue our trip south about 38 miles to an anchorage on the Manatee River.

The Sunshine Skyline Bridge across Tampa Bay

The path today took us through a number of bridges with bridge heights that necessitated our taking down our antennas so that we could sneak under them and others at which we had to request openings. It was an interesting passage through a well-marked waterway with many beautiful homes on its shores.

Finally we entered enormous Tampa Bay with its Sunshine Skyline Bridge and then headed across the ship channel through some choppy waters to our anchorage just off the Bradenton Yacht Club in the Manatee River. The boats were rafted together for a while, but in the interest of safety and because of the breeze, the wakes, and the current, *Freedom* eventually broke off and anchored a little away from us for the night.

[9] *See notes on page 254*

Nov. 28 — 55 miles to Englewood, Florida[10]

Even though *Reflection* had a washer-dryer combo aboard, it was only meant for light-capacity items, so with a week's worth of sheets, and towels, Pat and Sallyann were on a search to find a marina with a laundry facility where we could stop.

Sallyann located Royal Palm Marina, 55 miles along our route, and we arrived there at about 2 p.m. Doing laundry then became our activity for the next six hours because Sallyann and Pat did several loads each, in the marina's one washer and one dryer. No one else had a chance because the New Jersey girls had the machines commandeered!

Pat toasting the outside laundry

Andrew and I entertained ourselves by having beers at the Tiki Bar and watched several televised football games there between carrying loads of clean wash back to the boats. We also supplied Sallyann and Pat with beverages at the outside laundry facility as we watched a fabulous sunset. It's tough being the captains!

Nov. 29 — 25 miles to Cabbage Key, Florida[11]

We did not leave our slip until 11 a.m., and the day's trip was glorious. The inland waters were smooth, the sky was a clear blue, the sun was shining, and we were finally warm!

Many dolphins jumped and played around our boat, while pelicans dove for fish. With island beach music playing on our CD player, we had a relatively short 25-mile trip to Cabbage Key, where we planned to dock for the evening and have dinner.

 The Cabbage Key Inn is located on a 38-foot Indian shell mound surrounded by 100 acres of tropical vegetation. There are no cars on the island and not even a paved road. The Inn is rumored to be the place that inspired Jimmy Buffett to write "Cheeseburgers in Paradise," and its walls and ceilings are covered with decades of dollar bills several layers thick that patrons have signed. Some say there are more than 50,000 of them.

The walls at the Cabbage Key Inn covered in money

Rather than being a Key West style bar, the inn was quite lovely with fireplaces, a screened porch, and old-fashioned deck chairs. On the other hand, the menu was pricey, they had no Rose's Lime Juice for our gimlets, and the food, in our opinion, was just all right. We were on an island where everything had to be brought in by boat, so that is what we paid for — the island ambience and beautiful view. No matter what, it was a wonderful day.

Nov. 30 — 53 miles to Naples, Florida[12]

Our original plan was to go to Fort Myers Beach, but after hearing some looming bad weather reports about heavy winds and rain arriving during the middle of the

[12] *See notes on page 254*

week, we were reluctant to put ourselves in the position of getting caught in Fort Myers for a number of days if conditions became unsuitable for us to be able to travel south on the Gulf.

Freedom *traveling alongside us on the Gulf of Mexico with a smooth sea*

Many beautiful homes line the waterway into Naples.

There is no inside route to Naples from Fort Myers Beach; you must travel outside on the Gulf of Mexico. Today's conditions would be just what we wanted, so we quickly changed our plans and untied our boats at 7:30 a.m. It would be more favorable to make the jump now, and if the weather stayed foul, we could still move on through an inside route to Marco Island, if necessary.

It was again a beautiful morning, and the conditions were calm and smooth. I managed to cancel our slip reservations in Fort Myers Beach, then Sallyann and Pat made phone calls to various marinas in Naples, and we were finally able to arrange for the boats to stay in Naples at the Naples City Docks.

We stopped in Fort Myers Beach to take on fuel at Ballard Oil Company, where the diesel fuel was priced significantly less than we had seen in a long time. At noon, we headed out Matanzas Pass into the Gulf, which was absolutely beautiful and the complete antithesis of our trip last week. After 24 miles, we headed into Gordon Pass and up the Naples River, which was bordered by one beautiful home after another. By 4 p.m., we were all tied up and settled in. Andrew and Sallyann came over for happy hour, and we enjoyed a beautiful Florida sunset.

 Naples was founded during the late 1880s. Throughout the 1870s and '80s, stories in various magazines and newspapers described the area's mild climate and excellent fishing, often likening it to the sunny Italian peninsula. When promoters described the bay as "surpassing the bay in Naples, Italy," the name stuck. Today, Naples is a shopper's and diner's dream with numerous upscale shops and restaurants along its Fifth Avenue and Third Street shopping districts.

Dec. 1-6 — Naples, Florida

We spent six days here in a slip at the Naples City Docks waiting for a good weather window to safely make the final Gulf crossing to our winter homeport in Marathon, Florida. Some days had been sunny and warm, but they were also unfortunately too windy for travel, while others were just plain windy and rainy as various fronts passed over us.

During our stay here, we shopped at the Tin City complex of stores in town, had lunch at the Riverfront Café, and had dinner at The Boathouse on the waterfront. We had some quiet evenings aboard by ourselves when we caught up on our reading and cable TV, but on others, we had pizza delivered, partook in Andrew and Sallyann's turkey pot pie, and shared several happy hours with them.

Andrew and I had also gone on a few long bike rides to procure a replacement starting solenoid for our starboard engine (the cause of our problem before we crossed the Big Bend) and a bike basket. Sallyann was also happy to discover a bakery within walking distance, and every day she took Tut out for at least one stroll on his leash. Pat was pleased to have more leisure time to make phone calls, write email, place Christmas gift orders, and sign Christmas cards to send out.

The offending part — This little $9 starting solenoid almost stopped us from making the Big Bend crossing.

We also kept in touch with Richard aboard *Holiday VII*, who had led us down the Tenn-Tom Waterway to Mobile, Alabama. Richard and his wife, Carol, went home to Memphis for Thanksgiving and returned to their boat in Gulfport, Florida, this week. They were on their way to meet us here, and all three boats planned to leave together tomorrow for our various marina locations in Marathon. At this point, we had not determined whether we would complete the 100-plus-mile crossing in one or two days, but we were all looking forward to finally getting to our headquarters for the next several months.

Dec. 7 — 110 miles to Marathon, Florida[13]

In the morning, we at last got the weather window we had been waiting for to comfortably make the 110-mile Gulf of Mexico crossing to our winter home at Banana Bay Resort and Marina in Marathon. We left the Naples City Docks at

---

[13] *See notes on page 254*

6:40 a.m., and by 7 a.m., we cleared Gordon Pass and entered the Gulf. At the beginning, the breeze blew lightly out of the south with a slight northwest swell, but the wind and wave conditions lightened even more during the day as the sun shone brightly, and the temperature eventually rose into the low 80s. Small sea birds dove in our bow wave to catch fish, and dolphins, pelicans, and flying fish escorted us through the blue green waters of the Gulf.

Approaching our winter home at Banana Bay Resort and Marina in Marathon, Florida

What an absolutely wonderful trip it was, and by 2:30 p.m., we started to see the outline of the Keys and the Seven Mile Bridge that connects Marathon to the lower Keys emerging on the horizon. Along the way *Freedom* followed us slightly behind or alongside, and *Holiday VII*, which had left a little later than we did, traveled about 8 miles behind. We were all in frequent radio contact, and we were able to warn our buddy boats about the many crab pots we had to avoid along our route.

As *Reflection* and *Freedom* approached Marathon, we broke off onto different headings that would take us to separate marinas for the first time since Oct. 29, when we had started out from Rogersville, Alabama, together. We said a poignant goodbye to each other over the radio, even though we would only be 1.5 miles apart throughout the winter. Having spent 40 days and traveled 1,268 miles together in all kinds of conditions was significant, and we had experienced lots of fun and adventure with them along the way!

*Reflection **at rest at Banana Bay***

As we made our turn into the entrance of Banana Bay Marina at 4:30 p.m., we saw the dockmaster, Billy, waiting for us with some of our new marina neighbors to welcome us into our slip and to take our lines. Finally, after almost an hour of setting up lines, electric cords, and the cable TV, we were at last settled into our slip to my satisfaction. Although we were extremely tired after our long day, when Pat and I sat down on our aft deck to see the sun go down over the Gulf of Mexico, we reveled in the absolute beauty of this wonderful place, and were so thankful for all the blessings God had given us to make the trip and our winter stay here possible. Dreams really do come true!

Notes:

(1)
Fairhope — Eastern Shores Marina and the Fairhope Yacht Club (which has reciprocity for recognized yacht club members) have transient slips. It is a short taxi ride to the town with shopping and restaurants.

(2)
Roberts Bayou — The entrance is narrow, so follow the buoys into the cove beyond, and anchor in about 7 feet of water. You might want to set a float above your anchor so that other boaters can see where it is set in the small anchorage. Pirate's Cove Bistro is a short, dinghy ride away. Slip depths at Pirate's Cove are shallow, and in

our opinion, the food at the restaurant is a bit pricey with the portions on the small side.

(3)
Destin Harbor — After passing under the highway bridge, turn to port, and follow the channel along the bridge to the narrow harbor entrance. Once inside, there is plenty of room to anchor in 10-foot-plus water depths.

(4)
Burnt Mill Creek — Anchor in 5-6 feet of water just off Graze Point, and use caution because the spot is exposed to all southern winds.

(5)
Panama City Marina has reasonable transient rates, gives a BoatUS discount on slips, and has a nice laundry facility. There is a Chinese food buffet on the highway that can be reached via the town trolley, and pizza delivery to the boat is also available here.

(6)
Pier 98 Marina on Pitt Bayou has reasonable fuel prices.

Port Saint Joe Marina is located 5 miles off the Intracoastal Waterway, has a friendly staff, reasonable transient rates, an America's Great Loop Cruisers' Association discount on slips, and a restaurant on the premises with several others nearby. Chinese food delivery is available to the marina (if you are lucky), a supermarket is two blocks away, a liquor store is one block away, and courtesy bicycles and tricycles can be obtained at the marina.

(7)
Carrabelle Beach Anchorage is protected from northerly winds, while Shipping Cove on Dog Island is protected from southerly winds. East Pass is wide and deep, but if you are transiting at night, beware of three unlit green buoys marking the southwest side of the channel.

Before venturing out into the Gulf, check for wind forecasts at:

- *www.windfinder.com/forecasts/uswave_wave_height_direction_caribbean93.htm*
- *www.stormsurfing.com/cgi/display.cgi?a=gom_height*
- *You might also call (850) 942-8833 and speak to a meteorologist from the National Weather Center in Tallahassee, Florida.*

There are thousands of small buoys marking crab and lobster pots along the west coast of Florida. Avoid approaching the coast before 10 a.m. so that the sun's reflection on the water does not obstruct your view of the buoys.

(8)

Clearwater — Clearwater Pass is wide and clearly marked with buoys. Transient rates in Clearwater and along the west coast of Florida can run up to $3.50 per foot.

(9)

Bradenton — If you are traveling past Tampa Bay, take the Sunshine Skyway Channel (about 6 feet deep) that runs just west of the Sunshine Skyway instead of the Intracoastal Waterway. That will cut several miles off your trip.

Manatee River Anchorage — The river entrance just off Tampa Bay is well marked. Anchor in 9 feet of water just inside McKay Point. There is protection from the north but exposure to the south.

(10)

Englewood — Royal Palm Marina has a friendly staff, a small outside laundry facility, and a tiki bar that was converted into a restaurant. The slip rates are competitive, considering where you are, with easy access to Intracoastal Waterway.

(11)

Cabbage Key — Follow the channel west from Intracoastal Waterway marker "61." Proceed slowly. There is electric service, but no water at dockside, and a restaurant on-site. Friendly staff members will help you tie up. Slip rates and the restaurant prices are a bit on the pricey side, but you are on an island.

(12)

Ballard Oil Company (239-463-7677) in Fort Myers Beach charged up to 80 cents less per gallon for diesel than the other marinas in the area and had the lowest price we had found anywhere on Florida's west coast.

Naples — Naples City Dock has a friendly staff, transient rates that are $1 to $2 per foot less than others in the area, multiple-day discounts, a laundry facility on the premises, and many restaurants, a deli, a convenience store, shopping, and the beach all nearby.

(13)

The Florida Keys — Be aware of crab and lobster pot buoys as you approach the Keys. Watch your depth sounder closely, especially near shore. Going aground here can be expensive in repairs to your boat and in fines. Dockage and fuel prices in the Florida Keys are some of the highest on the Loop. "Paradise" is expensive. Arrange for dockage months in advance because marinas quickly fill up for the winter.

Chapter 13

"Just Another Day in Paradise"

Dec. 8-April 30 — Marathon, Florida

Aside from making two short trips back to New Jersey to check on things there, we spent nearly five months here in Marathon, and it was the best winter of our lives!

> Marathon's city limits encompass 13 islands in the Florida Keys. Among them are: Knight's Key, Boot Key, Key Vaca, Fat Deer Key, Long Point Key, Crawl Key, and Grassy Key.
>
> Although the Weather Channel often incorrectly refers to Marathon as Marathon Key, there is no Marathon Key. The name Marathon dates back to the building of the Florida East Coast Railroad through the Keys. The name got its origins from the railroad workers who worked night and day to complete the railway. When many of them complained that the work had become a real marathon, the name stuck. Today, Marathon is a vacation destination well known for its sports fishing on the Gulf of Mexico and Atlantic Ocean sides, plus its nearby bountiful reefs make it a popular diving, snorkeling, spear fishing, and lobster tickling area. It also has of one of the last untouched tropical hardwood hammocks in the Keys located at the Crane Point Museum, and, as we can attest, it is a wonderful place to spend the winter.

Enjoying the northern snowy months in the Florida Keys was something that Pat and I had always wanted to do, and we were not disappointed. The area has the laidback attitude and the beauty of the Bahamas but with all the additional advantages of being in the U.S. — and the phones usually work!

It did not take long for us to feel right at home. We took full advantage of our time here: becoming members of the Museum of Natural History of the Florida

Keys, joining the Marathon Yacht Club[1], volunteering to bread fish at the Marathon Seafood Festival, going to Mass and enjoying the beautiful gardens at San Pablo Catholic Church, attending plays at the Marathon Community Theater, taking several trips to Key West, snorkeling, and catching the "Keys Disease" — symptoms that include being in the sun with a cocktail in your hand and not a care in the world. It was wonderful!

The pool at Banana Bay Resort and Marina

This is a fully grown Key deer (about the size of a large dog).
Key deer are a miniature species of deer that are unique to the Florida Keys.

---

[1] *See notes on page 260*

Loading the starting gate at the annual Pig Races, held in Marathon to raise money for a local charity

Boot Key Harbor with its 226 moorings, located on the Atlantic side of Marathon

We also had our share of company from up north. Once your friends and family find out that you are in the Keys for the winter, you will have visitors — and we did. My relatives, Pat's relatives, and a number of our friends came down to get out of the cold and into the warmth, and we were delighted to have them!

Throughout the winter, maintenance chores on *Reflection* also kept me occupied. I even got to work on the porcelain goddess a few more times. However, I think my days of intimacy with her have ended because I discovered a simple and inexpensive way to keep her operating efficiently[2]. Thank heaven!

After this wonderful hiatus, however, it was time to return to our northern home, so we planned to leave Marathon and Banana Bay Resort tomorrow to begin our final leg of the Loop. Late in the afternoon, Pat and I walked to a point at Banana Bay that looks out over the Gulf and toasted our stay here while we watched the sunset for the last time. We had not even left yet and were already missing the place, but we have reserved our slip here for next winter and will be back!

Admiral Pat as we arrive at the Annual Marathon Seafood Festival,
where we volunteered to bread fish

2 See notes on page 260

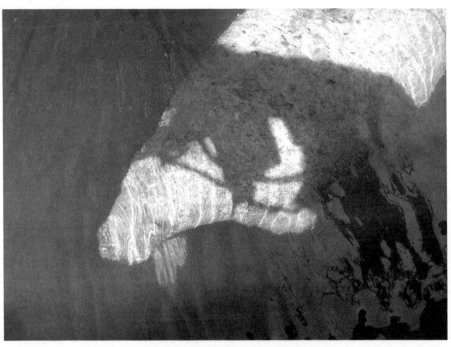

A manatee visits us in Banana Bay

A baby pelican waiting for a free meal

Notes:

(1)

If you are going to be spending the winter in Florida or are traveling along its coasts, consider joining a yacht club that is a member of the Florida Council of Yacht Clubs. Doing so can be to your advantage. Besides being able to participate in your own club's activities, members of Florida Council of Yacht Clubs-affiliated clubs offer extended reciprocal privileges, such as getting your first night's dockage free when visiting other member clubs and being able to use their restaurants and facilities. If you will be staying in Marathon for the winter or have an interest in learning more about the Marathon Yacht Club, contact me at reflection.loop@verizon.net.

(2)

The secret to improving the function of a slow-emptying head (non-vacuum) is as follows:

1. *Turn off the intake water.*
2. *Pump enough white vinegar through the system to displace all the water.*
3. *Let it sit for at least 24 hours.*
4. *Open the water intake, and flush the vinegar out.*

You should find that things move along quite well after this process.

Chapter 14

"Homeward Bound"

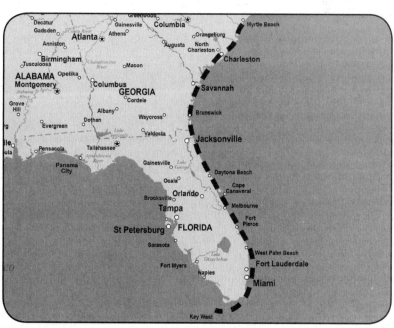

May 1 — 43 miles to Islamorada, Florida[1]

We left our southern home here in Banana Bay at 10 a.m. with air temperatures in the low 80s, water temperatures in the low 90s, and clear skies with winds out of the northeast at a brisk 15 to 20 knots. Though it was hard to leave this special spot, we did so knowing we would return next December.

As *Reflection* left the dock, only the maintenance men, Larry and Tony, were there to see us off because most of the other boats had already left for northern climates. The colors of the water were beautiful as we headed up the Gulf side of the Keys,

---

and we carefully watched our depth sounder because of the many shallow areas around here. We planned to make the first day out a short one by going only 27 miles to our chosen anchorage at lovely Matecumbe Bight, where we pulled in around 1 p.m., had lunch, and took naps.

Dolphins playing in **Reflection**'*s wake*

Around 4:30 p.m., I told Pat that I wanted to start up our generator to keep our refrigerator and other appliances powered up for the pleasant evening ahead. Then, we got the first surprise of our Loop completion: The generator was only putting out 25 volts of AC power instead of 120 volts!

I had no idea how we were going to get out of this one. It was late on a Saturday afternoon, all the marinas in the area would be closed soon, and if we could not find one that was open where we could access electric, we were in deep trouble. Acting quickly, we started looking in our local guidebooks for a marina in the nearby area where we could pull in and get electric power for our fully stocked refrigerator and freezer (with hundreds of dollars of newly purchased food), get my beloved ice maker going, and possibly find generator repairs.

We made numerous phone calls, and finally found one marina about 7 miles away to help us. We immediately picked up anchor and started heading in that direction; however, traversing the shallow channels in the area took local knowledge. The marina's dock assistant gave us one set of directions on the phone, but then when we realized he had sent us up the wrong channel, we called back. He then said he was in the process of leaving for the evening but that he would give us the marina owner's phone number so that he could give us additional directions.

We then had to head back a number of miles, and the time was getting later. The directions and shallow channels were so convoluted that the marina owner finally came out in his own boat to lead us in and sounded the depths ahead of us on our way into hidden Watermark Marina, where it was low tide.

We came in carefully through a channel that was extremely narrow and shallow with water depths only 1 to 2 inches below our keel. I almost expected to see Humphrey Bogart dragging *The African Queen* around the next turn. We eventually entered a marina that was not much wider than our own entrance channel at home in Seawood Harbor. With the sun about to set and after *Reflection* was tied up, we then found out that the power connections at this brand new marina, which was still under construction, were not completed! That had been our reason for coming here! So now the owner and I had to scour the premises for extra power cords, and we even jury-rigged an outlet so that we could plug in for the electricity we needed. After thanking the marina owner for all his help (We paid for it, but it was cheaper than losing all our refrigerated goods, and he did not have to come out on a Saturday night.), at about 8 p.m. we were finally settled in. Pat and I realized that the odds of our finding a generator mechanic on the weekend were less than zero, so we decided we would wait until Monday to make our calls and adjusted our plan of anchoring out the next night to finding another marina slip instead. We had learned to be flexible on the Loop!

May 2 — 35 miles to Key Largo, Florida[2]

I got to practice my boat maneuvering skills in the morning as I turned *Reflection* on a dime in a tight spot so that we could exit going forward instead of backing out of the marina. Next, we got to practice our navigation skills as we made our way out of the shallow channels without going aground. Luck was on our side.

The wind was still blowing out of the northeast as we headed to Anchorage Resort and Marina, a spot familiar to everyone who has ever entered the Keys via the Jewfish Creek Bridge because it is the first marina on the right in Key Largo.

At 33 miles long, Key Largo is the largest and most northern island in the Florida Keys archipelago, and its original Spanish name was Cayo Largo, meaning Long Key. It became famous as the setting for the 1948 film "Key Largo" starring Humphrey Bogart, Lauren Bacall, and Edward G. Robinson, although the picture was filmed entirely on a sound stage in Hollywood except for some background shots. The movie was the initial inspiration for Pat and me to visit the Keys more than 25 years ago. Key Largo is a popular tourist destination that calls itself "The Diving Capital of the World" because the living coral reef a few miles offshore attracts thousands of scuba divers and sport-fishing enthusiasts each year.

We had no idea that Anchorage Resort and Marina and Gilbert's Resort across the creek would be "hopping" that much on a late Sunday afternoon! Boats of all sizes were coming and going from the docks and the tiki bar, and the music was loud, if nothing else. It was fun, however, watching everyone enjoying themselves, and we had a pleasant evening aboard as we continued to ponder solutions to our generator issue.

We contacted our friends Bo and Cyndi from whom we had bought our boat, and they said that it would be fine for us to bring the boat to their dock in Palm City on Wednesday, a day earlier than planned, for our visit with them. Bo gave us the phone number of a Westerbeke dealer in his area that might be able to do repairs, and we also hoped to have a fuel truck delivery of diesel fuel made at their house for *Reflection.*

Once we passed under the Jewfish Creek Bridge on our way north,
we would be leaving the Florida Keys behind us.

May 3 — 43 miles to Miami, Florida

We left Key Largo at 8 a.m. for our 43-mile trip to the Coral Reef Yacht Club in the Coconut Grove area of Miami.

 Starting about 1825, several waves of immigrants established Coconut Grove. By 1873 the area saw an influx of Americans from the northeastern states and some British, who were no doubt trying to escape from the cold in England. In 1882, the first hotel on the South Florida mainland, the Bay View Inn (later known as the Peacock Inn) was located in Coconut Grove. From that point on, it was well on its way to becoming a resort destination. Until 1925, Coconut Grove was an independent city, and then it was annexed by the city of Miami. The Grove, as the locals know it, is sometimes known as Miami's Food Court because of its many and varied restaurants. It is also home to The Kampong, an 8-acre tropical garden that is part of the National Tropical Botanical Garden and is the location of The Barnacle Historic State Park.

The skies were somewhat overcast as we traveled north across the sounds and Biscayne Bay, and we were surprised to see how few boats were out on the water. We seemed to have the place to ourselves.

It was good to see the Miami skyline as we approached the yacht club, and Tony, the dockmaster, was there to help us tie up. Because we are members of the Marathon Yacht Club, we have full reciprocal privileges at all the other clubs in the Florida Yacht Council and some reciprocity at others listed in the American Registry of Yacht Clubs. These privileges can include docking, dining, and access to the bar, pool, golf, and tennis facilities that are particular to each club.

This club was lovely. Unfortunately, the facilities were closed on Mondays, but we were able to dock here with no fee. I spent the afternoon on the phone, but finally we got a verdict from the Westerbeke dealer in Stuart, Florida, that our generator was not worth fixing, or so we thought. Though the news was grim, I immediately started making additional inquiries, and after doing so, we decided that we would wait until we got home to buy a used or rebuilt one. The only change Pat and I would have to make to our trip itinerary was that now we would have to travel from marina or yacht club to marina or yacht club on our way north because without a working generator, anchoring was out. The Admiral then got out her guidebooks, and by evening, we had a revised plan for our journey home.

May 4 — 47 miles to Boca Raton, Florida[3]

Reflection left the dock at Coral Reef at 7 a.m., and I maneuvered her out of a tight spot with large boats in front and behind her. She is a big girl who needs her room, but after having traveled thousands of miles, we handled her pretty well, even in awkward spaces.

Looking off the Intracoastal Waterway down the Miami River

We made our way through bridges, and again, there were few vessels around on our passage through Miami.

Spain claimed Miami in 1566, and within a year, a Spanish mission was built there. Not much went on until 1836 when Fort Dallas was built and became a site of fighting during the Second Seminole War. A woman, Julia Tuttle, conceived the Miami we know today, and it is the only major city in the U.S. that has that distinction (The captain thinks that's why the city has so many shopping malls!). In the late 1800s, she convinced railroad tycoon Henry Flagler to expand his Florida East Coast Railroad to the region, and because of this, she became known as "the mother of Miami." For more than 100 years, Miami has continued to grow, and its current population is more than 5.5 million residents. In 2009, Miami was ranked as the richest city in the US.

[3] *See notes on page 291*

The Intracoastal Waterway through Miami

We spotted some of Reflection's *bigger friends as we passed through Fort Lauderdale.*

Pat enjoyed traveling the Intracoastal Waterway up to Boca Raton, and we could have made a commercial for "Homes of the Rich and Famous" as we passed many multimillion-dollar mansions and hundreds of luxury apartments and condos along the way.

 The Spanish were the first Europeans to come to the area, but why they named it Boca Raton is somewhat of a mystery because the literal translation of those two words is "mouse mouth." We had learned, however, that the word "Raton" in Spanish can also be used to describe an inlet and that Spanish sailors also used the word "Boca" (mouse) to describe rocks that gnawed at a ship's anchor cable. Luckily, whatever the origin of the name, it was never translated into English because no one would consider moving to "Mouse Mouth, Florida." That name surely would not fit the cultural center and chic shopping community it is today with the Boca Raton Museum of Art and the National Cartoon Museum (formally the International Museum of Cartoon Art), and for shoppers, the Town Center at Boca Raton with its numerous upscale shops and restaurants.

We arrived at the beautiful Royal Palm Yacht and Country Club around 12:30 p.m. The dockmaster got us settled in at our slip, which was across from several gorgeous homes, and we spent the rest of the afternoon getting ready to see our friends Florence and her daughter and son-in-law, Andrea and Ed, along with their daughters, Melissa and Kaitlyn.

One thing that traveling the Great Loop has allowed us to do is to catch up with old friends from around the country. Pat and Florence have known each other for more than 30 years, and they taught and carpooled together for more than 15 years. She and her family are close friends to us, and we often visited them throughout the Christmas holidays when she first moved to Florida.

Our guests arrived at 6 p.m., and after cocktails and munchies aboard, we went to the Lemon Tree in Boca Raton for terrific Thai food. As usual, Ed knew the owner, so our meal was special. He was a great host, and we had a wonderful evening being with everyone.

May 5-7 — 72 miles to Palm City, Florida

This day, we traveled 72 miles to the home of Bo and Cindy, the previous owners of our boat, in Palm City, Florida. We left the Royal Palm Yacht Club before 7 a.m. to travel through a series of several bridges, adjusting our speed so that we would arrive at each for its scheduled opening. Again, the homes we passed along the way were simply phenomenal. Each home was larger and more beautiful than the next, but despite their obvious opulence, most were already closed up for the season.

One of the many watering holes along the waterway — Captain George loves its name.

*The Lighthouse at Jupiter Inlet — Here, the water color changes
from a tropical blue-green to dark green.*

By 4 p.m., we called Cyndi and Bo to tell them we were entering their lagoon system. It was nostalgic for us to bring *Reflection* back to the dock where we first saw her and to have them see her for the first time since we left here on April 11, 2008. We were delighted to visit them and see their new boat, *Voyageur*, a striking Mainship 34. As usual, their new boat was kept in pristine condition, and it was a wonderful sight to see our two boats tied up stern to stern. They came aboard for a tour of the improvements we had made to *Reflection* and for cocktails and a Chinese takeout dinner, and we spent a wonderful evening with them trading stories about our various travels and our busy lives.

The next day, Bo and I did a walkthrough on *Reflection*, and even though it had been more than 27 months since we had bought the boat, I always respected and valued Bo's opinion on various aspects of our vessel. We also had a delightful time with Jessica, Bo and Cyndi's daughter, who stopped by for a visit in the afternoon. It was all followed by a quiet evening aboard.

The following day, after a few days of suspecting a virus on our computer, I made some calls to get a tech aboard to check it out. We managed to make a trip to the grocery store and to do two wash loads in Cyndi's laundry before John from Fast Tek arrived at 9:40 a.m. Within minutes, he informed us that we needed to buy a new computer, which was another trip surprise! He met me a few hours later at a local Best Buy to purchase one and then spent time late in the afternoon transferring our old information onto the new computer. He arrived back at *Reflection* at 6:30 p.m. and worked with me for an hour so I could get acclimated to the new laptop. After he left, we took Bo and Cyndi to the Harbour Ridge Yacht and Country Club for dinner. Also in the Florida Yacht Council, its clubhouse and grounds are grandiose and impressive, and we enjoyed a fabulous dinner with terrific food and wonderful friends at this beautiful facility.

May 8 — 43 miles to Vero Beach, Florida

Bo and Cyndi helped us cast off our lines from their dock at 7 a.m., and they made promises to visit us at our home in New Jersey during the summer. We then headed out on today's route to Vero Beach.

 Vero Beach is the location of the Dodgertown Sports Complex, where the Brooklyn/Los Angeles Dodgers' baseball team held their spring training camp from 1948 until 2008. It is now used for baseball and football tournaments, concerts, monster truck rallies, and other events. Vero Beach is located between Florida's two climate zones: To the north, the climate is considered to be subtropical, and to the south, it is tropical, so when you are here, you can take your pick as to where you are in the world.

There are three major industries in Vero Beach: the Piper Aircraft Company, citrus, and tourism. Like most of the coastal cities of Florida, it also has its share of beautiful beaches, restaurants, fishing, and water sports.

We had a lovely ride north on this beautiful, sunny day, and *Reflection* arrived at The Moorings Yacht Club around 1 p.m. We were the only boat there at the dock, which was located right next to the pool and club area. Again, it was a stunning location, and the dockhands who took our lines even brought us ice water and lemons on a tray after we were tied up. We felt like we were hot stuff!

Pat and I rested in the afternoon and then got ready to host our friends Gus, Linda, and Nancy for cocktails aboard the boat. They all live here at The Moorings during the winter months, and we were all members or officers of the Bristol Sailing Club (a local club located near our home in New Jersey) at one time and had known one another for many years.

After a tour of *Reflection* and happy hour aboard, they hosted us for dinner at the Yacht Club, followed by a driving tour of Vero Beach, a town that appears to be a lovely community in which to live. We were happy to spend time here with our friends, and they all looked like living in Florida for the winter months agreed with them.

May 9 — 44 miles to Indian Harbour Beach, Florida

As we got ready to leave the dock in the morning at 9 a.m., we were delighted to have Linda and Gus come to see us off. It was another beautiful day on the water, and despite the strong winds that blew out of the southeast there were boats with families beached at the many islands that dotted the Waterway. They must have been celebrating Mother's Day — Florida style.

At 2:30 p.m., we pulled into stunning Eau Gallie Yacht Club with its vibrant blue-roofed white buildings, and it was bustling with activity. There were many families having Sunday brunch, some swimming in the pool, and others simply enjoying being on their boats. Unfortunately, Pat was feeling a little under the weather with allergy symptoms, so we stayed onboard for dinner and retired early.

May 10 — 39 miles to Titusville, Florida[4]

Though we had traveled this area of the Waterway two years ago on our first trip from Florida to our home, some parts looked familiar, but some did not. At that time, we had crew aboard with us, and we were doing a much faster pace of 100

---

[4] *See notes on page 291*

miles a day, so some of it went by in a blur. This time, we stopped and smelled the roses by going only 50 miles or less each day.

Reflection arrived at Titusville Municipal Marina around 12:30 p.m.

Although Spain acquired Florida in 1821, the Seminole Wars delayed the eventual settlement of what would become Titusville for quite a long time. It was not until 1867 that Confederate Colonel Henry T. Titus arrived in the area with the intention of building a town on land that his wife, Mary Hopkins Titus, owned, and by 1870, he had erected The Titus House, a large, one-story hotel next to a saloon. At some point later, a man named Captain Clark Rice wanted to call the new town Riceville, so Henry Titus, being a sporting man, challenged him to a game of dominoes to decide the name. Titus won.

Beginning in the late 1950s, the development of Cape Canaveral and later the Kennedy Space Center on nearby Merritt Island caused Titusville to become a bit of a boomtown. With the resultant rapid growth in its economy and population, it eventually acquired the nicknames of "Space City, U.S.A." and "Miracle City".

The large structure in the center is the Assembly Building,
and to the left is a launch tower at the Kennedy Space Center.
As you can see, NASA does not like anyone to get too close to its toys.

After we settled in, I went into the dockmaster's office, and the personnel there tried to convince me to extend our stay because a NASA space shuttle launch was scheduled to go off in a few days. The marina was planning a dock party for the event, and the staff told me that when a shuttle goes off, the whole marina shakes. Unfortunately, our schedule did not coincide with NASA's, and we had already committed to being in Georgia by Friday. As much as we would have liked to see the liftoff, we just could not be everywhere. When I returned to the boat, we wrote out mail, paid bills, worked on the blog, and enjoyed a pizza delivery while watching "Dancing with the Stars." It was just like being at home.

May 11 — 47 miles to Daytona Beach, Florida

Today's destination was Daytona Beach.

 The Timucuan Indians, who lived here in fortified villages, originally inhabited the area where Daytona Beach is located. However, after contact with the Spanish, the first Europeans to come here, their culture died out. During the 18th century, the British then took control of the area from the Spanish, but then Spain, an ally of the patriots, eventually kicked them out after the American Revolution. In 1804, Samuel Williams received a land grant of 3,000 acres from Spain, which encompassed the area that would become Daytona Beach. Williams built a slave labor-based plantation here, which his son Samuel Hill Williams abandoned after it was burned down during the Second Seminole War. In 1871, Mathias Day, Jr. from Mansfield, Ohio, purchased a large tract of land on the William's Plantation and built a hotel around which the town rose, but unfortunately only a year later, he went bust. Although he had lost his land, the local residents still decided to name their new town in his honor. Thus Daytona was born.

Daytona began to make its mark in 1902 when automobile and motorcycle races began running on its wide beach of smooth, compacted sand that was ideal for racing. It continued until 1959 when the Daytona International Speedway was built. Today, there are motor-related events held there each year, including the Daytona 500 NASCAR race, the Rolex 24 sports car race, the Coke Zero 400 NASCAR race, and Daytona Beach Bike Week. Plus, there is spring break for college students.

We had a lovely ride north again with light boat traffic, unlike our inaugural trip up the Intracoastal Waterway two years before. Daytona Beach was busy and crowded at that time, and we remembered having had vessels of all sizes zigzagging around us, but today we almost had the waterway to ourselves.

The winds continued to be out of the southeast, and the temperatures were in the low 80s. The day's destination was our last yacht club in Florida — the Halifax River Yacht Club. It turned out to be a beautiful large facility, and the dockmaster and his assistant welcomed us at our slip. I then got a personal tour of the club, and we were given an extensive booklet about the Halifax River Yacht Club and the surrounding area. We could have had dinner in the lounge or dining room, but we opted to have a quiet dinner aboard because it was a "Dancing with the Stars" results show night, and I could hardly control my enthusiasm …(zzz).

The Halifax River Yacht Club

May 12 — 53 miles to Saint Augustine, Florida[5]

We left the dock at 6:40 a.m. for a 53-mile trip to Saint Augustine.

 Spanish explorer Ponce de Leon, who claimed the region for Spain while reportedly looking for the Fountain of Youth, first explored the area around Saint Augustine in 1513. The city was founded on Aug. 28, 1565, the feast day of Saint Augustine of Hippo, when Spanish explorer Pedro Menéndez de Avilés landed here. It is the oldest city in the continental U.S., and it predates the Jamestown settlement in Virginia by more than 40 years. The French, British, and Spanish battled over who would control Saint Augustine for the next 250 years after its founding, but in 1821, the U.S. took over, and in 1845 the control was finally settled when Florida became a state. Today, the city is a popular tourist attraction and a "Mecca" for history buffs wanting to learn more about its Spanish colonial buildings and its 19th-century architecture.

The weather continued to be the same — sunny and beautiful — and except for having to be extremely watchful of the water depths near several spots that were shoaling in the proximity of the closed Matanzas Inlet, the trip was smooth. We arrived at the Saint Augustine Municipal Marina around 1 p.m., and I had to carefully bring the boat into the dock because the current was ripping through from the southeast. It was a different docking experience from the nail-biter of our first trip here two years earlier. Today, once I maneuvered *Reflection* into the slip, the dockhand efficiently caught our lines from Pat using our successful personal docking system in which Pat first throws some light lines that we later replace with our heavy ones. It works for us.

We headed to the A1A Alehouse for dinner and sat down again at the same bar we had drinks at two years ago when we were bringing the boat home on our maiden voyage with her. While reminiscing about that night, I asked the barmaid if she would be willing to play a joke on my cousin, Ed, who was with us on that trip. She said sure, and we placed a call to Ed at his home in New Hampshire. When he answered, she pretended to be one of the patrons who remembered Ed from that original visit. We are not sure if Ed appreciated the joke, but we sure did, and Pat and I had a bunch of laughs as he stuttered his way through a short conversation with our accomplice. Afterward, we walked around town and had drippy, but excellent, ice cream cones before returning to the boat a few hours later.

The Lightner Museum contains relics of America's Gilded Age.

A typical street in Old Saint Augustine

May 13 — 62 miles to Fernandina Beach, Florida[6]

I again played the wind and the current as we backed away from the dock and headed out under the Bridge of Lions to our last stop in Florida, Fernandina Beach.

Fernandina Beach has the curious distinction of being the only municipality in the U.S. to have flown eight different national flags. The French were the first to plant their flag here, when in 1562, French Huguenot explorer, Jean Ribault, arrived here and named the island Isle de Mai. In 1565, the next group to come along was the Spanish, who drove off the French and murdered everyone on the island. In the early 1700s, Georgia's founder and colonial governor, James Oglethorpe, renamed it Amelia Island in honor of Princess Amelia, King George II's daughter, even though it was still a Spanish possession. In 1763, after their victory in the Seven Years War, the island was turned over to the English by treaty. However, the Spanish got it back again in 1783 at the end of the American Revolutionary War. In 1811, surveyor George J. F. Clarke laid out the town of Fernandina and named it in honor of Spain's King Ferdinand VII.

Then, things started to get a little nutty. In 1812, insurgents known as the Patriots of Amelia Island seized the island and raised a North American Patriot flag, which they soon replaced with the American flag. In 1813, the Spanish came back and managed to kick out the Americans. Then, thinking that it would be a good idea to protect their interest in the area, they erected Fort San Carlos on the island in 1816. Later, in 1817, Scottish-born South American freedom fighter Gregor MacGregor led 55 musketeers to seize Fort San Carlos, claimed the island on behalf of "the brethren of Mexico, Buenos Aires, New Grenada, and Venezuela," and raised the Latin American Patriots' Green Cross of Florida flag. Not long after MacGregor got there, the Spanish again returned and routed him, except that they could not gain complete control of the island because of the presence of American irregular forces that Ruggles Hubbard and Jared Irwin organized. Hubbard and Irwin later joined forces with the pirate Luis Aury, who laid claim to the island in the name of the Republic of Mexico. However, that did not last for long because U.S. Navy forces drove Aury from the island, and President James Monroe held Amelia Island in trust for Spain.

The saga continued on Jan. 8, 1861, two days before Florida's secession, when Confederate sympathizers took control of the area and claimed it for the Confederate States of America. However, just more than a year later, on March 3, 1862, the Union forces, consisting of 28 gunboats, restored federal control to the island and finally raised the American flag. The last time I checked, it was still flying there. Today, Amelia Island and Fernandina Beach are the homes of many upscale resorts, world-class spas, championship golf courses, exclusive restaurants, historic sites, and annual festivals.

As we headed north toward Fernandina Beach, the scenery began to change with much more marshland appearing. We eventually crossed the Saint John's River near Jacksonville and spotted the first large commercial ship we had seen since Miami. When *Reflection* arrived at Fernandina Harbor Marina, a capable dockhand again greeted us and caught our lines. Pat and I appreciated his skill because in this area of big tidal ranges and fast-running current, getting the boat tied up quickly is important.

The marina was busy with vessels of all sizes docked here, including a coastal cruise ship and a private vessel even larger than the cruise ship! We dodged a big group of tourists apparently coming back from the ship's shore excursion as I was assisting Pat up the steep ramp to the laundry facilities. Then I talked with some sailors who had just come down the Intracoastal Waterway from Georgia. They said that we should go offshore the next day, if possible, because the insects known locally in Georgia as May Flies (which are not flies, but, in my opinion, some kind of flying darts that like to drill into human flesh) were out in force in the marshes, which would make the inland journey uncomfortable. After hearing that bit of news, we decided that going out into the Atlantic Ocean tomorrow would be the preferable route to take.

Docked at Fernandina Beach, this unique cruise ship travels mostly the inland waters of the U.S. and Canada.

May 14 — 42 miles to Brunswick, Georgia[7]

Reflection left the dock before 7 a.m., and within 2 miles, we crossed the border into Georgia and then headed out the Saint Mary's River Inlet. The wind was out of the southeast, and we were headed into an incoming tide, so I pumped up the engines as we headed out, but when Pat started getting splashed by spray up on the flybridge, I decided it would behoove me to back off the throttles a little. If the Admiral is not happy, the Captain is not happy!

Once out of the inlet, we eventually made our turn north and began to take the waves on our stern quarter, which made for more motion than we would have preferred, but at least the trip to Saint Simons Inlet was only 22 miles away. I told Pat, "At least there are no bugs out here!", but that was not a comfort to her as *Reflection* rolled fore and aft and side to side through the choppy seas. The conditions finally improved again as we headed into the inlet past Jekyll Island and up the Brunswick River.

The Lighthouse at Saint Simons Inlet

I planned to fill up with fuel at Ocean Petroleum in Brunswick because this location was well known for having good fuel prices, but unfortunately we had to wait at idle in the river for almost an hour while two other vessels that had tied up before us fueled up. We finally got in there, refueled, and then headed farther up the river to Brunswick Landing Marina.

 The settlement that would become Brunswick began in 1738 as a tobacco plantation owned by British colonists. It was incorporated in 1856 and took the name Brunswick after the duchy of Brunswick-Lüneburg in Germany. During World War II, Brunswick played an important role in the war effort by producing nearly 100 Liberty ships at the JA Jones Construction Company. The first ships took more than 300 days to complete, but the last ship took only 34 days from start to finish. Imagine the organization and cooperation needed to build a ship in just 34 days! Today, Brunswick, with its deep-water port, supports thriving seafood and shipping industries, and pulp and wood products, bulk cargoes, and tourism are prominent segments of the local economy.

When we arrived at the marina, the dock mistress and her agile female assistant got us quickly docked around 1:30 p.m. Pat then cleaned the inside of the boat while I sprayed off the salt from our ocean trip, and then I caught a cab to go to the grocery store while Pat did another load of wash in the marina's lovely boaters' lounge.

It must be apparent by now that the Admiral never allows dirty laundry to pile up; she takes advantage of using convenient laundry facilities every chance she gets. Our friends George and Linda were coming aboard the next day in Savannah, so we wanted everything onboard to be shipshape for their arrival, and when all our tasks were completed, we walked across one of the town plazas to a lovely restaurant, The 4th of May, for a dinner of local southern dishes. On our return, we retired early in anticipation of a big travel day the next day.

May 15 – 82 miles to Savannah, Georgia[8]

This day's destination was the Savannah Yacht Club, just on the outskirts of the city of Savannah.

 Founded in 1733 by British General James Oglethorpe, the city of Savannah became the colonial capital of the Province of Georgia and later, the first state capital. Although attacked by federal troops during the American Civil War, Savannah was spared the destruction that took place in other southern cities, thus leaving many of its historic homes and buildings intact.

Today, Savannah is a mix of modern and historic buildings with an industrial center and an important Atlantic seaport. Each year, millions of visitors come to Savannah to enjoy the city's architecture and historic buildings, and its downtown area, which includes the Savannah Victorian Historic District, the Savannah Historic District, with its 22 park-like squares, is one of the largest National Historic Landmark Districts in the U.S.

At 6:40 a.m., we untied our lines and headed back down the Brunswick River to Saint Simons Inlet again. Our trip out to the ocean was calmer than the day before, and the waves seemed a little smaller and more on our stern, which made the motion easier. That was good because we had 60 miles to travel to Wassaw Sound.

Throughout the course of the day, the seas got calmer, and the warm sun made the ocean sparkle. As we approached the sound, we had to keep our eyes out for the uncharted inlet markers, which were placed quite a distance apart. Their spacing was not exactly the best of assistance for mariners like us who were unfamiliar with the area or for navigating through the shoals on each side of the inlet. It was not an easy task. It was just a "joy" to enter an unfamiliar inlet while straining your eyes to find the scattered buoys which are supposed to guide you in! This was definitely not one of our favorite things to do! Happily, we were able to eventually spot them all, and *Reflection* made her way in safely. Then, we headed up the busy Wilmington River toward the yacht club.

The Savannah Yacht Club — elegance in the old south

There were many vessels of all types out on the river, including many sailboats of various classes involved in Saturday racing regattas. We successfully maneuvered out of everybody's way, pulled into the dock at 2 p.m., and immediately phoned our friends to tell them that we had arrived. Having started out from New Jersey a day earlier, they had stopped overnight in Myrtle Beach, South Carolina, and picked up a rental car after dropping off their own car at the Myrtle Beach Yacht Club earlier that day. They said that they would not get to us until about 4 p.m., so that gave us time to shower, dress, and straighten up the boat. We then called Andrew and Clare, friends we had met two years ago here in Savannah, who had made the arrangements for us to dock there tonight, and invited them to come aboard for cocktails and munchies at 6 p.m.

After George and Linda arrived with their luggage, George returned the rental car to the airport, and Linda unpacked. Because of heavy traffic, we finally all convened on our aft deck at 6:30 p.m. It was so good to see our friends, and we ended up trading sailboat stories and going over some of our adventures on the Loop. We ended up going to one of the Savannah Yacht Club's lovely dining rooms for dinner, and it was obvious that Andrew and Clare were well-known club members by seeing all the people with whom they chatted and the wonderful attention we received from the staff at dinner. The food, atmosphere, and camaraderie were excellent, and Andrew was a more-than-gracious host by treating us to dinner. It was a truly fabulous evening!

May 16 – 46 miles to Beaufort, South Carolina[9]

Reflection was on her way to the Port Royal Landing Marina near Beaufort at 8 a.m., and our leisurely trip gave George and Linda a chance to get their sea legs on the 44-mile journey through the "Low Country." George is an amateur photographer, so his cameras were always "at the ready." The course wound through many twists and turns as we made our way through miles of marshland, past Hilton Head Island, and eventually Parris Island.

One of the many historical homes we saw in Beaufort

Finally, we arrived at the marina around 1 p.m., but after we were tied up, we experienced the bouncing that opposing wind and tide can create. At any rate, we got off the boat, borrowed the marina's courtesy car, and drove into Beaufort.

Beaufort was founded in 1711, and it is the second-oldest city in South Carolina after Charleston. The city is recognized for its scenic location and its impressive antebellum architecture. Like Savannah, although occupied by Union forces during the Civil War, it was spared, leaving most of the original structures unharmed. In spite of new development during the 20th century, Beaufort has retained much of its historic character through its renowned architecture and historic preservation efforts. The city celebrates several festivals during the year including: the Water Festival, a two-week extravaganza in the middle of July, the Shrimp Festival in October, and The Beaufort International Film Festival held in March, which screens independent-made films.

We found the Visitors' Center and then went down to the riverfront to board a carriage ride tour around this lovely city. The architecture of many of the homes dates back to the 1700s because it was largely saved from the destruction of the Civil War. The townspeople are also proud of the many movies that were filmed here, including "Forrest Gump." After our tour, we headed to the small outdoor restaurant at the marina for an early dinner and enjoyed the rest of the evening relaxing aboard.

An Angel Oak Tree, which is indigenous to coastal Carolina —
Some have been known to live up to 1,500 years.

May 17 – 71 miles to Charleston, South Carolina[10]

We began the day's 69-mile trip at 7 a.m. and again made our way through miles of marshland with Indian names for rivers, creeks, islands, and cutoffs like: Ashepoo, Coosaw, Toogoodoo, Stono, Wadmalaw, and Wappoo. We saw many dolphins playing in our wake and often diving underneath our bow, but so far, they had proved elusive to George and his cameras because they seemed to hide as soon as he picked up a camera to capture a picture.

It started to drizzle as we approached Charleston, and the wind was blowing in the upper teens. However, I was able to bring us safely into the dock at Charleston City Marina with the assistance of my capable crew and a quick-moving dockhand. Though again we had a swift running current, conditions eventually improved when the wind died down. Unlike our first trip along the Intracoastal Waterway, we had developed enough skill so that white-knuckle docking had pretty much become a thing of the past. After getting settled in, it was time for cocktails, dinner, and a pleasant evening aboard.

May 18 – Charleston, South Carolina

 Charleston was founded in 1670, was originally named Charles Town, and was located on the west bank of the Ashley River. In 1680, the city was moved to its present location, and it adopted its current name in 1783. It is known as "The Holy City" due to the prominence of its churches and to the fact that it was one of the few cities in the original 13 colonies to provide religious tolerance, as long as you were not Catholic. (Tolerance could only go so far!) In 1995, the city was recognized as the "best-mannered city" in the U.S., and the distinction lent credibility for the establishment of the first Livability Court in the country. (Be nice or else!) Charleston is steeped in history from the colonial era through the American Revolution, but it is most noted for the firing on its Fort Sumter that started the Civil War. History buffs, this is your kind of town!

The Admiral and I spent some time in the morning taking care of necessary business items and making phone calls, but afterward, we were all ready to take the marina's 11 a.m. shuttle bus into town. Because it was George and Linda's first visit to Charleston, we suggested that we take another narrated carriage ride to give them an overview of the historic district. It turned out to be a good idea, and when it was over, we headed to the market area with its several buildings full of merchandise stands. We then had lunch at an Irish pub, walked around a bit more, and then took the shuttle back to the marina. We bought a few breakfast items at the marina store and then headed out to our boat for a quiet evening aboard.

Dock Street Theatre, the oldest theater in the U.S., located in Charleston.

May 19 — 69 miles to Georgetown, South Carolina[11]

Our destination of Georgetown Landing Marina was a 69-mile trip, so we started out at 7 a.m. We made our way past Isle of Palms, Goat Island, and through many miles of the Cape Romain Wildlife Refuge. It was through this area that we finally broke out the fly swatters and bug spray, and at one point we even went down below to operate the boat from the lower station. If the bugs were here, summer could not be far behind.

We arrived around 2 p.m., rested, and had cocktails aboard, followed by dinner at the restaurant on the marina grounds. The food was excellent, and we had a lovely view of the waterway. The marina is a hub for tournament fishing boats, and the sight of all their out-riggers in the air made a lovely evening sight at sunset. Again the current ran swiftly here, and we were glad that the wind had died down so we would not bounce too much during the inevitable opposing wind and tide cycle.

May 20 — 29 miles to Myrtle Beach, South Carolina[12]

Before heading out, I walked to the local convenience store to get us hot dogs for lunch and some additional breakfast items, and after breakfast aboard, we took a cab into Georgetown.

Some historians claim that American history began in Georgetown in 1526 with the earliest settlement in North America by Europeans with African slaves. It is believed that the Spanish founded a colony in the area. However, it did not last. The colony failed for a variety of reasons, including disease and a revolt of the African slaves. Those who remained failed as farmers. They eventually decided that enough was enough and sailed away.

Things got going again when, in 1729, Elisha Screven laid the plan for Georgetown and developed the city in a 4-by-8-block grid. Today, the grid is referred to as the Historic District of the city and maintains the original street names and many of the original homes. Georgetown played an important part in the American Revolution with its port supplying General Nathanael Greene's army in the latter part of the conflict. Georgetown, like some of the other towns we had visited, was also mostly spared the ravages of the Civil War, thus leaving most of its antebellum structures and outlying plantations intact.

On our cab ride into town, we found out that our driver was one of the town council members, and for the entire ten-minute trip, he regaled us with local stories and his opinions on politics. We started out at the Visitors' Center and again opted for a narrated tram tour provided by Swamp Fox Tours to get an overview of the town, which is the third oldest city in South Carolina, and once rivaled Charleston as South Carolina's major port.

During its boom time of indigo and rice farming, Georgetown developed into a town with truly beautiful architecture, and many of its homes are marked with building plates from the 1700s, 1800s, and 1900s.

We enjoyed our tour immensely, including the visit to an African Methodist Episcopal Church, learning about General Francis Marion, a revolutionary war hero (aka Swamp Fox) who eluded the British and rescued American prisoners, and listening to narratives about the French Huguenots who settled the area and those specific to particular homes. Enormous oak trees and palmettos lined the streets, and Pat, in particular, fell in love with the town. We will be sure to stop again and tour the revitalized downtown shopping area when we travel south in the fall.

Our group returned to the boat at noon, untied our lines, and headed out to the Intracoastal Waterway. We made our way up the lovely Waccamaw River, which we remembered from our trip two years earlier. Traveling on the river, we could see oak trees with Spanish moss along our way and speculated about the rice plantations that existed there years ago. Our destination was Osprey Marina in Myrtle Beach, South Carolina, a stop on a sheltered turn-off only 20 miles away.

One of the many historic homes in Georgetown

The first Europeans came to the Myrtle Beach area in the second half of 18th century and attempted to start a plantation growing indigo and tobacco. However, the sandy soil produced poor yields and low-quality crops. Before the American Revolution, the area along the future Grand Strand was uninhabited. About that time, several families received land grants to settle here, but most did not last long. The last remaining family was all but wiped out in a hurricane in 1822, and the survivors decided it was time to go, so they abandoned the area. The region regressed back to its natural state until 1899 when the Conway Seashore Railroad came into the area to transport timber from the coast to inland customers. On weekends, the railroad and lumber employees would take train flatcars down to the beach, and they became the first Grand Strand tourists. By 1901, The Seaside Inn was opened nearby, and the area was on its way to becoming a vacation destination. Today, it hosts more than 14.6 million visitors annually. People come to Myrtle Beach for its oceanfront, golf courses, amusement parks, an aquarium, retail shops, and more than 1,900 restaurants.

We made good time traveling to Osprey Marina and pulled into its gas dock at 3:15 p.m. Even though we had filled up with fuel at Brunswick, Georgia, only six days ago, I wanted to top off our tanks again because Osprey's prices were also good. While I was doing that, Pat somehow slipped on the steps coming down from the flybridge and fell down hard on her behind onto our back deck. Though shaken and in pain, she immediately applied ice to her neck and tail area and was well enough to have pizza for dinner and to play a game of Train Dominoes with everyone that evening. Sometimes, you just have to party through the pain!

May 21 – 29 miles to Little River, South Carolina[13]

Our *Reflection* crew took a relaxed approach to getting started in the morning, and the Admiral was especially moving slowly as she nursed aches from yesterday's fall. However, we finally got underway at 9 a.m. for a 27-mile trip to the Myrtle Beach Yacht Club. The journey was scenic, and everything was going along well until we got a call on the radio from a boat from Cinnaminson, New Jersey, that wanted to pass us. Waterway boating etiquette dictated that we should slow down, move out of the way slightly, and allow the boat to pass. However, we forgot that we were in an area known as the Rock Pile, a stretch with rock ledges on the sides of the channel. Unfortunately, when we moved over, we bumped a piece of the ledge — not a nice sound or feeling! Pat and I looked at each other with dread, and after having traveled thousands of miles without damage, we were hopeful that *Reflection* would come away from the incident unscathed — but that was not the case.

At the time of impact, we were running on the port engine only. We frequently run on only one engine when traveling along at 7 knots, which is our speed most of the time. However, when I started up the starboard engine as well, there was a strong vibration coming from that side. My stomach went into a knot, and things got quiet on the boat. We all knew we had a serious problem, but how serious it was, we could not tell.

We limped carefully into the Myrtle Beach Yacht Club only a few miles away. While guiding *Reflection* into the entrance channel, I was concerned about my lack of maneuverability in this confined area. As we approached the dock, I engaged the starboard engine but used it sparingly while docking so I would not cause any more damage to the propeller and shaft assembly. The docking went without incident, and we were glad to be tied up.

The dockmaster suggested that we contact Rod, a local diver who lived aboard his boat in the marina, to evaluate the problem. Within an hour, Rod arrived and went to work. Although the visibility in the water was limited, he could see that

---

[13] *See notes on page 292*

the prop was bent, and fortunately, he was eventually able to get it off. Rod then took it to be repaired at a local prop shop that afternoon. We decided to have him put on the two spare four-blade props that we carried aboard, but because the hour was getting late, Rod would have to continue the repair job the next day. Because George and Linda were also leaving us the next day, we had a farewell dinner at the marina's restaurant with hopes that our repair would be quickly completed.

George and George waiting for the diver to surface with the damage report

May 22 – Little River, South Carolina

Linda graciously drove Pat to the supermarket in the morning, and we waited for Rod's return with the fixed prop and for him to make the transfer of the spare ones onto the shafts. Things moved slowly, so George and Linda, who were waiting to see the completion of the job, finally had to leave so that they could get to their hotel in Richmond, Virginia that night at a reasonable time. We had enjoyed a delightful week having them aboard and hoped that we might have possibly tweaked their interest in trawler cruising.

A few hours later, Rod finally completed the prop transfer job, and it was time to start up the engines to see how things sounded. Then, we experienced our third trip surprise! Despite the change of props, *Reflection* still had a major vibration on the starboard side, which could only mean that the shaft was bent. We were not "happy campers" because that meant our boat would have to be lifted out of the water for repair. We contacted Anchor Marina, which was only about a mile away. They had a travel-lift large enough to haul us out, but because it was late Saturday afternoon, nothing could be done until early Monday morning. Rod was willing to continue to work with us and agreed to meet us at the boatyard after the boat was taken out to help me take the shaft out for its eventual replacement or repair at that time. The weather that afternoon also deteriorated, and we encountered the first heavy rain and thundershowers on our entire trip north. With the weather matching our mood, we had a quick fried chicken dinner aboard and licked our wounds. All we could do was to wait for Monday and hope all would go well.

The captain watches as the diver takes the replacement propeller down.

Notes:

(1)

There are two routes from Marathon to Miami: Florida Bay (inside route) and Hawk Channel (outside route). The Florida Bay route, although more sheltered than the Hawk Channel route, has numerous shallow spots. If you draw more than 4 feet, use caution. Be careful when traveling through side channels off the Intracoastal Waterway route because they are often shallow and the charts might be unreliable.

(2)

Key Largo — Anchorage Resort and Marina has transient dockage at competitive prices for the area and is located on the Intracoastal Waterway.

(3)

With rare exception, all the bridges north of Miami along the Florida Intracoastal Waterway are on an opening schedule. Consult published guidebooks for times. Be careful along the route because most of it is a "No Wake" zone.

(4)

Titusville Municipal Marina has a friendly and helpful staff, transient rates that are reasonably priced for Florida, a laundry facility, and restaurants nearby. It is directly across from the Kennedy Space Center.

(5)

*There is shoaling in the Matanzas Inlet area of Intracoastal Waterway. See **http:// cruisersnet.net/category/all-other-news/icw-problem-areas** for all Atlantic Intracoastal Waterway Problem Stretches (Norfolk, Virginia, to Miami, Florida).*

Saint Augustine Municipal Marina is located on the Intracoastal Waterway immediately south of the Bridge of Lions. A strong current runs through the marina, so be careful docking, especially in a cross wind with the current running. Transient rates are average for the area, and it has a laundry facility on-site with many restaurants and attractions nearby.

(6)

Fernandina Harbor Marina is right on Intracoastal Waterway with floating docks and a large tidal range. It has a friendly and helpful staff, transient rates that are average for the area, a laundry facility, and about 20 restaurants nearby.

(7)

Beware of the Georgia Intracoastal Waterway because it has large tidal ranges and swift currents. There are several sections that have less than 4 feet of water at low tide, so see the Cruisers Net website for details. Take the ocean route, if possible.

Ocean Petroleum in Brunswick consistently has the lowest diesel fuel prices in Florida or Georgia. Call them at (912) 265-2275.

Brunswick Landing Marina is a full-service marina with transient rates that are average for the area. It has a free laundry facility, nearby restaurants, some shopping and is a short cab ride to a supermarket.

(8)
Wassaw Inlet — The buoys between R"2W" and G"9" are uncharted and spread far apart, use extreme caution transiting this area.

(9)
Port Royal Landing Marina has a courtesy car, a laundry facility, a restaurant on the premises, a friendly, helpful staff, and is fairly close to historic Beaufort and shopping.

(10)
Through Charleston City Marina is exposed to harbor traffic, it has transient rates competitive for this area, a laundry facility, a small convenience store, and a free shuttle to the downtown/historic district.

(11)
Georgetown Landing Marina is located just off the Intracoastal Waterway, has reasonable transient rates with a BoatUS discount, a laundry facility, convenience store, and restaurant nearby and is a short cab ride to the historic district.

(12)
Osprey Marina is located just off the Intracoastal Waterway. It is sheltered, has reasonable transient rates with a major discount after a three-day stay, low fuel prices, a BoatUS discount on fuel, and a laundry facility and restaurant on the premises (breakfast and lunch). A local restaurant will also pick you up.

(13)
Rockpile — Use extreme caution when traveling between Miles 347 and 353 on the Intracoastal Waterway. The rocks just outside the channel are unforgiving, so stay in the middle. Before entering the area, call a Security on channel 16 because you do not want to be caught in the area with a tow coming the other way as there is no room to hide.

Myrtle Beach Yacht Club welcomes all boaters and has transient rates that are average for the area, plus a BoatUS discount. There is a laundry facility and restaurant on-site.

Chapter 15

Tying Up the "Loop" Ends

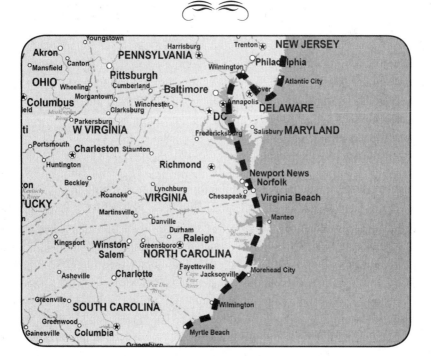

May 23 — Little River, South Carolina

It was a quiet day aboard as I prepared the boat to move tomorrow. Pat cleaned and packed up clothes, important papers, and other essentials so that we could get off the boat while it is out of the water and move to a hotel room. Luckily, there is a Hampton Inn close to the boatyard, so the only issue was not knowing how long we would be staying there because we did not know how long the repair process would take.

We were not missing any good weather on the water because there had been more thunderstorms in the afternoon, and more were forecast for that night and the next day to be followed by another coastal low coming in from the Bahamas and potentially working its way up the coast with strong northeast winds that week. Maybe we were just not meant to be in the Cape Hatteras area now. All we know is that everything happens for a reason and works for the good, so we expect a good outcome from the whole experience. How bending a prop and shaft would result in a good outcome, however, was beyond my comprehension.

May 24 — Little River, South Carolina[1]

We got a call from Anchor Marina early in the morning telling us that we could come right into their travel lift at 8:45 a.m. We pulled out of Myrtle Beach Yacht Club at 8:20 a.m. and *Reflection* was quickly and efficiently lifted out of the water and blocked up on jack-stands by 9:15 a.m. There, I had my first look at how much the shaft was bent. It was hard to believe that our slight bump on the rock ledge could have caused such damage to the propeller shaft, and it was severe enough that I had my doubts that it could even be straightened.

Before I worked on the shaft, one of the marina workers drove us over to the hotel, and we were checked into our room immediately. While Pat stayed at the hotel, I returned to the boat to work with Rod on removing the shaft. First, we had to sand the shaft smooth to remove any marine growth that had stuck to it. That was necessary because we were going to have to slide the shaft through several bearings that support it underwater. Next we unbolted the shaft coupling from the transmission. Once the coupling was off the shaft, we were finally ready to pull the shaft out. Then the real fun began! We applied liquid soap to the shaft, which had two consequences: It lubricated it so that it would slide through the bearings, and it made it slippery and difficult to pull it out. Slowly, it started to move, and it began to come out of the boat and pass through the underwater bearings. However, the farther it came out, the more Rod and I had to support it. The 14-foot, 2-inch thick piece of solid stainless steel was heavy. After what seemed like forever, it finally was out. What first seemed like a simple task (yet I often think that there are no simple tasks on a boat) turned out to be a monumental job that took most of the day.

After it was removed and the owner of a local prop shop inspected it, the verdict was that it would have to be taken to a larger shop in Wilmington, North Carolina, for repair if possible, or else we would have to have a new one fashioned — an expensive proposition. Rod got a trailer to move it, and he was planning to drive it to Wilmington early the next morning to see if it could be straightened.

I was filthy and exhausted when I got back to the hotel, and we opted to have pizza delivered to our room rather than to go out for dinner. It was a good idea because I could barely walk. It made Pat happy because she got to watch the "Dancing with the Stars" dance finals — which quickly put me to sleep.

May 25 — Little River, South Carolina[2]

While eating breakfast we got an early morning phone call from Rod, who was already at the Wilmington prop shop with our shaft. The verdict was that they could straighten it this time. I was relieved, but if it were hit again, we would have to spring for a brand new shaft. The good news also was that they would have it ready in a few hours if Rod would stick around and wait for it, which he was willing to do. Things were now going our way! I then went down to the boatyard to work on some other small repairs and clean the bottom of the boat while it was out of the water.

When Rod arrived at the marina in the late morning, we managed to get the now-straightened shaft back into the boat with a fraction of the effort it took to get it out. The last piece of the puzzle now fell into place when the boatyard said that they could launch us the next day so we could be on our way again the following morning. We were eager to get moving so that we could see our godson, Chris, and his new bride, Lindsey, in Wrightsville Beach, North Carolina. Our plan was to arrive in our homeport of Seawood Harbor sometime between June 8 and June 12. That was when we would cross our wake and complete the Loop.

In the evening, we went to Captain Poo's Bar and Grill, which is on Anchor Marina's property. The place was hopping! It reminded us of the dances we used to go to in our high school years in the 1960s, but now everyone there was in their 60s and up. The music was good, everyone was singing and dancing, and it was 35-cent wing and taco night. We had a good time and laughs as we ate, "people watched," and celebrated our repair. On returning to the hotel, we (Pat) finished off the evening by viewing the results show of "Dancing with the Stars" on TV. It was a wonderful night!

May 26 — Little River, South Carolina

Because *Reflection* was scheduled to be launched around high tide late in the day and Pat discovered that our hotel had a coin laundry, she took advantage of their facilities to do our wash while waiting for me to come back from the marina after doing the finishing touches on our vessel. We asked for a late checkout, and the hotel was glad to accommodate us, but we still had to wait around in

---

[2] *See notes on page 321*

their lounge area until the marina's crew was ready. Rod also came back to get his check and to see how everything was going, and then we all went back to the marina for the launch.

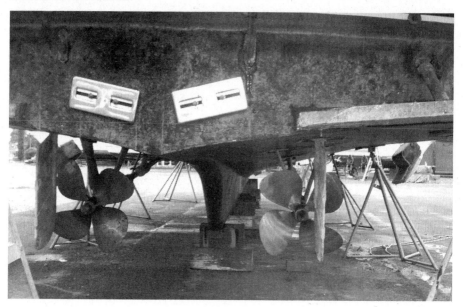

With new props and straight shafts, we are ready for the launch.

Reflection has her own wood blocks that hang over the sides to protect her fiberglass exhausts from being squeezed by a travel-lift's straps when she is lifted. The starboard block was put in place, however, the yard staff wanted to use their block on the port side. I do not like to tell people how to do their job, so I said all right. Just as the slings were tightened and *Reflection* was getting pulled up, we heard a loud crack, and one of the staff started yelling! When we ran over to see what had happened, we saw that the block on the port side had rolled, and the fiberglass exhaust on that side was crushed. My heart fell into my stomach. To say the least, this was not supposed to happen.

The marina staff was extremely embarrassed and apologetic, and within minutes, they began to make repairs. However, the job would take time, and it was already near 5 p.m. Then it started to rain. We knew we would have to spend another night at the Hampton Inn and would be delayed another day because of the additional repair. So we got our bags, which we had not even unpacked, off the boat, and went back to the hotel. I thought of returning to Captain Poo's for dinner, but neither one of us was in the mood for any kind of celebration, so we settled for cocktails and Domino's Pizza in the same hotel room in which we had spent the past two nights.

As we start to be lifted, we heard a crunch.

May 27 — Little River, South Carolina

Last evening and this morning, I had several conference calls with Bo, the previous owner of our boat. I got some additional tips on how the boatyard should correctly lift *Reflection* with her blocks, and then I discussed them with the yard manager. I also found out that the marina staff had stayed and worked on the fiberglass repair until 9 p.m. the previous night, and we appreciated their efforts in attempting to remedy the mishap in a professional manner. In the early afternoon, we got a call from the yard that they were again ready to launch "our girl." As we quickly left the hotel for what we hoped would be the final time, a marina staff member picked us up and took us by golf cart to the launch site.

By the time we reached our boat, she was already in the slings and being moved to the launch area. We got the "kid glove" treatment because she was slowly, carefully, and gently lowered into the water, and then we were assisted aboard. Everyone held their breaths as we started up the engines and backed out of the travel-lift and into the dock area at the marina. The engines sounded good, and the new props and shaft had no vibration. We were then happy boaters once more! It, indeed, was a good day, so Pat and I again celebrated with drinks and dinner at Captain Poo's in anticipation of finally continuing our journey tomorrow.

Reflection being gently lowered into the water, and this time there was no crunch

Reflection sitting back in the water where she belongs

May 28 — 65 miles to Wrightsville Beach, North Carolina[3]

We pulled out of Anchor Marina at 6:30 a.m. for our 65-mile trip to the Seapath Yacht Club in Wrightsville Beach, where our godson, Chris, and his new bride, Lindsey, were scheduled to meet us in the evening.

Development first started in Wrightsville Beach with the building of the Carolina Yacht Club in 1853. Continued growth in the area was spurred along when a train line was constructed from Wilmington to the beach in 1888. The line was later converted to electric streetcars, which began the era of the beach trolley, but by 1940, the automobile had derailed the trolleys. In 1905 the Lumina Pavilion opened. It housed an entertainment center with a large dance floor and attracted numerous entertainers, including most of the famous big bands, until it closed in 1973. Today, the biggest attraction is the beach with its many hotels and seaside restaurants that beckon tourists to the area.

It was a pleasant ride north to Wrightsville Beach as we passed a number of inlets, and then we encountered the Cape Fear River with the current going against us. *Reflection* handled every situation well, and I was happy with the smoothness of our four-blade props.

The last floating (pontoon) bridge on the Intracoastal Waterway —
The high bridge will soon replace it.

---

[3] *See notes on page 321*

The floating bridge in the open position, allowing us to pass through

As we got closer to Wrightsville Beach, it was obvious that Memorial Day weekend had started because there was much more boat traffic in the area, and slip space at the yacht club suddenly became scarce. Chris and Lindsey, who live in nearby Carolina Beach, arrived at the boat a lot later than they had hoped because of traffic delays, but we were just happy to see them.

They were married on May 1, but we had not been able to attend their wedding because of our trip, so we were thrilled to have them aboard for a separate celebration, to give them their wedding gift in person, and to take them out for dinner. We asked them to bring some wedding pictures, and after dinner, we went back to the boat so that Pat could "ooh" and "aah" over every single one. They are a lovely couple, and we know that they will be happy together.

May 29 — 57 miles to Swansboro, North Carolina[4]

We were on our way this morning at 7:35 a.m. to make the opening of the Wrightsville Beach Bridge, which only opens once an hour, on the hour. It was the first of four bridges we would encounter that day that would only open at certain times. This forces the boater to plan his or her speed and timing with precision. If you are late for an opening, your wait could cost you an hour of

---

[4] *See notes on page 321*

your trip, and if you are too early, you will have to waste fuel while idling, or else anchor, if you can. Luckily, we were good at figuring all this out, and we made our way through smoothly.

Along the waterway in this area, you see some interesting things, such as a house with a full-size statue of a giraffe in its yard and another home on a small strip of land that is painted the brightest shade of shocking pink. I cannot imagine what the owners were thinking. Well, at least it gets everyone's attention!

You see everything on the Intracoastal Waterway,
including a house with the statue of a giraffe.

Our destination today was Swansboro, North Carolina.

Swansboro was first incorporated as a town in 1783. It takes its name from Samuel Swann, who was a Speaker in the North Carolina House of Commons and a local resident. In 1818, the first steamboat constructed in North Carolina, the Prometheus, was built here, and Swansboro has earned the reputation of being "The Friendly City by the Sea," a title that seems to be correct as far as we can tell.

By the time we arrived at Dudley's Marina on the waterway for fuel and dockage, there was holiday boat traffic with much accompanying wakes as people traveled in and out of nearby Bogue Inlet. We did manage to tie up and get fuel, but we were not thrilled with the bouncing at the marina's face dock. One of our fenders got caught between the boat and a piling and exploded! Having an exploded fender, compared to having a bent propeller and shaft, is a minor inconvenience, and we had to keep things in perspective. Later on, we borrowed their courtesy vehicle, used it to make a quick trip to the grocery store, and loaded up on a week's provisions. Pat and I relaxed for the rest of the afternoon and evening, and luckily, the boat traffic eventually died down.

May 30 – 58 miles to Oriental, North Carolina[5]

The fishermen started pulling in early that morning at the marina for fuel, so we took that as our signal to start moving. Our trip took us past busy Morehead City, Beaufort Inlet, and the city of Beaufort. Small boats loaded with families and friends were everywhere, and we dodged so many of them that we thought that we were back in New Jersey transiting Barnegat Inlet. Luckily, we have had practice!

Our friends Andrew and Sallyann, aboard their boat, *Freedom*, were staying at our dock at home for the weekend. They started out from Kentucky, and though they left Florida ahead of us, they have many more legs of their trip to finish before they "cross their wake", whereas we will be finishing our trip on the Loop shortly. Since they were in the New Jersey area, we invited them to stay at our dock, but we advised them not to transit out of Manasquan Inlet until Tuesday, so that they do not have to encounter the "crazies" coming in or out from the ocean on this holiday weekend.

After many more miles, the scenery opened up when we entered the Neuse River (the widest river in the U.S.) near Oriental and the beginning of wide Pamlico Sound.

 Various native people who fished and farmed first settled the Neuse River area before Europeans came here. During the colonial era, the area had an infamous resident Edward Teach, better known as Blackbeard, living in Bath just north of town. From the beginning of the 20th century, Oriental's economy was based on lumber, fishing, and farming, but in the early 1960s, the last sawmill closed. Luckily, it was about that time that sailors found Oriental, and the number of sailboats that call Oriental their homeport went from four to more than 2,000 today. This is a curious fact because there are only about 900 residents in the town, but it is the abundance of sailboats that allows Oriental to call itself "The Sailing Capital of North Carolina."

We finished our 58-mile trip at lovely River Dunes Harbor Yacht Club, which is part of a planned community of homes and condos on sheltered Broad Creek off the Intracoastal Waterway. The facilities, docks, and setting are lovely. We spent a quiet evening aboard, got involved in watching a *Godfather* movie on TV, and ended up staying awake much later than we probably should have.

May 31 — 43 miles to Belhaven, North Carolina[6]

Our destination today was Belhaven, North Carolina.

Belhaven is a small town of friendly people with a few shops, a hardware store, and restaurants. The area is most notable for its abundance of wildlife, including whitetail deer, black bears, rabbits, squirrels, quail, swans, and varieties of ducks and geese. It is not exactly a mega-city!

As we left River Dunes and made our way into the large waters of the Pamlico River, we had to keep our eyes open for the many crab pots in the area that were hard to see in the bright morning sunlight.

The Intracoastal Waterway path then led us north into the Pungo River and many miles later to a 90-degree turn near the town of Belhaven, which we had earlier considered as a destination. However, after reading about the storm barrier in front of its town docks, which only offers moderate protection from wind and waves, we decided to go on to the Dowry Creek Marina located a little farther north because of its shelter from the southerly winds that pick up almost every afternoon.

It was a small rural marina that a woman runs herself, and we tied up with the assistance of the boaters who stayed there. They have a small pool and clubhouse, and we were invited to a late afternoon get-together there, but we opted to have our own Memorial Day dinner of barbecued ribs aboard.

Since leaving Little River, South Carolina, where we had our repairs made, I noted to myself that things had been tranquil as far as weather and boat operation were concerned. That is just the way I like it!

[6] *See notes on page 321*

June 1 — 53 miles to Columbia, North Carolina[7]

We cast off our lines before 7 a.m. and continued north up the Pungo River while reminiscing about our anchorage in this area two years earlier. *Reflection* soon entered the 20-mile long Alligator-Pungo Canal, a narrow manmade waterway that is quite scenic but where the boater must also be wary of the many stumps and snags located along its banks and must stay in the middle of its channel. Considering our recent prop and shaft adventure, we were careful en route.

The Alligator-Pungo Canal — Observe the stumps and snags.

There were sailboats motoring slower than we were on this stretch, but we were always considerate and called each on the radio requesting permission to make a slow pass with minimal wake. Each of them was gracious as expected, and we ended up becoming a forward lookout for the vessels behind us as we spotted and moved around a number of deadheads in the water.

One of the more "charming" aspects of traveling through the canal was the water color: It was as dark as black coffee, and it was not a product of man-made pollution. Its color comes from the natural tannins of the trees and vegetation from the marshes through which the waterway cuts, but it left its mark on *Reflection* in the form of a dark tan discolor on the bow, which is better known as "waterway stain".

We then finally entered the wide Alligator River and headed for the Alligator River Swing Bridge that is close to the entrance of the somewhat notorious Albemarle Sound. Our destination was the Alligator River Marina in Columbia, North Carolina, just beyond the bridge.

---

[7] *See notes on page 321*

The only historical site near Columbia is Somerset Place, an antebellum plantation dating back to 1785 that was the home of the Collins family and their 300-plus slaves of African descent. A visit there offers a view of plantation life during the antebellum period.

When we made our turn west into the channel that leads to the marina, we rocked and rolled our way into the harbor because we had the wind hard on our beam. Conditions calmed down immediately as we cleared the breakwater, and we were tied up safely only a short time later.

Many additional transient boats made their way in there all afternoon because it was the only fuel stop and dockage for 86 miles. Pat and I started playing a game of Train Dominoes late in the afternoon and only took a break around 6 p.m. to pick up burgers at the marina's grill. There, we met a couple that hoped to do the Loop next year in their newly purchased Monk trawler, *Journey*.

Tom and Melissa live in Swansboro, North Carolina, and because he is a Harbor Host for the American's Great Loop Cruisers' Association, he invited us to call them on our way south in the fall. It was only Melissa's fourth day on the boat, and Pat was stunned to learn that her responsibility onboard was taking care of the engine room! That was quite a turnabout from most cruising couples, but because Tom had knee problems, Melissa was quite willing to take on the job. We traded stories with them and another gentleman who was captaining a $1 million Regal powerboat from Florida to Stamford, Connecticut, and then we returned to the boat to continue our game.

June 2 – 73 miles to Great Bridge, Virginia[8]

We left the marina at 6 a.m. for our 73-mile trip to Atlantic Yacht Basin in Great Bridge, Virginia.

Great Bridge gets its name from the American Revolutionary War Battle of Great Bridge, which took place on December 9, 1775 and resulted in the removal of British government from Virginia. Though the battles of Lexington and Concord are historically more memorable, the Battle of Great Bridge was strategically the most important colonial victory over the British.

The winds were light, and the sun was coming up when we left, but as we traveled across the mighty Albemarle, we noticed several dark cloud banks, and then the

---

[8] *See notes on page 321*

wind picked up from the northwest — not the direction that had been predicted. Conditions got lumpy, and the clouds got darker, but we made the crossing safely and without any rain.

In 2008, we had taken the Dismal Swamp Route north, but on this trip we decided to follow the sparsely populated Virginia Cut route, which is 3 miles shorter and would take us up Coinjock Bay, Currituck Sound, and the North Landing River nearer Cape Hatteras and the Outer Banks. Our decision was also based on the fact that we could go through several timed swing bridges today, and with the marina's location being only 12 miles from Norfolk, we would then have to go through only one lock and a few timed bridges the next day, which would allow us to arrive in Norfolk early tomorrow.

After we tied up at the marina at 2 p.m., from our slip's vantage point, we watched the boats that were waiting for the Great Bridge Bascule Bridge to open (once an hour), and then the Lock opening up right after it. It was a busy spot, and we were glad we had decided to wait to go through until the next morning. Besides, we had to finish off our Train Dominoes game!

June 3 — 13 miles to Norfolk, Virginia[9]

At 7:45 a.m., I called the Great Bridge bridge tender and told him we were pulling away from the dock at Atlantic Yacht Basin for the 8 a.m. scheduled opening. That would then coincide with the opening of the last lock on our journey (No. 104), the Great Bridge Lock. Once we got through the bridge, we tied up quickly at the lock and were then lowered only 2 feet — quite a difference from some of our other locking experiences!

After the lock opened, we were grouped together with two other powerboats and one sailboat for our last timed bridge openings, with only two more highway and three railroad bridges through which to pass. We eventually went through the series of bridges pretty well, except for an approximate half-hour delay for a train with 99 coal cars at the Norfolk Southern Bascule Bridge. Admiral Pat counted off every car as they went over the bridge, and I can tell you, she is precise!

The area soon became industrial with many shipyards and other marine facilities along the way. We then stopped at the Ocean Marine Yacht Center in Portsmouth for fuel and then headed across the Elizabeth River to Waterside Marina in Norfolk, where we arrived at 11 a.m. It had taken us three hours to go just 12 miles.

---

[9] *See notes on page 322*

Great Bridge Lock, Lock 104 — the final lock on our Great Loop adventure

 Norfolk was named after Norfolk, England, the birthplace of Adam Thoroughgood, a former indentured servant who became an influential landowner in the area in the mid-1600s. Norfolk grew in the late 17th century when Half Moone Fort (in the shape of a half moon) was constructed and a 50-acre parcel of land was acquired in exchange for 10,000 pounds of tobacco. It was incorporated in 1705, and in 1736, George II of England granted Norfolk a royal charter as a borough. By 1775, it was the most prosperous city in Virginia based on its import and export operations with Great Britain. That tradition continues on today because Norfolk (port of Virginia) is one of the largest ports in the U.S., handling nearly 50 million tons of cargo each year.

Once *Reflection* was tied up, I took the opportunity to clean the outside of the boat during the afternoon while Pat worked on our blog and made phone calls, and in the evening we walked into the Waterside Festival Marketplace. We had been there many times before, but we were surprised to see how quiet it was that night. Many of the restaurants appeared closed, and we finally went to the Outback Steakhouse. We had a nice dinner, and eventually, the restaurant filled up with a mostly young crowd, but as for the rest of the establishments, we could not tell if they were only open on the weekends or if being closed was a sign of financial difficulties.

The cruise ship Enchantment of the Seas *making a U-turn in front of our dock, so it could head out of the harbor*

As we returned to the boat, I began thinking about our Great Loop journey, and I was beginning to feel sad that in a few short days the adventure of a lifetime would be over. Sure, it will be nice to be home, but I still could not get enthused about ending this trip. Maybe it is the wanderer in me, because I just wanted to keep on going. I did not want it to end.

June 4 — 62 miles to Deltaville, Virginia[10]

After an easy departure from Waterside Marina at 5:40 a.m., we headed out into the Elizabeth River. This passage is interesting because the sides of the river are lined with commercial ships of every description and with the numerous U.S. Naval warships that are stationed at Norfolk Naval Base, the largest naval installation in the world.

Patrol boats that guard the berthed Navy ships strictly enforce a security zone, and it is fascinating to hear some of the ship crews talking on the radio about their intentions to pull out to sea or vice versa. We even heard one ship talking to a recreational vessel to get out of the way as it was pulling in. Any smart person would not want to be in the way of one of these destroyers or aircraft carriers!

[10] *See notes on page 322*

A U.S. Naval ship in one of the many dry docks located along the waterway

The container ship CMA CGM New Jersey passes us slowly in the busy port.

We had a pleasant crossing of the Hampton Roads area, where the Monitor and Merrimac had their Civil War sea battle, and then we entered the wide lower Chesapeake Bay. Our trip north was tranquil, and we arrived at Dozier's Regatta Point Yachting Center in Deltaville on the Rappahannock River at 2 p.m. It was a lovely facility with a pool, captains' lounge, courtesy car, newspaper, and continental breakfast in the morning, and we planned to spend more time there on our trip south in the fall.

 Deltaville is a small, unincorporated community of between 500 to 800 full-time residents. The numbers swell into the thousands in the summer months due to the sailing and fishing opportunities in the nearby waters of the Chesapeake Bay. The town's main industry was originally boat building done mostly for commercial bay watermen. That era is long gone, and today, its economy is based on farming and the operations of marinas that dot the area.

That afternoon, we got *Reflection* and ourselves cleaned up for the much-anticipated visit of our dear friend, Judy. Judy has lived in this area for the past 20 years, and she and her deceased husband, Jack, have always held a special place in our hearts. They were mentors to us when we all lived in Brick, New Jersey, and were fellow members of the Bristol Sailing Club, an organization we had joined more than 30 years ago.

She and her friend, Agnes, arrived at 6 p.m. for cocktails, and despite their mutual knee and hip problems, they were able to climb aboard and take a tour of *Reflection*. We caught up on all our mutual activities, and one could not meet two more amiable, upbeat, active senior ladies than these two. It was then time to go out for dinner, and Agnes, at the age of 91, was our driver. She knew her way around the rural roads, and we had an enjoyable dinner at Cocomo's, a local watering hole.

We returned to the marina about 10 p.m. and said our goodbyes to Judy and Agnes with hugs and kisses all around and made plans to see them again in the fall and hopefully in Florida next winter.

June 5 — 62 miles to Solomons, Maryland[11]

Because we (especially Pat) are early-morning risers, we pulled away from the dock that morning at 6:20 a.m. for our 62-mile trip to Solomons Harbor Marina. The winds were supposed to be out of the southwest at 10 to 15 mph, but it was more westerly, which meant we again were taking the waves on our stern quar-

---

ter to port beam, giving us a rocking motion. The conditions were manageable, however, and after we passed the Potomac River, the waves lightened up, the sun shone, and all was right with the world.

Passing Point No Point Lighthouse on our way north

As we approached the Patuxent River and the Patuxent Naval Air Station, a large Navy transport jet was practicing a series of takeoffs and landings right over our boat. On one of the maneuvers, Pat almost jumped out of her skin as the plane came roaring in for a landing only hundreds of feet over our flybridge. I kept shouting for her to take a picture, since the plane was so close that we could wave to the pilot as it approached!

U.S. Navy transport right above us — what a roar!

A little while later we listened to the Marine Weather on the radio. The next day's weather forecast sounded somewhat questionable: small craft warnings and winds out of the southwest with gusts up to 25 mph and strong thunderstorms. We would monitor the situation and decide whether to move on tomorrow or stay put in Solomons for another day.

When we got tied up at the marina, we found out that the dockmaster, Bill, had also been in Marathon, Florida, for a number of months during the past winter, just as we had. It is such a small world. Pat then headed to the hotel's laundry facility, and I headed to the grocery store to do some shopping. Solomons has long been one of our favorite stops on the Chesapeake.

 The community known today as Solomons or Solomons Island was originally called Bourne's Island in the 1600s and then Somervell's Island in the 1700s. Shortly after the Civil War, a businessman from Baltimore, Isaac Solomon, built a cannery here, and his name stuck. Besides the cannery, boat building, which supported the work of the local fishermen, became a thriving business in the 19th century. Solomons played an important part in World War II because it was the location for training more than 60,000 troops in mostly amphibious operations. Ironically, many of the servicemen who trained here were sent to fight at the Solomon Islands in the Pacific. Today Solomons is a boater and tourist destination with marinas, seafood restaurants, gift shops, a boardwalk, a sculpture garden, and the Calvert Marine Museum.

June 6 — Solomons, Maryland

Because the weather forecast for the day still predicted small craft warnings for winds out of the southwest with gusts to 25 mph and thunderstorms with possible tornadoes for later in the afternoon, we thought that it would be wiser for us to stay in port. However, we chose to amend our itinerary and make a 100-mile run to the Chesapeake & Delaware Canal the next day because conditions would improve by then. The Admiral was becoming anxious for us to get home and "cross our wake," while I would have liked our journey to last a little longer. Maybe I was not looking forward to all the jobs facing me at home!

After a quiet morning, we walked to The Captain's Table restaurant for an early Sunday dinner. I had their fabulous she-crab soup, and we even ordered another quart to take back to the boat with us. We had eaten here many times throughout the years and have always enjoyed their down-home cooking and casual atmosphere. The predicted thunderstorms did appear in the late afternoon, and we were even under a tornado warning for about 45 minutes, but we escaped the major wrath of the system, and happily, things calmed down as the evening wore on.

June 7 — 100 miles to Bear, Delaware[12]

We left the dock at 5:40 a.m. for our 100-mile trip up the Bay. The winds were predicted to be out of the northwest at 10 to 15 mph with sea heights of 3 feet, and both wind and waves would diminish as we continued north. Things were fine as we left the harbor and entered the Patuxent River, but as we rounded the point and entered Chesapeake Bay, the wind was from the northeast, and we ended up taking the wind and waves directly on the nose. It was not the most pleasant travel situation, yet we forged ahead that way for about five hours while passing the Cove Point Light and the prehistoric Calvert Cliffs along the way.

The Calvert Cliffs — sandstone strata filled with fossils

Conditions eventually calmed down past the Annapolis Chesapeake Bay Bridge, and it continued to get nicer as we headed north up the Bay through the Elk River and then into the Chesapeake & Delaware Canal.

 In the early 1600s, a mapmaker working for the Dutch proposed a canal connecting Chesapeake Bay to the Delaware River, but it was not until 1764 that a survey of possible water routes across the Delmarva Peninsula was made, and a route from the Chester River to the Delaware River was proposed. Nothing happened until 1788 when regional businessmen, including Benjamin Franklin, raised the issue of constructing the waterway again. However, the actual construction of the canal did not begin until 1804, including 14 locks to connect the Christina River in Delaware with the Elk River in Maryland, but the project was halted again for twenty years due to a lack of funds.

When it comes to civil projects, things have not changed all that much. Construction finally got going again in 1824, and by 1829, the C&D Canal was open for business. When completed, it was 14 miles long, 10 feet deep, and 66 feet wide, with four locks. Through numerous improvement projects, the canal today is at sea level, and is 35 feet deep with a width of 450 feet. Further improvements are in the works.

Looking east as we pass under the Annapolis Chesapeake Bay Bridge

We arrived at Summit North Marina in Delaware at 4 p.m. and had dinner aboard with an early bedtime because the next day would be another big travel day. There was only one more state to go. The end was near, and I had mixed emotions about it.

June 8 – 110 miles to Atlantic City, New Jersey[13]

Reflection left the dock at 5:37 a.m. for our destination of Atlantic City, 110 miles away. It was a lovely, but cool, morning as we continued to make our way through the C&D Canal. Things soon got interesting when I saw flames and smoke coming up from a fishing pier along the canal! I immediately called the Delaware Bay Coast Guard to report the sighting and then had several more transmissions with

---

[13] *See notes on pages 322-323*

them to give our longitude and latitude coordinates and the exact location of the pier so that one of the local fire companies could respond to the blaze.

After leaving the canal, we then entered the Delaware River with the imposing Salem Nuclear Power Plant in sight. It is not our most favorite scenic view, but it is a favorite fishing area for many. (No, the fish do not glow at night!) We had an easy trip down Delaware Bay with the wind at our back, and then *Reflection* entered the Cape May Canal at 11 a.m.

 The Cape May Canal is a 3-mile sea level waterway that connects the New Jersey Intracoastal Waterway and the Atlantic Ocean through Cape May harbor to Delaware Bay. The U.S. Army Corps of Engineers constructed it during World War II to provide a protected route to avoid German U-boats operating off Cape May Point, and it is the final link connecting the Intracoastal Waterway starting in Manasquan, New Jersey to Delaware Bay.

Looking back at the Cape May Ferry terminal

We were back in New Jersey waters for the first time in more than a year. As we entered the canal, we passed the Cape May Ferry Terminal to port. Naturally, one of the ferries chose that moment to signal that it was about to back out of its slip, but we snuck past it and then continued on slowly because we were entering a dredging area. Suddenly, we heard on the radio, "Trawler ahead of me, trawler ahead of me, what are your intentions?" Pat wondered if he was talking to us. We took a look around, but we did not think so because all we saw was a small trawler approaching us on our bow, and the announcer did not identify where he was. Suddenly, we heard another repeat of the previous announcement. I then got on the radio, told the caller our location, and asked if he was calling us.

The elderly captain immediately responded and demanded that we move aside because he felt that he needed more room to pass us. When I informed him calmly that we had to continue on our course due to the uncharted shallows just off our starboard side and stated that we had plenty of room to pass each other safely port to port, the other captain uttered a number of profanities at me. He then gave me the one-finger salute, which I returned. It was so good to be back in New Jersey again! Now we felt at home!

We continued though the canal and into and through Cape May's harbor. We had visited Cape May on numerous occasions in the past, so we decided to skip it this time.

The town of Cape May was named after a Dutch captain, Cornelius Jacobsen Mey, who explored and charted the area between 1611 and 1614. Notice how his name is spelled because he was "honored" by the spelling of the town as May.

By the mid-1700s, Cape May had become a tourist destination for vacationers from Philadelphia, and today the U.S. government recognizes it as the country's oldest seaside resort. Its popularity continued to grow through the 18th century, and it was considered one of the finest resorts in America by the 19th century. In 1876, a massive fire destroyed 30 acres of the town center, thus the homes that were rebuilt were to almost all in the Victorian style of the era. Through preservation efforts, Cape May today is known for its large number of well-maintained Victorian houses, the largest collection of its kind in the U.S., second only to San Francisco. In 1976, the entire city of Cape May was officially designated a National Historic Landmark, and it is the only city in the U.S. with such a designation.

Making our way out the wide Cape May Inlet into the Atlantic Ocean, we marveled then at the color of the seawater that was a tropical blue-green color, similar to the waters we had seen in Florida. It was an absolutely clear, beautiful day with winds out of the northwest and 2- to 3-foot seas. We had a pleasant trip north, and we noticed a change in the familiar landscape of Atlantic City's skyline that we could see from many miles away — an absolutely huge new casino/hotel being built near the Showboat casino to be called Revel. We entered the Absecon Inlet (Atlantic City Inlet) and tied up at Gardner's Basin Marina by 4:15 p.m.

The Atlantic City skyline near the end of our day

 Because of its location along the New Jersey coast just 60 miles southeast of Philadelphia, Atlantic City presented itself as a prime potential resort town for developers. In 1853, the first commercial hotel, The Belloe House, was opened. During the following year, the Camden and Atlantic Railroad train service began, and Philadelphia tourists started coming in. In 1870, the first boardwalk was constructed to help hotel owners keep sand out of their lobbies, and since then, the boardwalk has expanded numerous times. That same year, the first road from the mainland to the city was completed, requiring a 30-cent toll. New Jersey has loved toll roads for more than a century. They are a tradition!

By 1874, almost 500,000 passengers a year were coming to Atlantic City by rail, and soon, two more rail lines were added to handle the crush of tourists. Throughout the next several years, larger and larger hotels were constructed, and several entertainment piers, including the famous Steel Pier, were added. It was now common for guests to visit for weeks at a time. By the 1920s, tourism was at its peak, and during Prohibition, liquor flowed freely, and gambling regularly took place in the back rooms of nightclubs and restaurants. After World War II, the city began to decline because with affordable automobiles, tourists started coming only for weekends instead of for weeks. The glory days of Atlantic City were all but gone, but in 1976, legalized gambling came to the city. Today, it is a gambling resort second only to Las Vegas.

After relaxing for a while, we decided to stay on the boat rather than to go out for dinner. Pat and I elected to play Train Dominoes and to eat appetizers and small pizzas accompanied by celebratory cocktails for our last night onboard because the realization that the next day would be our last day on the Loop was setting in.

June 9 — 63 miles to Brick, New Jersey (Seawood Harbor) — Home Port[14]

We were up early and were anxious about the tide heights because based on the weather forecast, we had decided that we would return home by the Intracoastal Waterway route that twists and turns through the somewhat shallow marshlands of southeastern New Jersey, rather than by the outside route up the Atlantic Ocean and into Barnegat Inlet.

Dawn breaks, and all is calm as we start our last day on the Loop

Because the winds were predicted to pick up from the southeast gusting to 25 mph, and rain was also in the forecast, the inside route seemed to be a better choice. *Reflection* left Gardner's Basin at 5:10 a.m., and the scene was lovely as we entered the Intracoastal Waterway with the dawn sun breaking through the clouds over the ocean. The predawn sky was one of the most magnificent and awe-inspiring we had seen on the entire trip, with streaks of yellow, orange, and red painted across the eastern sky. We made our way carefully through the channels, always making sure that we were within the channel markers so as not to go aground. Our depth sounder alarm went off several times, but we were always able to find deeper water.

A number of our fellow loopers had problems in the Little Egg Inlet area, but we did not because we observed the markers and did not rely solely on our GPS chartplotter but on our actual visual sightings of the buoys and day-markers. Hardly any boats were on the water, and our trip past the many summer homes on Long Beach Island was quite pleasant.

After about four hours, I phoned our neighbor, Ernie, to ask him to make sure there were lines on our dock and to tell him that we expected to make it home by 11 a.m. A little while later, we made the turn into our home waters of Barnegat Bay. We were nostalgic about the amazing adventure that we were completing, and then we talked about all the enjoyable things we could do this summer with our boat in our local area.

It now became quite overcast in the western sky, but it looked like we would still beat in any showers. As we passed day-marker "20" and began heading toward the entrance channel to our community, I had mixed emotions about crossing our wake and completing the Loop. I wondered what Pat would say if I suggested we not pull in and just keep going around again. I decided not to press my luck and kept quiet. Finally, our own channel into Seawood Harbor was in sight. Unfortunately, the condition of our community's inlet from the bay had gotten worse since we had left because a sandbar was building up and narrowing the channel, and shoaling was continuing to make the depths tenuous.

I maneuvered *Reflection* carefully to our dock and then blew her horn to announce our arrival in our lagoon. We were greeted by one of our neighbors, Jackie, who ran out of her house, waving and yelling, "Welcome home!", and Ernie, and his dog, Casper, who gave us his version of a warm "Hello" by running up and down our docks barking excitedly!

At exactly 10:58 a.m. and after 5,474 miles, we "crossed our wake" and completed the Loop at our wonderful home where we had started the trip on June 6, 2009. Later that evening, we had a festive arrival celebration with our neighbors, whom I called our support crew. We then made champagne toasts to each other and to *Reflection* as an acknowledgement of how truly grateful we were to God for not only blessing us with each other, our boat, and this exciting travel adventure, but also for the great people we had met, as well as the old friends we got to see along the way.

Ours was truly a fantastic journey, not only because of the places we went, but because it also enabled us to learn a lot about ourselves as individuals and also as a couple. Our vessel and we were tested at various times and under a variety of circumstances, and we had passed the tests! Our world had grown, and we returned home with new strengths and abilities that had developed from our confidence, trust, and love for each other.

Here are a few of our trip statistics:

Miles traveled: 5,474
Days on-board: 324
Number of states visited: 16
Locks passed through: 104
Gallons of fuel used: 3,547
Number of towns/villages visited: 98
Great Lakes sailed through: Lake Ontario, Lake Huron, and Lake Michigan
Length of stay in Canada (Ontario Province): 5-1/2 weeks
Length of stay in Marathon, Florida: 5 months
Number of friends made: Too many to mention.

Was this a trip of a lifetime? Yes, or until we say, "Let's do the Loop again!"

The Admiral and the Captain holding their Gold Burgee from the America's Great Loop Cruisers' Association, signifying the completion of America's Great Loop

Notes:

(1)

Anchor Marina — If you are going to be stuck somewhere for an emergency repair, this is the place. It is a well-equipped boatyard run by professionals at a reasonable price. If they should make a mistake, they fix it, fix it right, and do it quickly. We highly recommend them.

(2)

Captain Poo's Bar and Grill at Anchor Marina is a fun place to eat and drink right on the Intracoastal Waterway.

(3)

Cape Fear River — Its currents can be swift and its waves steep with an opposing wind and tide.

Seapath Yacht Club is open to the public and is located just off the Intracoastal Waterway. It has a laundry facility, restaurants nearby, and transient rates which are comparable for the area.

Bridges — With rare exceptions, all bridges in North Carolina are on a schedule, so time your trip carefully.

(4)

Dudley's Marina has reasonable transient rates and a courtesy car, but it can be bouncy on holiday weekends.

(5)

River Dunes Harbor Yacht Club has transient rates that are reasonable for the area and is located a short trip up Broad Creek off the Intracoastal Waterway. It has a courtesy car, a restaurant on premises, and a laundry facility. It is sheltered and quite new.

(6)

Dowry Creek Marina is a small, friendly marina with reasonable transient rates for the area. It has a laundry facility and a pool, and it is a short distance off the Intracoastal Waterway.

(7)

Alligator-Pungo Canal — Stay in the middle of the canal, and keep on the lookout for debris and deadheads.

Alligator River Marina has transient rates that are reasonable for the area with a laundry facility and a small general store/restaurant. It is easily accessed from the Intracoastal Waterway.

(8)

Atlantic Yacht Basin has transient rates that are comparable for the area. It is a full-service marina with a laundry facility right on the Intracoastal Waterway.

(9)
Great Bridge (bridge and lock) — The bridge and lock work together with openings on the hour. If possible, tie up to the south side of the lock because it has considerable padding.

Top Rack Marina in Chesapeake, Virginia, has free dockage if you dine at the on-site Amber Lantern restaurant, and good fuel prices. Call ahead at (757) 227-3041.

Avoid traveling during the commuter rush hour because several bridges between Norfolk and Great Bridge have restricted openings at these times. Even at other times, expect delays.

Waterside Marina has reasonable transient rates with BoatsUS and America's Great Loop Cruisers' Association discounts. It has a laundry facility and shopping, restaurants, and the Norfolk Naval Base nearby. If you have time, take the Base tour. Other museums and sites are also within a short distance.

(10)
Dozier's Regatta Point Yachting Center has reasonable transient rates with an America's Great Loop Cruisers' Association membership discount. It has a laundry facility, a courtesy car, and a pool, and it is only a few miles off the Chesapeake Bay on Broad creek off the Rappahannock River.

(11)
Solomons, Maryland, is a great place to stop on Chesapeake Bay. It is located a few miles off the Bay on the Patuxent River, and many marine services and a West Marine store are available here. It is well worth the trip.

Solomons Harbor Marina has transient rates that are comparable for the area with a multi-day discount. It has a laundry on-site, and the post office, restaurants, and an Immediate Care Medical facility are nearby.

Captain's Table restaurant is a short walk from the marina and is one of our favorites. It is reasonably priced and features good homestyle Chesapeake Bay cooking.

(12)
The Chesapeake and Delaware Canal is a sea level canal with barge and ship traffic. Stay clear of commercial traffic.

Summit North Marina has transient rates on the high side, but they are the only game in town. It has a laundry facility and a restaurant and is a full-service marina. There always is room for one more boat. Call (302) 836-1800.

(13)
Cape May Canal — As you enter the canal from Delaware Bay, be aware of ferry traffic. Stay to the port side of the channel past the ferry terminal because there are

shallows to starboard. Use extreme caution passing through the railroad bridge a few miles up the canal. It is narrow, and the current might be swift.

Cape May Inlet is wide and deep. It might have confused seas near the mouth, but things should calm down within a mile or two of leaving the inlet.

Absecon Inlet (Atlantic City Inlet) is wide and deep, but not all the buoys are charted.

Gardner's Basin Marina has transient rates that are reasonable for the area, but there is water and 30-amp electric only. It is a short trip to downtown Atlantic City via the Jitney minibus service (a bus stop is located in front of the marina). An aquarium and two restaurants are on-site.

(14)

Here are some guidelines for a trouble-free and enjoyable trip through the New Jersey Intracoastal Waterway:

Do not exclusively follow your chartplotter or the magenta line. They are merely guides.

Do follow the buoys and day markers; they mark the best water. In areas where buoys are used, they are often moved, and additional ones are added as necessary. Follow the numbers and colors. For example, if your chart shows three green buoys in a line but you observe that one is way off to one side, it is probably there for a reason.

Do not cut corners. Do not pass buoys on the wrong side.

Do stay in the middle of the channel except when passing other boats. If your depths are looking shallow, look behind your boat at the last mark you have passed, and make sure you are in the channel.

Avoid traveling the waterway on weekends. The boat traffic at those times can be more than you will want to encounter.

Do not let the charted depths north of the Route 37 Bridge in Barnegat Bay scare you. There is considerably more water in the channel than the chart shows.

The last bridge on the New Jersey Intracoastal Waterway heading north is a railroad bridge crossing the Manasquan River. Use caution when transiting the area because the opening is narrow and the current can be strong.

Some areas along the New Jersey Intracoastal Waterway can have low water depths less than 5 feet. If you are concerned about your draft, pick your day and take the ocean route.

The majority of the bottom is soft mud. If you are going slow and find yourself touching the bottom, you can get yourself off with little problem.

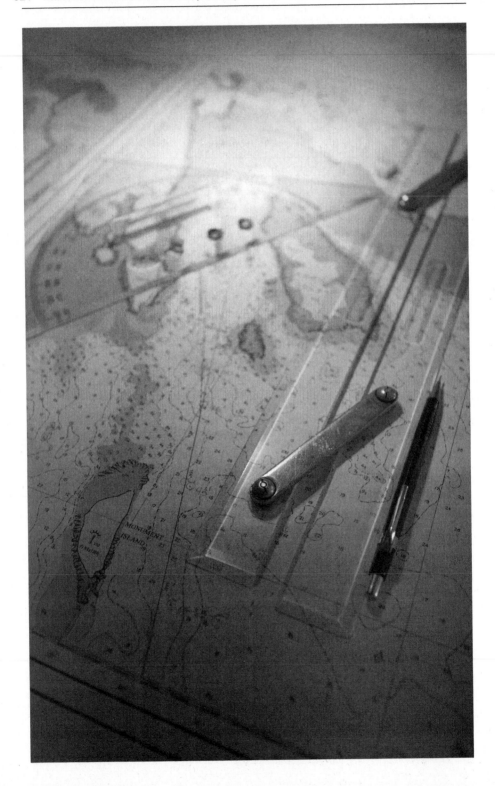

Glossary

Nautical Terms Used
Aboard *Reflection*

Admiral — The wife of the Captain. She is sometimes known as the First Mate, but is *actually* the one in charge of the boat. There is truth to the saying, "If the Admiral is not happy, no one aboard is happy!"

Aground — Description of a boat sitting with its keel on the bottom of a body of water, an unplanned event that could ruin a boater's day or a longer period of time, depending on the amount of damage done.

America's Great Loop Cruisers' Association — An association for boaters who share navigational and cruising information specifically about the eastern North American waterway connection route and for those who dream about one day making the journey. Members are quickly identified by their burgee, which has a map of the Great Loop journey embellished on it.

Anchor — (1) A metal object attached to the boat by a line or chain that is cast overboard to keep the vessel in place by attaching itself to the bottom (and hopefully staying attached to the bottom) until the captain decides to bring it back onboard. (2) To hold fast to the bottom preferably without slipping, so the captain can get a good night's rest.

Anchor Light — A white light used after dark in the rigging of a boat, usually at its highest point to signify that the boat is riding at anchor.

Unfortunately, some boaters like to live life dangerously and choose not to show such a light, thus risking a collision at night with another passing vessel.

Anchor Out — A term used to describe staying overnight on a boat while it is anchored. With any luck, when you awake in the morning, the boat is still in the same place as when you went to sleep.

Anchorage — A safe place out of boat traffic to stay overnight at anchor; however, the word "safe" is a relative term.

Beam — Describes the breadth of a vessel (and sometimes a person) at its widest point.

Bilge — The lowest interior compartment of a boat or ship. It often contains stagnant water and other slimy stuff and is one of the Captain's "favorite" places to make a repair.

Bimini Top — Canvas supported by a frame over the steering station of a boat, which provides protection from sun and rain. There is no connection with the island of Bimini in the Bahamas.

Bollard — A thick, short post made of steel on a ship, wharf, or in a lock that is used for securing lines (some folks resemble bollards).

Bow — The "pointy" end of the boat.

Bow Thruster — A small propulsion device located in the bow of the vessel to assist in maneuvering in confined spaces. Ideally, it helps you cause less damage when docking than you would have without it.

Buoy — A floating navigational aid. It can become a navigational hazard, however, on flooded rivers when it becomes submerged.

Burgee — A small flag mounted on a boat displaying the colors of the yacht club or nautical "gang" to which you belong.

Captain — The husband of the Admiral and the one who *thinks* he is in charge of the boat.

Channel — The deepest section of a waterway. Straying out of it could cause a number of problems (see Aground).

Chart — A nautical paper map that is especially useful when your electronic charting devices decide to quit working.

Cleat — An anvil-shaped piece of hardware on a vessel or a dock to which a line can be fastened and hopefully stays fastened.

Crew — A group of friends or relatives who come along for a boat ride. If you are lucky, they might help out.

Day-marker — A fixed aid to navigation. If not passed on its proper side, your boat might go aground, thus resulting in your vessel becoming a new day-marker, and a warning to other boaters not to be as stupid as you were.

Deadhead — A submerged waterlogged stump, not a dense member of the crew, or a follower of a famous rock band.

Depth Sounder — An electronic device that displays the depth of the water and warns you that you are about to go aground.

Dinghy — (1) A small open boat carried by a larger boat as a tender. (2) A term to describe a person who is not playing with a "full deck."

Docking — Maneuvering a boat to a structure (dock, seawall, etc.). It can sometimes be an act of sheer terror.

Draft — The amount of water depth required to float a vessel and an important number to know (see Aground).

Engine Room — An area below deck where the propulsion machinery is housed. It is a bit damp, cramped, and an excellent place to bloody your knuckles with a low overhead (ceiling) at just the right height to cause minor brain damage when the Captain tries to stand up. Lots of "colorful" words can often be heard coming from this area.

Fender — An inflatable device hung off the side of a boat to protect the hull from damage, often referred to as a "bumper" by the nautically challenged among us.

Floating Dock — A dock that is attached to piles in such a way that it can move up and down with the rise and fall of the water level. This is the Captain and the Admiral's favorite kind of dock.

Flybridge — (1) The highest navigational deck on a boat, and often an open space (2) A place where the Captain can steer the boat and in rough seas can get a saltwater shower at the same time. (3) A place where flies like to collect when traveling through Georgia and New Jersey.

Forward — (1) The direction toward the front of the boat. (2) The usual direction in which you might want to proceed.

Galley — The boat's small kitchen from which many amazingly delicious large meals appear.

GPS Chartplotter — An electronic device that displays the boat's position on a nautical map but which can also get you into trouble if you focus too much on the device and not what is in plain sight (see Aground).

Great Loop — A circumnavigation of Eastern North America by water, sometimes incorrectly called the "Great Circle Route."

Happy Hour — A pre-dinner gathering of the Captain, the Admiral, the Crew, and other like-minded people to discuss the day's events, and perhaps tomorrow's plans. Snacks and an adult beverage accompany it, but depending on the happenings of the day, there might be the need for several adult beverages.

Head — A marine toilet or the compartment where the toilet is located. The origin of the term is somewhat clouded, but here is one explanation: Sailors returning from shore leave who had too much to drink frequently found themselves with their head in the bowl as they held the "porcelain goddess" in order to purge. Fortunately, this Captain has not found it necessary to hold the "goddess" in many years.

Helm — The steering station on a boat or ship. The person, whether male or female, who is at the helm and steering the boat is called the helmsman, not the helmsperson. (So much for political correctness!)

Helmsmanship — The ability to steer the boat in such a way that it does not go aground or strike any object.

Holding Tank — A storage container on a boat for toilet water. Depending on who is aboard, some boats might need larger tanks to hold more than others because they can fill up quickly.

Ice Maker — The most important mechanical device onboard the boat. No ice equals no cold drinks, and no cold drinks equals no happy hour, and no happy hour equals an unhappy captain.

Intracoastal Waterway — An inland water route that follows much of the Gulf and Atlantic coasts. It is often winding and shallow.

Keel — A structure that runs along the centerline of the bottom of the boat that adds stability. It is the first thing that finds the bottom of a waterway when going aground.

Line — Another term for rope. However, in boating, if you call a line a rope, everyone will know you are a rookie.

Loopers — Boaters who are "on the Loop" or who have completed the Great Loop journey. They can often be found traveling together as buddy boats, are known for giving strong assistance and support to one another, as well as for having terrific dock parties and happy hours.

National Oceanic and Atmospheric Administration NOAA — A federal government agency. Among its many responsibilities are weather, sea conditions, and tide and current forecasts. Unfortunately NOAA does not always know, and when their predictions are off a bit, it can make for a very interesting day on the water.

Packing Nut — A threaded hexagonal nut around the propeller shaft that contains packing (waxed cotton wadding) to prevent water from entering the boat. It can cause lots of excitement aboard when it does not prevent water from entering the boat.

Piling — A pole-like structure made of wood, steel, or concrete, often used with a line in the securing of a boat to a dock. It is also something else a boat can hit while docking.

Port — (1) The left side of the boat when looking forward. (2) A safe place where ships or boats can dock. (3) A sweet red wine that might be consumed in big quantities depending on how the docking procedure went.

Prop — (1) A short and commonly used version of the word, propeller. (2) To hold up – for example: the Admiral had to prop up the Captain after the party last night.

Pump Out — A vacuum device that empties the holding tank hopefully into a sewer rather than all over your boat.

Radar Arch — A sometimes-hinged, arch-shaped structure near the boat's highest point, which supports the vessel's radar and other antennas. It often requires bridge openings for it to clear without damage.

Raft-up — The tying up of two or more boats together at anchor for the purpose of social interaction, i.e. "party-time."

Rudder — A vertically hinged plate mounted at the stern of the boat for the purpose of steering, ideally, in a straight line.

Salon — The living room on a boat sometimes mistakenly called a saloon.

Skinny Water — A shallow depth of water through which a boat can barely pass, not a place for "Skinny Dipping".

Starboard — The right side of the boat when looking forward.

Stateroom — An often-exaggerated term for a small sleeping cabin.

Stern — (1) The wide end of the boat. (2) The expression on the faces of the Coast Guard or the Marine Police if they have to stop and board your vessel for an infraction.

Stink Pot — A term used by sailors for any powerboat.

V-berth — Two sleeping berths located in the bow of a boat in the shape of a "V." Bodily placement is with the occupants' heads at the top of the "V" and feet at the bottom, however, without a filler piece to close the wide, deep gap at the top, cuddling becomes difficult, if not impossible, though this is sometimes desirable, depending on the sleepers.

VHF (Very High Frequency) Radio — A device for boaters to communicate with the Coast Guard in an emergency and with each other. Unfortunately, it is also sometimes used for mindless chatter.

Wake — Waves created by a boat moving through the water. The faster the boat travels, the larger the wake. The larger the wake, the more nearby boats rock, sometimes violently. This often results in the waked captains wanting to attend the offending captain's "wake" (memorial before a funeral).

Authors' Biographies

eorge Hospodar first began his nautical life by purchasing a 14-foot sailboat, *Rum Dum,* in 1970. His wife, Pat, joined him in 1971, and together they have cruised more than 33,000 miles aboard their two sailboats, *Adventuress* and *Temptress,* and on their motor yacht, *Reflection.* Boaters for over 40 years, they have extensively explored the coastal waters from Nantucket to Norfolk including Chesapeake Bay, and for several years they were cruising editors for "Waterway Guide." Since 2008, they have traveled up and down the Atlantic Intracoastal Waterway numerous times, and have completed the America's Great Loop waterway trip through the U.S. and Canada.

George graduated from the New Jersey Institute of Technology with a Bachelor of Arts degree in Computer Science and spent a majority of his career as a consultant in the design, programming, and installation of financial systems for the banking industry. He is a past commodore of the Bristol Sailing Club of Bay Head, New Jersey, was the owner of a marine canvas business, served on the Board of Directors of the New Jersey Marine Trades Association, and is a past president of the Chesapeake Marine Canvas Fabricators Association. George has been a 100-ton U.S. Coast Guard licensed captain for more than 20 years.

*P*atricia Hospodar holds a Bachelor of Arts degree in Music Education from Rutgers University, a Master of Arts degree in Education from Seton Hall University, and has done additional post-graduate study at Rider University's Westminster Choir College. She retired after 36 years of service as a music educator in the Irvington (NJ) Public School System, where she was the community and Essex County Teacher of the Year and an award-winning middle school choral director whose choirs performed in a wide variety of venues, and in numerous choral festivals and competitions in Canada and the U.S.

George and Pat are members of the Marathon Yacht Club and are lifetime members of the America's Great Loop Cruisers' Association. They currently divide their time between their home on Barnegat Bay in Brick, New Jersey, and their "adopted" home aboard *Reflection* in Banana Bay Marina in Marathon, Florida.

Index